PELICAN BOOKS
A495
# ARCHAEOLOGY IN THE USSR

A. L. MONGAIT

A. L. MONGAIT

# ARCHAEOLOGY IN THE
# USSR

*Translated and adapted by*
M. W. THOMPSON

**PENGUIN BOOKS**
BALTIMORE · MARYLAND

Penguin Books Ltd, Harmondsworth, Middlesex
U.S.A.: Penguin Books Inc., 3300 Clipper Mill Road, Baltimore 11, Md
AUSTRALIA: Penguin Books Pty Ltd, 762 Whitehorse Road,
Mitcham, Victoria

—

*Arkheologiya v S S S R* first published 1955
This translation first published in Pelican Books 1961

—

This translation copyright © M. W. Thompson, 1961

—

Made and printed in Great Britain
by Cox & Wyman Ltd
London, Fakenham, and Reading

# Contents

# List of Plates

# List of Text Figures

All the figures are from the original Russian edition, with the following exceptions: Figs. 1, 2, 18, 20, 22, and 26 were specially drawn by the translator; Fig. 8 was supplied by the author; Figs. 11 and 21 were taken from *Ocherki Istorii S S S R*, I, Moscow, 1956, Figs. 15, 16, and 17 from *Kultura Naseleniya Gornovo Altaya*, S. I. Rudenko, Moscow, 1953, and Fig. 28 from *Sovetskaya Arkheologiya* XVIII, Moscow, 1953.

# Author's Preface
## to the Penguin English Edition

IN the initial stages of the development of archaeology scholars classified antiquities not on a world scale but only by reference to their own particular country, and spoke of 'the antiquities of Italy' or the 'Bronze Age of Northern Germany' and so on. With the accumulation of archaeological material it became clear that the limits of distribution of the various archaeological materials did not correspond even in a general way with contemporary political or even ethnical and linguistic frontiers. The recognition of the unity and interdependence of the manifestations of human culture, the historical sense that came into being in the study of ancient objects in the second half of the nineteenth century, made it necessary for archaeologists to look beyond their national boundaries. It became clear that archaeology could not cope with the great historical problems set it while it was confined within national frontiers. Archaeology is one of the most international of sciences and the mutual interchange of information amongst the scholars of various countries plays a significant part in its development.

Russian antiquities were for a long time little known to students of other countries. The cause of this was probably the lack of knowledge of the Russian language (the difficulties in the study of which were for some reason considered insuperable), and a certain doubt in the achievements of Russian scholarship, occasioned by a lack of knowledge of the facts. Meanwhile over the vast area of Russia, where antiquities of practically all periods and numerous peoples occur, already in the nineteenth century a large number of discoveries had been made that were of significance for world archaeology as a whole.

Foreign students first became interested in the archaeology of the steppe areas of Eurasia, where very important historical events took place and where the movements of nomads sometimes decided the fate of ancient kingdoms.

The spectacular discoveries of Scythian remains made in Russia became the subject of research of many foreign historians, among them the remarkable English scholar, E. H. Minns. But on the whole Russian archaeology attracted little attention outside Russia. It is only since the Second World War that a number of specialist works have appeared in Europe and the U.S.A. in which Russian archaeology has played a predominant part. Amongst scholars contributing to this in the first rank must be named V. G. Childe. Nevertheless it is a matter of surprise how little is known beyond the frontiers of the U S S R of the archaeology of this country even by specialists, let alone by the general public. Matters are worse when information is published about Soviet scholarship in works written not for a scientific but for a political purpose, and which to this end distort facts, devote little attention to scientific discoveries, and inaccurately describe the points of view of Soviet scholars and the objectives of research in the U S S R. The foreign reader is therefore warned to suspect the reliability of a politically tendentious book whose author attempts to discredit the science of a nation against which he manifests feelings of spite and to sow discord and hinder unity among scholars of different countries.

Archaeology ought to serve to bring different peoples closer together; it is based on the recognition of the unity of the laws of development of society; it demonstrates the cultural unity of mankind and deals with ancient civilizations of which contemporary peoples are the heirs. Archaeology has often been used for quite contrary purposes. We must not forget how not long ago the Nazi *Germanenforschung* sought to find grounds to justify the political annexations of the German Empire. In Germany before 1945 a pseudo-science was nurtured which, mingling and confusing ideas with facts, sought to prove the superiority of one people over others. This tendency was peculiar not only to Germany and still has not disappeared: archaeological arguments even now serve to support excesses of chauvinism. Archaeologists should refute such speculations in their science for they bring discredit to the whole subject. Translations of scientific books advance the unity of scholars of different countries and lead to widespread knowledge of scientific achievements. Soviet publishing houses are acquainting readers with foreign archaeological literature and Russian translations have appeared in the last few years of books by English scholars: V. G. Childe, J. G. D. Clark, J. D. S. Pendlebury, and others. It is a pity that foreign translations of Soviet archaeological literature appear very rarely.

I am therefore very grateful to the publishers of Penguin Books for undertaking the publication of my book *Archaeology in the U S S R* in an English edition. The fact that this was the first such book controlled its form and content. It had to place before a wide circle of readers discoveries which previously had been known only to specialists, and at the same time to provide all the necessary reference material that is needed by the specialist. So the book contains many

facts, the results of research, but it is not a history of Soviet archaeology. The methods used by the archaeologists who discovered these
facts are described summarily, in general outline.

The course of Soviet archaeology has not been smooth and
straight; success has been achieved by searching, overcoming mis-
takes and difficulties. Soviet scholars received a broad scientific
inheritance, but their problem was not only to reorganize this
inheritance sensibly but also to extend the scale of work and reinter-
pret the existing data in a new way. Parallel with the new practical
tasks was the problem of selecting from the inheritance of foreign
and Russian theory that part which was consistent with the point of
view of Soviet archaeologists, whose work is based on the principles
of historical materialism, so that they could work out a theoretical
basis for their archaeology.

Before the Revolution Russian archaeologists, in spite of some
success in the development of their own methods of research, on the
whole were in the sphere of influence of west European scientific
methods, but today we may speak of the existence of a Soviet
archaeological school.

I repeat once again that little is said about the history and theory of
Soviet archaeology in my book. It deals for the most part with the
results of the researches of Soviet archaeologists; the actual process
of research is in the majority of cases not described in the book. In
order to pursue this further, as well as to acquaint himself more
closely with Soviet archaeology, the reader must turn to the list of
references at the end of each chapter.*

Five years have passed since the appearance of the Russian edition
of this book, so for the Penguin edition I have again read through
the text and introduced several additions and changes.†

(*received in London July 1959*)

A. MONGAIT

* Not included in this edition. The references are all in Russian and
readers who know Russian will find them in the original edition. T.

† Dr Mongait's corrected copy of the Russian edition was received after
the English translation had been completed. All the necessary corrections
of fact have been made, but in some cases the original form of the Russian
edition has been retained where the author had made an alteration of word-
ing. For example 'bourgeois' has been retained instead of 'foreign' in the
emended copy. Dr Mongait also kindly supplied a number of replacement or
substitute photographs for those reproduced in the original Russian edition,
of which the following appear in this edition : Plates 1b, 3a, 4, 8, 12, 13a 15,
16a, 16b, 24. T.

# Translator's Foreword

ARCHAEOLOGICAL discoveries in different parts of the world have aroused great interest, but they have not normally been associated with the Soviet Union, which is often regarded as a country too busy with plans for industrial or engineering expansion to spare time to study the past. Yet the Soviet Union has since the Revolution been the scene of very great archaeological advances which in some ways match its achievements in industry, agriculture, and other fields. One of the difficulties in following Soviet archaeology has been the lack of books that give a general picture of work there. The last few years, however, have seen a spate of general books published in the Soviet Union on periods, areas, or even world history which have allowed us to appreciate the volume of work undertaken in that country.

In 1954 a book by Artsikhovsky was published entitled *The Foundations of Archaeology*. It was a textbook approved by the Ministry of Higher Education for use in the historical faculties of universities and at pedagogical institutes, and confined itself to archaeology within the U S S R, 'the only country in the world from whose antiquities it is possible to construct a general course in archaeology'. It started with the Palaeolithic Age and ended with the emergence of Moscow. In the following year Mongait's *Archaeology in the U S S R*, which is translated here, was published by the Institute for the History of Material Culture of the Soviet Academy of Sciences. It covers the same field as Artsikhovsky's book with a very similar choice of material, but differs in that it deals only with post-Revolutionary work and also is specifically intended for the general reader. It is also much more lavishly illustrated. In 1956 the authoritative *Outlines of the History of the U S S R, I*, appeared, edited by Mongait and Tretyakov, with the different sections written by the leading Soviet experts. It does not however go beyond the Classical Period. Of these three books Mongait's seemed the best choice for translation in this series, mainly because it is written for the general reader but also because it includes accounts of the interesting discoveries from medieval Russia. It is unfortunate that it does not deal with pre-Revolutionary work, but there is the consolation that there are already two large works in English dealing with this subject.

It is hoped that this book will introduce the general reader to the rich archaeological remains of the U S S R covering a vast area of space and time, and also to the great labours of Soviet archaeologists in their exploration. Even the reader not interested in archaeology may find that the book throws light on some aspects of the Soviet Union of which he had not been aware.

The book is divided into ten chapters. The first is a general introduction with some account of archaeology in Russia before and since the Revolution. The following nine chapters need not be read consecutively. Chapters 2–5 are arranged chronologically. For the general reader the main subjects of interest are the earth-houses of the palaeolithic mammoth hunters in Chapter 2, the extraordinary Tripole villages in Chapter 3, the rich burials discovered at Trialeti in the Caucasus described in Chapter 4, and the exciting frozen burials from Pazyryk in the Altai Mountains (one of the most important discoveries in modern archaeology) in Chapter 5. Chapters 6–8 deal with areas in the extreme south of the Union either actually colonized or strongly influenced by the Assyrian, Greek, and Persian civilizations that they adjoined. It is impossible to mention all the exciting discoveries from there but the Urartian metal objects from Karmir Blur and the Arabic, Chinese, Sogdian, and Turkic documents from the castle on Mug Mountain are especially noteworthy. Chapter 9 deals with the early history of the East Slavs and though of considerable interest may be difficult for the general reader. Chapter 10 deals with the towns of Kiev Russia and has the added interest that it is Mongait's own field of study. In view of the present interest in medieval archaeology in this country it will have an especial appeal to certain English archaeologists. The Mongol Tartars overwhelmed south Kiev Russia rather as the lava of Vesuvius overwhelmed Pompeii with the corresponding advantage to the archaeologist. In the north at Novgorod the water-logged conditions have been exceptionally favourable for preservation and Soviet archaeologists have been rewarded with very unusual organic finds such as the timber roads and the birch-bark documents.

This book is not a full translation of the original. Chapters 1 and 9 comprise slightly over two-thirds and the other chapters three-quarters or seven-eighths of the original. The omitted parts are of political or ideological character, and also contain many proper names of persons and places and a few more complicated or repetitive passages dealing with archaeology proper.* A few insertions have

---

\* Dr Mongait's book received a long and severe but very fair review in *Sovetskaya Arkheologiya*, 1957 (3), pp. 289–99. I have introduced certain modifications and corrections as a result of this but otherwise except for a slight toning down of certain passages there is no alteration of the phraseology. The major alterations advocated in the earlier chapters must (as the reviewers say) await Mongait's second edition. Dr Mongait has very kindly supplied the corrections and additions that he has used in an English edition

been made but are enclosed in square brackets followed by the letter T. for translator. The chapter divisions are the same but some of the titles have been altered, while the system of subdivision in the chapters does not occur in the original except in Chapter 1. Unless it is stated to be otherwise, most of the figures and plates are from the Russian edition. Many of the prints from which the blocks for the Russian edition were made have now been dispersed but Dr Mongait has very kindly sent those that remain and some additional substitutes, from which a selection has been made for this edition. The translator wishes to record his gratitude to Dr Mongait for his assistance in this matter.

## GEOGRAPHICAL BACKGROUND

In order to reduce the burden of foreign names in the text a large number of names of places, persons, expeditions, and so on have been omitted. No disrespect to either persons or places is intended. To help the reader who is not familiar with the map of Russia a rough-and-ready system has been adopted of giving in brackets a very approximate position of the important sites with reference to fifteen or so well-known Russian towns shown on the accompanying map (Fig. 1). The size of this book does not allow the inclusion of large- scale maps but the reader will find that it will repay the trouble if he spends a few minutes looking at an atlas map of Russia before he reads the book.

The main feature of the Russian landscape are the four zones that traverse it from east to west: the open tundra in the north, the broad forest zone south of this, the open steppe, and the more interrupted zone of desert in the extreme south (Fig. 2). The forest zone is very variable in different parts, and the deciduous mixed forest area on the west forming a great triangle pointing east has played an important part in Russian history. The steppe zone on the south is also rather variable passing from wooded or parkland steppe, feather-grass or proper steppe, to desert steppe. Owing to a light and unreliable rainfall agriculture over much of the steppe is a hazardous occupation and throughout historical times the inhabitants of the steppe have been nomadic pastoralists.

The conflict between nomads and settled peasantry forms the dynamic of Russian history, and as nomads may be unfamiliar to English readers it is worth devoting a little more attention to them. They were not tied to cultivated fields and to this they owe their

published in 1959 in the Soviet Union, some of which have been incorporated into this translation.

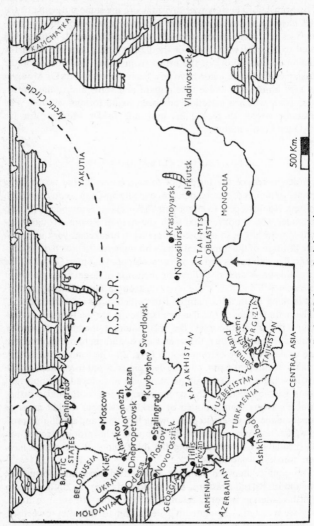

1. Soviet Union, administrative map.

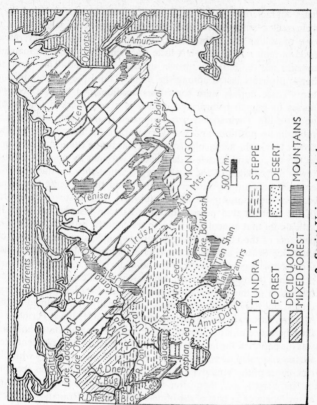

2. **Soviet Union**, physical map.

TUNDRA

FOREST

DECIDUOUS
MIXED FOREST

STEPPE

DESERT

MOUNTAINS

500 Km.

Barents Sea

Okhotsk Sea

R. Amur

R. Lena

Lake Baikal

MONGOLIA

Altai Mts.

R. Yenisei

R. Irtish

Lake Balkhash

Ten Shan

Pamirs

R. Amu-Dorya

Aral Sea

Ural

Caucasus Mts.

Caspian Sea

R. Dvina

R. Don

R. Volga

R. Ural

Lake Ladoga

Lake Onega

Baltic

R. Dnepr

R. Bug

R. Dnestr

Black Sea

main characteristic, mobility. Throughout the historical period they were skilled horse-riders, and upon their horse gear much of their love of colour and elaborate decoration was lavished. They often lived in tents which have left little trace and their most permanent remains are the barrows thrown up over their dead. This form of burial probably lasted among the nomads until the eighteenth century. These burials were sometimes accompanied by sacrifices of horses or human beings, and cruelty is a very marked feature of nomadic life. Their society was dominated by men, with women in a subordinate position, and was very warlike. In many parts of the Soviet Union the archaeologist's spade has borne eloquent testimony to the savage and senseless destruction wrought by nomads on the towns and villages of the settled peoples that they conquered. The contrast between the farmer Scythians and the nomadic Scythians made by Herodotus in the fifth century B.C. is the first written record of the contrast that persists through Russian history, but there is little doubt that in neolithic times in the contrast between the Tripole peasants of the Ukraine and the barrow builders of the east end of the Black Sea we are seeing something analogous. Early written history records wave after wave of the nomadic tribes moving west along the steppe (Sarmatians, Alans, Avars, Khazars, Pechenegs, etc.). The formation of the Kiev state in the tenth century led to a counter-attack, but Kiev Russia was repulsed and finally overwhelmed by the Mongol Tartars in the thirteenth century. The Medieval Period saw the emergence of a number of vast ephemeral nomad states and this was the period of the largest, that of Genghis Khan. For two centuries Russia was ruled by nomads of the Golden Horde, and only with the emergence of the Muscovite state in the fifteenth century was she able to free herself, and then after four centuries of relentless pressure absorb the greater part of the nomad area into the Romanov Empire. Very large areas of the Union are still inhabited by peoples living a nomadic life but the great expansion into the lightly inhabited areas of industrial schemes, the reclamation of the 'virgin lands', and so on will probably in the long run lead to the disappearance of this way of life except perhaps among the reindeer herdsmen of the north.

Soviet workers normally divide the Union into European and Asian parts on the line of the Urals, the river Ural, and the Caspian Sea. This is partly a matter of convenience and partly to show real differences between the two areas. The Asian part is a good deal more mountainous than the European part and of course experiences a much more rigorous climate. This no doubt hindered the development of agriculture in early times as it does today. The great mountain barrier on the south has to a great extent isolated it from permanent influences from this direction and the fact that the area was ultimately conquered from the west emphasizes the geographical fact. Central Asia, the area south of the Aral Sea, has been an important outlet through which nomads have flowed south and the influences of the more settled agricultural peoples have radiated north. This area was sandwiched between the nomads in the north and the empires that arose from time to time on the south, and the formidable defences found on the archaeological sites of this area are a testimony to this perennial conflict. On the west side of the Caspian Sea the Caucasus has played a rather similar part, but the very mountainous nature of the country has allowed its inhabitants to preserve their ancient languages and culture in a more intact state. The European part of the U S S R on the other hand lacks the natural barrier of the Asian part and it has experienced strong and permanent influences from various directions, from the south (Greeks), east (nomads), and north (Vikings).

The appearance of an ethnographic map of the Soviet Union with its multiplicity of different and apparently hopelessly heterogeneous groups may well induce dismay. The key to the map is a linguistic one, for it is upon differences in language that these divisions (and to some extent the administrative divisions of the U S S R) are based. Clearly if two people cannot understand each other's speech there is something very different in their background. Over a hundred languages are spoken in the Union but happily these fall into a few main subdivisions. We may mention the peripheral groups first. In the extreme north-east are the Palaeo-Asiatics whose languages and way of life have been compared with those of the North American Indians. In the Caucasus, especially Georgia, a bewildering multiplicity of languages are spoken (sometimes in only one or two villages). The Caucasian languages have no known affinity with other languages (except possibly Basque). There are then several peripheral Indo-European languages: Iranian (Ossetian in the Caucasus, Tajik in central Asia) and Armenian in the south, and the Baltic languages (Lithuanian and Latvian) in the north. In early historical times Iranian languages were much more widely spoken in south Russia than now (e.g. Scythian, Parthian, Sogdian), but these languages have been lost through the westward movement of Turkic speakers into this area in medieval times. This leaves the three main groups: the Finno-Ugrians (or Uralians) in the north, the Altaians on the south and east, and the Slavs thrust forward like a wedge from the west between the two. Many of the Finno-Ugrians and Altaians are primitive agriculturalists or entirely nomadic while the Slavs have been settled farmers from the earliest recorded times. The Finno-Ugrians impinge on the east of the deciduous forest and occupy the pine forest and tundra as far east as the Yenisei. They include Estonians, Finns, Mordvins, Mari, Komi, Udmurts, and so on (the Magyars, another group in Hungary, took to the steppe in early times). On the whole the Finno-Ugrians have played a fairly passive part in Russian history and have been thrust eastward by the advancing Slav peasantry. Very different are the Altaians, many of whom were steppe nomads in historical times. They occupy the forest and tundra east of the Yenisei as far east as the Palaeo-Asiatics (nomadic Tungus and Yakuts) and to the south of this occupy most of the steppe and desert zones extending beyond the frontiers of the Soviet Union (Mongolia and Turkey). Most of the southerly Altaians in the Union are speakers of Turkic languages (Azerbaijani, Bashkir, Chuvash, Uzbek, Kazakh, Kirgiz, Turkmen) which constitute the most important linguistic group in the U S S R after Slavonic (modern Turkey owes its language to steppe invaders of early historical times). The Slavonic languages are one branch of the Indo-European languages and are normally divided into South (Bulgarian and Serbo-Croat), West (Polish and Czech), and East Slav. The East Slav languages comprise White Russian, Ukrainian, and Great Russian, the latter being the national language of the U S S R and spoken by over half the inhabitants as a first language.

The Soviet archaeologist has before him the formidable task of tracing the early history of these different linguistic groups and their multiplicity of subdivisions. In many cases the languages were not committed to writing before Soviet times, so in the absence of written documents the subject can only be studied archaeologically. When the groups are nomadic and have moved considerable distances the problem is one of baffling complexity.

## CHRONOLOGY

No attempt has been made to interfere with the dates given by Mongait. For Chapters 6–8 and 10 there is a reasonable chronological framework based on written sources, as well as coins, inscriptions, and so on from the sites. Mongait himself discusses the difficulties of chronology in Chapter 9. In Chapter 5 the sites by the Black Sea can be dated fairly well by Greek imports, but dating is difficult farther north or in Asia where proper Scythian finds are rare. For instance, estimates of the date of the famous Pazyryk barrows vary by two or three centuries.

In the prehistoric periods dealt with in Chapters 2–4 dating is very difficult. For the Palaeolithic Period dating is largely guesswork except that a date of c. 8000 B.C. is generally accepted for the end of the Wurm glaciation. Some of Mongait's dates for neolithic cultures of the north part of the U S S R may seem surprising. They are partly guesswork, but it should be remembered that the word neolithic is not used in the same sense in the U S S R as in the West. The people in question were not agriculturalists, at any rate in the early stages. Dating in the Neolithic and Bronze Ages depends on connexions with the early literate civilizations first of the Mediterranean and then from the Bronze Age of the Urals with China. The connexions are complicated and usually very tenuous. There is no proper typological framework of bronze tools for the Bronze Age and Soviet archaeologists have so far been content to define different cultures in various parts of the Union. Nearly all prehistoric dates are subject to constant revision.

## RUSSIAN ARCHAEOLOGY BEFORE THE REVOLUTION

The two main factors in the early development of Russian archaeology were the constant expansion of the Russian Empire and the rich grave goods that were found in many Russian barrows. The variety of different races (especially in Siberia) encountered by the early colonists aroused great interest among educated Russians, for instance, the very primitive people of Kamchatka described in the eighteenth century. English barrows very rarely yield valuable grave goods and have therefore been much less of a temptation to local inhabitants than those in Russia. Here the early colonists of the steppes soon discovered that the barrows often contained valuable objects, and the plundering of neighbouring barrow fields by bands or even organized parties of colonists was a frequent occurrence. The incorporation of the Black Sea coastal area into the Russian Empire at the end of the eighteenth century provided Russian archaeology with the sites which were to be its chief objective for the next century: the Greek cities on the coast and the Scythian barrows in the hinterland. The latter were rich in precious metals, jewellery, and metal objects, and in the east part of the area the burials were often accompanied by the sacrifice of numerous horses. The description of the Scythians by Herodotus at once gave the burials a special interest in a period when education was still largely classical.

In the thirty or forty years before the Revolution the scope of Russian archaeology became greatly enlarged. The search for Scythian barrows often yielded barrows of other periods, as was the case in the famous Maikop barrow. Medieval and Bronze Age barrows were dug in large numbers. In the Ukraine Tripole sites were discovered. In 1884 a two-volume work on the Stone Age in Russia appeared. In fact in most fields material accumulated fast. Some of the outstanding Russian archaeologists of the end of the period like Latyshev, Khvoika, Rostovtsev, Gorodtsov, and Farmakovsky were scholars of international repute. It is unfortunate that the language difficulty has prevented a full appreciation in the West of the great volume of work undertaken in pre-Revolutionary Russia.

The organization of archaeology in Tsarist Russia is important for what followed. The reader may understand this better if we compare the situations in Russia and in England in 1914. In both countries there were of course national museums. At this date in England state bodies to protect and record antiquities had just started, while the survey and marking on the Ordnance Survey sheets of antiquities, one of the corner-stones of British archaeology which had begun more or less accidentally a century before, was complete. In England, however, the state played a relatively small and ancillary part in archaeology. Excavation, such as there was, was carried out almost exclusively by private individuals at their own expense, while the chief function of the national and numerous county societies was to publish an annual journal in which reports on excavations and other articles appeared. In Tsarist Russia the position was quite different. There were of course some private excavations and some independent local societies, but archaeology was regarded as a proper function of the state. The main organ of archaeology was the Imperial Archaeological Commission which was a department of state, a part of the Ministry of the Court. It had its own headquarters in St Petersburg, carried out excavations, often of an ambitious nature, every year, and published several periodicals. The Imperial archaeological societies of St Petersburg and Moscow may perhaps be compared with English societies, since they controlled their own affairs, but they were really semi-official bodies. For example only a tiny part of the St Petersburg society's funds came from the subscriptions of its members. It depended on a substantial annual subsidy from the state and received special grants from time to time for certain pieces of research or excavation. The published correspondence with the Government reveals that without the subsidy the society could not have survived.

Two of the main features of Soviet archaeology were already present in Tsarist times: the predominant part played by the state and the emphasis on excavation and exploration, sometimes on an ambitious scale.

## SOVIET ARCHAEOLOGY

One result of the Revolution was the elimination of the old archaeological societies, leaving the Commission without a rival. In 1918 its name was changed to the Russian and later to the State Academy for the History of Material Culture, and in 1937 it became one of the institutes in the Department of History in the Soviet Academy of Sciences. This is one of the eight departments in the Academy and there are some half-dozen other institutes in it (of History, Slav Studies, Oriental Studies, Ethnography, Art History, and Sinology) as well as the Academy's Archives, the Scientific and Methodological Council for the Preservation of Cultural Monuments, and the Museum of the History of Religion and Atheism. In the early years there was a good deal of continuity with the Commission in personnel and work, and even now, in some names of periodicals and so on there are traces of continuity. I I M K, however, has a very different character from the older body. It now exercises general supervision and control of archaeology throughout the Union. Subordinate bodies comprise institutes in the Academies of Science of some constituent republics (especially active are those in the Ukraine and Georgia), departments of archaeology in the universities, and of course a multitude of museums. A young person who wishes to become an archaeologist studies history, which includes some archaeology at the university, and then if he shows the ability he continues as a post-graduate student. He may leave at a fairly early stage and enter a museum, or continue to a doctorate and then join the staff of I I M K or teach at a university. The highest achievement of a Soviet archaeologist is to become an academician, but this honour is a rare one.

Apart from being a supervisory and teaching foundation I I M K is also the main research body within the Union. Local institutes and museums of course undertake work within their own area, but in large-scale expeditions such as those at Novgorod or in central Asia (Khorezm expedition) I I M K takes the leading part. It publishes three periodicals and various volumes from time to time. As some of the periodicals appear more than once a year the volume of publication that issues from it is considerable. There is no equivalent body in England, but it combines the functions of the Ancient Monuments Board, the Institute of Archaeology of London University, and the Society of Antiquaries, although it has wider powers and perhaps places greater emphasis on research than any of these bodies.

It is not necessary to speak at length about the actual results of Soviet archaeology since that is the subject of this book. There is a certain amount of understandable exaggeration in some of the claims of Soviet archaeologists yet in many fields the achievement has been impressive. For example, between 1925 and 1935 scores of upper palaeolithic sites were discovered in Russia which did much to redress the balance between Western and Eastern Europe in this field of study. In the earlier periods in central Asia the achievement has been almost as great and in many other fields only slightly less so.

Both before and since the Revolution the main task of Russian archaeology has been to explore the vast territory of Russia and chart the remains of antiquity found in it. In the last few years, however, Soviet like Western archaeologists have concentrated their attention more on methods than on the mere discovery of new objects, more on the large-scale excavation of a single site than on the discovery of new sites. In Germany before the war the ample provision of state funds and the availability of labour due to unemployment led to a series of excavations in which the whole area of a site was stripped instead of simply a part being sampled. Naturally the information obtained, especially about the size and nature of the group inhabiting the site, was immeasurably increased. This German work has had a strong influence on English archaeology, although shortage of funds has made it difficult to emulate. Roughly speaking, the earlier and smaller the site the cheaper the work. In the Soviet Union the loess soils of the south are particularly suitable for this work and moreover contain upper palaeolithic and neolithic (Tripole) sites. With ample funds provided by the state Soviet archaeologists have been very successful in this type of work, although unfortunately Mongait does not show plans of the best examples in his book.

There can be little doubt that the most impressive excavation of Soviet archaeologists has been on parts of medieval Novgorod, one of the largest and most successful excavations ever carried out in Europe. Large-scale work began in 1951 and has continued since then (the results of the four seasons 1951–4 were very promptly published in 1956). In 1951–4 4,000 sq. m. were cleared to a depth of about 20 ft. About 150 technical and professional staff and 300 labourers were employed and elaborate electrical equipment was used for removing spoil. Something of conditions in the town were already known and for this reason an area had been chosen where it was reasonably certain that water-logged conditions had led to the preservation of organic remains. In the event the junction of the timber roads for the former Main and Serf streets was revealed. These were formed of boards laid crossways set on poles laid lengthways, and they had been renewed twenty-eight times between the mid tenth and mid sixteenth centuries. Except in the uppermost layers the wood was well preserved, and so with the associated log-houses (over 500) and objects of each period, a sequence of medieval remains was revealed that is quite unrivalled. The lower roads could be dated by coins and the upper by lead seals and birch-bark letters (two or three with references to historical personages). This rough dating could be further refined by correlating layers with large numbers of burnt log-houses with fires mentioned in the chronicles, which give the exact date and occasionally specify the area or street of Novgorod that was burnt. One of the main motives of the excavation was to find birch-bark letters and some 300 have been found so far. These are written in Russian and were found in layers from the mid eleventh to mid fifteenth centuries (in medieval England surviving correspondence was in Latin or Norman French until the fourteenth century). There can be no doubt that the success of the excavations at Novgorod (a town that has always held a special place in Russian affections) has given a strong and well-deserved fillip to the morale of Soviet archaeologists.

One of the main impediments to the advance of archaeology in the Soviet Union has been the bad quality of the excavation reports. In the 1930s especially reports appeared without plans or sections, or with these but with no scale, and the reader could form no idea of the site, even when it was an important one. (This failing of course has not been confined to the Soviet Union; it is common enough in the West.) Owing to the obsession with theoretical problems the record of the excavation was sometimes overlooked. Soviet archaeologists have become conscious of this since the war; indeed in the attacks on 'Marrism' and the archaeology of the 1930s this is a point that is often made. The result has been that in the last ten years or so Soviet excavation reports have been transformed and now often reach a high standard of excellence. For instance those on the Pazyryk barrows or the Novgorod excavations are a pleasure to handle.

## IDEOLOGY IN SOVIET ARCHAEOLOGY

Some political theories (like those assuming a 'social contract') depend on certain postulates about events in history, but most of these theories have never passed beyond the stage of discussion. Marxism of course also depends in the last analysis on a certain interpretation of history, but Soviet leaders have been confronted with the problem that they are not merely discussing Marxism but are actually putting it into practice. It became clear at an early stage that it was difficult if not impossible to transform a society, industrialize it, and collectivize its agriculture if the universities, schools, museums, and so on were disseminating views that indirectly questioned the necessity for such a transformation.

During the first ten years after the Revolution there was relatively little ideological interference with archaeology and the Government itself published books by Rostovtsev who was an *émigré* hostile to the régime. With the First Five-Year Plan and the general social upheaval of the period after 1928 all this changed. All the forces of Russian society were marshalled to support the new industrial and agricultural transformations. In archaeology recriminations, denunciations, and arrests followed in quick succession. A substantial but uncertain number of museum assistants, university lecturers, and other holders of archaeological posts were arrested. For the most part they were sent into exile from which some of them have subsequently returned. The arrests ceased by about 1935 since by this time Soviet archaeology had become entirely Marxist. The whole period of the 1930s was marked by attempts to replace the existing terms for periods and divisions into terms corresponding to those of Marx and Engels. Matters were further complicated by N. Y. Marr who directed G A I M K from 1930 to the time of his death in 1934. Marr had a Scottish father and a Georgian mother and was brought up in Georgia. It is not surprising that from an early age he showed an interest in languages, and he held the chair of Armenian at St Petersburg before the First World War. After the Revolution he became a Marxist and grafted Marxism on to his own 'Japhetic' theory of language. His linguistic theories, which became absurd towards the end of his life, need not concern us here. In 1950 Stalin in his book *Marxism and Problems of Philology* denounced Marr's views as non-Marxist. Marr's name, which had become attached to I I M K, was at once removed and he was denounced in editorials in the leading periodicals. In the following year leading Soviet archaeologists contributed to a book entitled *Against the Vulgarization of Marxism in Archaeology* in which the errors of Marrism were exposed. Mongait, who was then in his thirties, took an active part in the overthrow of Marrism.

The years following the death of Stalin have seen conscious efforts in archaeology as in other spheres of Soviet life to return to Leninism. After the Revolution a large number of local archaeological societies and study groups sprang up spontaneously all over the Union. They were regarded with suspicion by the Government and in the early 1930s were eliminated. This action is now spoken of with regret, and it is proposed that the societies should be refounded, but that this time they should be centred on the local museums. This will of course bring them into the hierarchy. It is suggested that local newspapers devote one page a week to their activities. It is hoped that they will assist in the compilation of a great corpus and map of antiquities in the U S S R, a project on which work has now begun. During the 1930s museums were compelled to show schemes illustrating the

Marxist development of society. Local museum curators are now exhorted to replace cardboard and ribbon displays with exhibitions of their own collections, especially those of periods well represented in the neighbourhood.

It may help the reader if we briefly describe the Marxist view of archaeology as held in the U S S R. In the Soviet view the most important object of study in history is the 'productive forces' or 'means of production', for it is upon these that 'social relationships' and thus the 'social system' depend. There are believed to be five systems which followed one another consecutively: the primitive social, slave-holding, feudal, capitalist, and socialist systems. The 'periodization' of known history into these five stages is one of the main preoccupations of Soviet historians. The first and last systems are classless while classes are the main feature of the three middle ones. The state did not exist in the first stage but was created at the beginning of the second stage by large owners as an instrument to protect their property. Development in different parts of the world was at an uneven rate. For example, the early Slavs and Germans missed the slave-holding stage and Soviet writers describe in exultant terms their overthrow of the Roman world, since this paved the way for the next stage. Many modern primitive peoples have of course never passed beyond the first stage. In this book we are only concerned with the first three stages and the words prehistoric, ancient, and medieval can be substituted for the Marxist primitive, slave-holding, and feudal without much loss of meaning.

The view that primitive society is classless has given prehistoric archaeology a special interest in Soviet eyes. Indeed Soviet archaeologists have been warned that they must not idealize this period, for it lacked all those material comforts which could only be obtained by passing through the three stages of class society. L. H. Morgan's *Ancient Society* published in 1877 and largely based on work among North American Indians aroused considerable interest at the time and was read by Marx who made notes on it. He did not live to incorporate its findings into his own political philosophy. This was done by Engels who, using Marx's notes and making considerable additions of his own, published in 1884 *The Origin of the Family, Private Property, and the State*. It is a basic textbook for prehistoric archaeology in the Soviet Union and is frequently quoted (less often now than twenty years ago). From this book a system of periodization was worked out in the 1930s which we adopt here from a school textbook of 1947. There are five stages: the primitive herd (lower palaeolithic), primitive community (upper palaeolithic), matriarchal clan society (neolithic), patriarchal clan society (Bronze Age), and the period of the break-up of tribal society (Iron Age). In the introduction to the authoritative *Outlines of the History of the USSR*, I (1956), the editors (Mongait and Tretyakov) discuss the whole problem and the controversies that have arisen especially with regard to the appearance of the matriarchal clan and conclude: 'From what has been said the authors of the present book have not considered it possible to subdivide their material on the basis of the periodization described above. They have used for this purpose the traditional archaeological periodization. . . .' The same is the case in the book translated here, as indeed in all contemporary Soviet publications. However, references to the Engels scheme are frequent in all Soviet archaeological work and the reader would be well advised to remember the system.

It will be remembered that the early Marxist regarded the state as an instrument of the ruling classes and envisaged a revolution starting in one country rapidly becoming international. This was, of course, the expectation of the early revolutionaries in Russia. However, events took a different course. The working out of socialism in one country has always been faced with the dilemma of applying in one state a political system designed for international use. The material successes of the five-year plans inevitably engendered patriotism, while the defeat of the German invaders gave rise to a great upsurge of national pride and self-consciousness in Russia. Furthermore the nationalist movements among the non-industrialized peoples of Asia and Africa have proved a much stronger ally for the Soviet Union than the international feeling for communism among the industrial proletariat in the West. The result has been that ideology has had to be modified to accommodate ebullient patriotism at home and strong nationalism abroad. The rigid application of the theories of Marx and Engels so characteristic of Soviet history and archaeology in the 1930s, and associated with the names of Pokrovsky (in history) and Marr (in archaeology), are now denounced as the 'vulgarization of Marxism', 'vulgar sociology', and so on because they fail to take account of national and racial variations and lead to a 'decolorization of the historical process'. The adjective 'colourless' is in very frequent use and is applied to archaeology that does not emphasize these variations between peoples.

Nationalism or patriotism is very conspicuous in all spheres of Soviet life and of course in archaeology. The independent growth of culture in all periods of Russian history and prehistory is emphasized, and foreign influences (Greek, Viking, Byzantine, Arab, etc.) either denied or minimized. Pre-Revolutionary Russian archaeologists are considered to be as good or better than Western archaeologists of the same period. Sometimes indeed the claims are bombastic to the point of being ludicrous.

Nevertheless it is probably wrong to pay too much attention to the negative aspects of Soviet nationalism; the positive aspects are more important. It has led to rehabilitation of pre-Revolutionary archaeology which in the 1930s was sometimes denounced as a form of exploitation. The elimination of Marrism and the rigid or absurd application of the Engels scheme has been of great benefit to Soviet archaeology. The Soviet archaeologist no longer experiences the ideological guilt of the 1930s and can stand before his national monuments with pride and satisfaction. Patriotism has certainly aroused a great interest in the past in the Soviet Union, in the past of Russia of course but also in the past of countries outside the Union.

Relations between archaeologists in the West and in the Soviet Union have not been very happy. Great interest was aroused by the outburst of activity in the years following the Revolution, but Western scholars recoiled before the arrests and flood of polemics in the 1930s. During the Second World War salutations were exchanged between Soviet archaeologists and the late Sir Ellis Minns, and it was hoped that more friendly relations might develop after the war. Unfortunately the last years of Stalin saw a rising tide of Soviet nationalism and Western archaeologists were denounced as 'colonialist', 'imperialist', 'clericalist', 'bourgeois', and so on. This reached a climax in 1951 when at a plenary session of I I M K at Tartu Mongait delivered a lecture entitled 'The Crisis in Bourgeois Archaeology' in which the leading Western archaeologists were denounced (mainly English, including Fox, Hawkes, Atkinson, Daniel, Wheeler). This lecture was apparently occasioned by the fact that these writers had failed to pay sufficient attention to Soviet work. Some of this bitterness underlies this book, but since it was written there has been an appreciable improvement in relations. For example, a distinguished Soviet archaeologist has become an Honorary Corresponding Member of the English Prehistoric Society, while Western publications are summarized or reviewed in moderate terms in Soviet periodicals. There has been a deliberate effort to establish contacts and so on. It is to be hoped that this translation may help in a small way to carry this welcome turn of events further.

It only remains for the translator to record the pleasure the translation of this book has given him, his admiration for the way in which the author has summarized a great mass of material mainly outside his own field of study, and of course his admiration for the work of Soviet archaeologists which has made the book possible. It is to be hoped that even greater triumphs await them in the field.

# Acknowledgements

I AM very grateful to Professor J. D. Evans and Miss S. A. Butcher who have read the typescript and made many helpful suggestions. Mr S. E. Rigold has very kindly read Chapters 6–10 and corrected a number of classical and other personal and place names.

M.W.T.

# Note on the Transliteration of Proper Names

CONSONANTS should be pronounced as in English, but it should be remembered that *zh* represents the sound of French *j* as in *Zh*ukov and that *kh* represents the sound of German *ch* (Wehrma*ch*t) as in *Kh*rushchev. Voiced consonants in a final position become unvoiced. This applies especially to *v* so that Rostov and Kiev are pronounced Rostoff and Kieff. The vowels are 'continental' and pronounced as in German or Spanish. *Y* is pronounced like English *i* in b*i*t. *E* is usually a soft diphthong sound something like Spanish *ie*, so that Dn*e*str, Dn*e*pr, or Ol*e*n are pronounced Dniestr, Dniepr, Olien. No attempt has been made to show either the position of the accent or palatalization since this would give the names a forbidding appearance.

There are many non-Russian place names in this book. In the case of Greek cities on the Black Sea the usual Latin form has been used (e.g. Chersonesus, not Russian Khersones). Classical names have also been used to some extent in central Asia (Chorasmia and Sogdiana instead of Khorezm and Sogd), but not in all cases (Amu-Darya, not Oxus). In the case of Turkic, Caucasian, and other native names, the Russian version has been used but *j* (pronounced like English *j*) has been substituted for *dzh*. Tiflis has been preferred to Tblisi.

In the case of names of cultures the nominative form of the place name has been used where it could be identified, thus *Andronovo* or *Abashevo* not the adjectives *Andronovskaya* or *Abashevskaya* cultures. Where the place name already has an adjectival ending this has been retained.

B

# Preface

THIS book is intended to be a popular scientific outline of the development of archaeology in the Soviet Union. Pre-Soviet researches are referred to only where it is necessary to understand the results achieved by Soviet archaeologists.

While describing the achievements of Soviet archaeologists in the different periods or in the various parts of our homeland, the author has not set himself the task of giving a full account of the discoveries, for this can be found in the specialist publications. He wishes to acquaint a wide circle of readers with the results of archaeological science sufficiently to show the general direction of work in this or that field and to illustrate this by examples of the more significant discoveries.

Not all important problems of archaeology have been studied with sufficient thoroughness, and various questions of theory remain unresolved. Historical deductions based on archaeological data are exceptionally difficult and often controversial. On a number of little studied problems differing opinions are held, so that the position adopted in this book on certain matters is not accepted by all scholars. In particular there is a wide measure of disagreement about the full extent of the area occupied by some cultures, and about their date. In such circumstances the author has simply attempted to report the existence of disagreement and to state the various points of view on the subject of controversy. Besides this in a number of cases the author writes 'Soviet archaeologists maintain . . .', when there is not in fact full unanimity among them on the subject. As it is not possible to describe all variations of opinion, the author allows himself to use the words 'Soviet archaeologists' when the views of the majority of them are being represented.

In spite of the popular character of the book, the author considered it necessary to provide reference material. The list of references appended to each chapter does not claim to be exhaustive* and it contains only works published since the 1917 Revolution, for this reflects the aim of the book: to show the achievements of Soviet archaeologists.

I consider it my duty to express my gratitude to all my colleagues who, by advice and by putting at my disposal diaries and records, made the task of writing this book easier.

* These references are omitted in this translation. T.

## Chapter 1

# INTRODUCTION

ARCHAEOLOGY belongs to that group of sciences which was born only recently and has developed quickly. Only a few decades ago its principles and methods were so uncertain that it was doubtful which branch of knowledge it belonged to. Sometimes it was assigned with anthropology to biology, sometimes with art criticism to the history of art. The rapid success of archaeology, however, gave it a place among the social sciences. Entire subdivisions of history were created on the basis of archaeological facts. Without these facts it would not have been possible to write the history of primitive society, that of the Ancient East or other periods of history. The most important facts established by archaeologists are included in school textbooks, and archaeology is studied in higher educational institutions of many countries. Special scientific foundations occupied with archaeological researches have sprung up, while the more outstanding discoveries and researches of archaeologists have attracted wide popular interest.

### ARCHAEOLOGY, THE SCIENCE

The word 'archaeology' is derived from the Greek words meaning 'ancient' and 'word' or 'science'. The literal translation 'science of ancient things' does not express the real purpose of the study. In past times it meant simply 'ancient history'. Many bourgeois archaeologists regard the task of archaeology as simply arranging in chronological phases the 'Stone Age', the 'ancient East', or 'classical art'. In some countries archaeologists concern themselves only with the antiquities of Greece and Rome.

Soviet scholars consider archaeology as a distinct branch of history, that is the science that concerns itself with the study of human development as a unified process controlled through all its diversity and contradiction by intelligible scientific laws (V. I. Lenin, *Collected Works*, xxii, 41). Archaeology depends on the classification of its materials, which is the very basis of its methods, but its task is the same as history's – the proper understanding of historical development. For the study of history there are two great groups of sources, written documents and material things. The latter represent the basic class of remains with which archaeological research is concerned, but the use of written sources is not excluded from archaeological work.

The duration of the period of the history of humanity from which written sources survive is just 5,000 years (from the earliest Egyptian records to the present day), but the duration of the period of pre-literate humanity is estimated to be between 400,000 and 700,000 years. Clearly this gigantic slice of history can be studied only on the basis of archaeological data. Recorded history forms only one-hundredth part of the whole history of humanity. Even in the later times, comparatively close to us, as for example the Middle Ages, archaeology can furnish valuable material, because written sources do not survive for the study of important periods of history, or because they do not deal with many aspects of the life of society.

It is difficult to conceive of clearer and more valuable historical sources than the Russian chronicles, for they include a mass of information of a historical, legendary, and literary kind; yet if we try to obtain from this source an account of the economy of medieval Russia, of the life of the people or the development of the towns, we do not get an overall picture. The chronicles were composed at princely courts or in rich monasteries, and so their authors, carrying out the orders of the feudal nobles, devoted themselves to political history and paid little attention to economics and to the people's manner of living. Even for a comparatively late period, like the ninth century and those following, with their very fine written records, archaeology can bring valuable assistance on just these matters.

Naturally the significance of the material remains grows proportionally to their antiquity. Unfortunately the quantity and variety of remains diminish also in proportion to the age of the period being studied.

One of the reasons for the success of archaeology is the speed with which the amount of material available has grown. The ground still holds an almost inexhaustible number of remains. By his field work the archaeologist can often substantially increase the amount of evidence for a given period in a comparatively short time. The greater part of the written sources bearing on a period are already known and new finds are rare, but the search for material remains daily brings important discoveries.

It is, however, necessary to observe that archaeologists frequently do bring written sources to light, in the form of inscriptions on objects revealed by excavation, and these may constitute important historical texts. In excavations whole archives of ancient documents are sometimes found, written on paper, clay, bone, or wood. So in central Asia were obtained records of the ancient Sogdians, Chorasmians, and Parthians. An outstanding discovery was the writing found on birch-bark at the ancient Russian town of Novgorod.

An eminent British archaeologist, the late V. G. Childe, wrote:

Archaeology produced a revolution in historical science by pushing back the horizon of history to the same extent as the telescope broadened the field of vision of astronomy. It lengthened a hundred times historical perspective into the past, just as in biology the microscope revealed the minute cells concealed in the external forms of large organisms. In short it introduced changes in the volume and content of historical science as great as radioactivity did in chemistry.*

There was a time when archaeology was regarded as a field of knowledge that assisted the study of history, and it was assigned a place with other adjuncts of the historical discipline such as numismatics, the study of seals, heraldry, palaeography, and the like. Archaeologists showed very quickly that their science can stand on its own feet and settle historical problems. Archaeology brought to light hitherto unknown societies and states, and extended human history backwards by hundreds of thousands of years. Archaeology won its right to an independent existence.

Archaeology in the Soviet Union forms an organic part of historical science. Soviet archaeologists helped to establish historical truth, solving a series of problems of the history of our country, formerly misrepresented by bourgeois historiography...

* *Progress and Archaeology.* Moscow, 1949, pp. 18–19.

Soviet archaeologists have helped to work out the history of many peoples, above all in our northern areas and in Siberia, who up to the 1917 Revolution had no writing and so had not known their own history. . . .

## ARCHAEOLOGICAL REMAINS AND THEIR SIGNIFICANCE

Material remains like ancient objects and settlements, the archaeologist's subject of study, constitute the material culture of the society that created them. Sometimes archaeology is called the history of material culture (the central archaeological foundation in our country is the Institute for the History of Material Culture of the Academy of Sciences of the USSR). It must be said that the name does not express precisely the purpose of Soviet archaeological science, which is in fact something much broader. It is to reconstruct the social life of the society being studied and even occasionally something of its spiritual life. No Soviet archaeologist calls himself a historian of material culture; he sets himself a much broader task.

Of all things preserved from the past the most important for the study of history are tools. . . . By using the material of which tools are made as a basis for classification, archaeologists have been able to divide the history of humanity into Stone, Bronze, and Iron Ages. From the first use of stone to the stone axe and from the stone axe to iron-using is a very long road of development, and it is by means of the remains of material culture that we are able to survey this road. Not only tools but also objects not falling within the category of Marxist means of production often clearly show this process of social development. . . .

Few ancient objects survive on the surface of the earth: the great majority are in the ground and have to be dug up by archaeologists. How did they get there? Archaeological finds were almost never deliberately buried, apart from a few exceptions: in times of misfortune, foreign invasion, and for other reasons, people sometimes buried valuable objects for safety. When these are found today they are called hoards, but they are rarely found and more often than not are found accidentally by ordinary people, only subsequently reaching the hands of

experts. The majority of objects found in the ground by archaeologists evidently came there through very different causes. (

Objects and buildings were of course originally on the surface,
but, lost or abandoned by their owners, they lay for century after
century in the same place. Gradually, as a consequence of
the erosion of the surface of the earth and of buildings,
floods, and the work of the wind, there grew over them a
layer composed of building debris, rotted organic material,
remains of burnt bone, charcoal, ashes, and so on. On the
ancient soil surface new deposits collected covering objects and
ruins. (Charles Darwin in his work *On the Formation of Humus
through the Activity of Worms* has assembled curious evidence
on the important part played by earthworms in the burial and
covering up of remains of the Roman and other periods in
England.) In the following periods people settled on these
deposits, neither knowing nor caring about the traces of past
life buried beneath them. So gradually in the course of centuries the layer of earth containing the objects of material culture of the past grew deeper.

Such a layer is called by archaeologists the cultural layer. Its
thickness is variable and is not directly proportional to the time
since its formation started. The thickest cultural deposits in the
USSR are found in various tells in Turkmenia (up to 34 m.),
in the fortified town of Tamansk (up to 14 m.), in Novgorod (up
to 9 m.). In Moscow the cultural layer is only 10 cm. thick in the
recently occupied parts, but in the centre, on the site of the
ancient city, it reaches 8 m. Sometimes in spite of the antiquity
of the site the cultural deposit is destroyed and levelled so that
it only reaches 20–60 cm., for example on some of the hill-forts
of central Russia. This is due to erosion, destruction by agriculture, and so on.

The layer below the cultural layer is called by archaeologists
the 'natural' or 'bed rock' (*materik* in Russian), and is, properly
speaking, the layer where there are no traces of human activity.

Cultural layers are studied in various types of settlements.
Remains of fortified villages or towns are called 'hill-forts' or
'camps' (*gorodishcha* in Russian), and other types of occupation simply 'settlements'. The following characteristics are helpful in referring a site to its proper category: camp or hill-fort,

site defended by earth or stone walls; settlement, open and undefended. For a settlement which existed before earthworks came into existence the word 'site' is used.

The archaeologist encounters only partially preserved remains of buildings, sometimes only foundations or traces of foundations. However paradoxical it may seem, the best 'surviving' sites for archaeological exploration are precisely those destroyed by war, consumed by fire, or overwhelmed by natural disasters such as volcanic eruption or earthquakes. In such circumstances the inhabitants were not able to carry away their possessions, many of which were left on the site, while partly burnt buildings are better 'preserved'. Medieval Russian towns destroyed by the Tartar Mongols in A.D. 1237–40 give a very clear picture not only of the destruction of the town but also of its preceding life.

Wood usually decays quickly in the ground, though it can survive in conditions of extreme dryness or wetness. This is the case for example at Novgorod, Riga, and Staraya Ladoga (in north Russia) where the wet conditions of the ground have preserved wooden objects, houses, and wooden roadways.

Best preserved of all are objects of stone, bone, and pottery (baked clay). Pot sherds form the main mass of finds on settlements, so that they constitute the main material for inferences and deductions by archaeologists, who pay special attention to them. They have been called 'the alphabet of archaeology in each country'.

At a time when archaeology had not yet sufficiently mastered its techniques it was called ironically 'the science of broken pots'. But even a broken pot can yield important information. Originally pots were made by hand, but with the emergence of class society and the specialized craftsman from village economy the use of wheel-made pottery spread. Thus by this single piece of information, the use of the potter's wheel, we can judge social life at a given time. But there are other important clues that a simple sherd can reveal. With the appearance of metal vessels, pots also appeared imitating their shape and form. Ancient tribes and peoples had their favourite forms of pot and personal ornament. The use of the word 'favourite' is unfortunate for the form was dictated by the use to which the pot was going to be put: ornament was not only for beauty but had, too, a magical significance. In the course of centuries ancient tribes made only insignificant changes in the forms of their pottery and in their ornaments, so that it is possible to follow their evolution and so grasp the sequence of events over long periods of history.

Traditional patterns are transferred from generation to generation irrespective of the place chosen for settlement, so that tribes moving to new places retained their former way of decorating their pots. Sometimes an ancient tribe is called after the form or decoration of its pottery in place of the real name that we do not know. One says that these were the 'corded-ware' tribes (corded ware is pottery decorated with cord impressions), or this was the 'bell-beaker' tribe. More often and more properly one speaks not of tribes but of 'the archaeological culture of corded ware'.

The term 'culture' is employed by archaeologists to denote a complex of archaeological remains belonging to the same period and area and characterized by the same general features. It is usual to name a culture after a single feature, often not in itself the main one but simply one that is clear and easily remembered: for example, by the decoration or shape of its pottery, the burial custom (thus the Timber-Frame culture is so called because its burials are in timber-framed pits), or by the locality where the most typical remains were first found, like the Romny culture, named after the town of Romny (Ukraine) near which a site yielding remains of this type was first excavated.

When we study the remains of ancient periods we notice significant differences between forms of burial, houses, types of objects, techniques, economy, and so on in neighbouring areas at the same period. If we plot them on a map we will see that for the most part a definite type of object will be confined to one recognizable area of distribution, a second to another, a third to yet another, and so on. When we prepare maps showing the distribution of tools, pottery, ornament, and so on from a single period in a specific area then it is found that one particular group of types of object is always found in one and the same area and always in a precise relationship with other objects. The complex of such elements is called an archaeological culture. How can such variations in objects and customs be explained among people at the same stage of development in the same geographical environment? It is clear that these differences are due to the differences between tribes. In this way archaeological cultures allow us to estimate the distribution of tribal settlements. No culture can be distinguished by a single trait, for one feature may be common to several cultures; the distinction of a culture must depend on an aggregate of features. Sometimes it can be regarded as the expression of a certain ethnic group.

For an example taken from the Neolithic Period of differing contemporary cultures within a small area we may turn to the comparatively small river Oka (near Moscow). Quite different techniques of preparing stone tools are found. In the area of modern Belev tools were made from large broad flakes of flint, in the region of Ryazan from small narrow flakes. Further downstream they were made from broad flakes, and lower still down-river on narrow knife-shaped flakes. Such distinctions can only be explained at this period by the settlement of distinctly separated tribes on the Oka. On this basis archaeologists distinguish the following neolithic cultures on the river: the Belev, Ryazan, Volosov, and Balakhna cultures (the names of the places where the finds were made).

Archaeologists who discover a new culture cannot always identify it with peoples mentioned in written sources, so that many ancient peoples simply have to retain their cultural name for want of their proper one. A culture by no means always corresponds with a definite ethnic group. Often peoples speaking quite distinct languages share a uniform or parallel culture, and on the other hand in primitive times quite unconnected tribes under similar social and geographical influences will show parallel features in their way of life and material culture. Such occurrences are called 'convergence'. Unfortunately it is sometimes not possible to decide whether the observed resemblance is due to convergence or to physical migration from one area to another.

The term culture has this basic use but is also used in another sense by archaeologists. It is applied not only to the remains of human activity found in one area, but also to certain stages in the progress of technique and development of human society which have common features in several parts of the world. Thus the most primitive stage of human culture, the Chellean (named after the town of Chelles in north France), is found in western Europe, Africa, and south Asia, as well as in Armenia in the USSR. When the archaeologist uses this term he does not mean that the people in these widely separated areas belonged to the same culture or that there was a sense of community between them. In this case the term only implies a similar general level of technique and certain other common cultural elements. So sometimes instead of Chellean culture one speaks of Chellean period or stage of development. The absence of a precise definition of the word culture and its significance forces the archaeologist who uses this term to define the manner in which he is using it.

In the study of archaeological cultures the excavation of graves is at least as important as that of settlements. Graves give the investigator a profusion of material, throwing light not only on past religious and burial habits but also on the every-day life of the time. Belief in a future life was the motive for placing in the grave objects which the deceased used in this life and might need in the hereafter. For this reason the grave was built like a hut, for the home for the future life had to resemble the one used in this. With a woman were placed embroidery, mirrors, ornaments; with a smith tools, moulds for casting metal or finished articles; with a warrior weapons; with a king all his treasures, wealth, slaves, and horses. From the grave goods much can be inferred about social and economic matters, although sometimes it is true the objects found in graves do not belong to real life: occasionally they were specially prepared for the funeral rite. More often they are cult objects, or, alternatively, objects used in real life but at a time long prior to the time of burial. The grave rites preserve traces of religious conservatism surviving in rituals but extinct in social and economic life. In this way the grave often shows the ethnographic connexions better than the settlement site. Moreover the graves yield skeletal material which allows the physical aspect of the people to be studied through each period in the area under consideration.

Graves may be either flat (with the burial in a pit) or with earth heaped up on top, that is burial mounds or barrows (*kurgany* in Russian). Flat graves are often very difficult to find because there are no surface indications. Barrows are well known, and not only to the archaeologist, for they sometimes project high above the ground (Pl. Ia). Especially remarkable are the huge barrows so conspicuous in our southern steppes, where they relieve the monotonous flatness of the countryside.

There are other types of monuments such as remains of workshops, mineral workings, and so on.

The archaeological site is hidden in the ground; how does the archaeologist become aware of its existence? Sometimes this is accidental, and a site is exposed through quarrying or erosion. The archaeologist learns of this through local inhabitants. The most important palaeolithic site in Siberia, Malta, was discovered by a peasant, but the information reached the museum at Irkutsk only through gossip. The important find of documents in the formerly unknown language of the Sogdians in an eighth-century castle on the mountain of Mug (east of Samarkand) was made by a shepherd. It was noticed by the local people that the manuscripts were written in a script that was unknown to them.

Besides studying accidental finds archaeologists make systematic searches, carefully working over each area and looking out for what they know to be likely signs. For example it is known that in central Russia tribes of the Early Iron Age constructed their hill-forts on promontories so that one side was protected by a river and the other two sides by a gully or valley. The archaeologist interested in this period will search these promontories and on many of them he will find the desired site. The search for camps and barrows is made easier by the prominence of their remains, but the search for settlements and open sites is more complicated. Nevertheless certain finds occur on the surface, especially pottery, showing the existence of a cultural deposit in that spot. Sometimes archaeologists do not just seek monuments of a specific period but wish to make a complete survey of certain areas and plot on a map both previous and new discoveries. The best results by far in this type of survey are achieved when it is carried out by the most 'primitive' method – on foot. Larger areas can be surveyed by car or aeroplane. Under suitable conditions aerial surveys give excellent results. For example, on aerial photographs fields sown with cereals sometimes show dark marks, delineating a vanished settlement. In antiquity people dug a defensive ditch around their settlement, throwing up the earth to make a defensive rampart, but in the course of time the ditch silted up through erosion from the sides. The deep soil in the vanished ditch provides better nourishment for the plants above it, so the plants grow taller and more thickly than normally. This explains the appearance of darker patches on the photograph. Air photographs taken over deserts often expose ancient towns and forts smothered by sand.

Aerial survey not only yields new discoveries but also shows a ground plan of the site at the same time. By using aerial photography the Khorezm Archaeological Expedition revealed hundreds of new sites in the desert, and mapped the roads and settlements.

The search for archaeological sites is also possible under water. On the beds of lakes, rivers, and the sea ancient objects and even considerable buildings are found. Coasts and riverbanks change through the centuries, and ancient waterside towns, especially their harbour areas, become partly submerged. Thus 'underwater archaeology', the search for antiquity with the help of divers, promises interesting results, and attempts at such work have already been undertaken in the USSR. Submerged coastal structures in Koktebel, Chersonesus (the Greek city), and at other points on the north coast of the Black Sea have been explored. In the river Bug near the village of Sabatinovok a dug-out canoe, which had been lying there for 500 years, was found and taken up.

Soviet archaeologists carry on their work in the mountains and deserts, in the southern steppes and on the coast of the Arctic Ocean, in central Russia and in the Far East; they search and investigate the ancient monuments of Pamir 4,000 m. above sea-level and work in the Sarakamyshskaya depression 90 m. below the level of the Caspian Sea (which is itself below sea level).

The possibility of new discoveries is really inexhaustible. 'Archaeological remains are not found only in the places where we look for them', said the eminent Russian archaeologist, A. A. Spitsyn.

All discoveries furnishing scientific information are protected by the State in the USSR. As the excavation of a monument leads to its partial or complete destruction, the methods of archaeological research require rigorous scientific supervision. Therefore excavations without special authority issued by the Institute for the History of Material Culture, or the equivalent body in the constituent republics, are forbidden. Of outstanding importance for archaeology are the Government regulations for the improvement of the protection of cultural monuments and 'The Position regarding the Protection of Cultural Monuments'.* These important pieces of legislation secured the protection of cultural, including archaeological, monuments and laid down the basic principles for their investigation.

Extensive and systematic excavations demand substantial financial resources. In the Soviet Union the State finances excavation through appropriate learned bodies.

* In 'The Position regarding the Protection of Cultural Monuments' it is laid down : 'all cultural monuments on the territory of the Soviet Union that have scientific, historical, or artistic significance constitute inviolable communal property and are placed under State protection.' Archaeological monuments are defined as 'ancient barrows, camps, pile dwellings, remains of ancient sites and settlements, of ancient towns, ramparts, ditches, traces of irrigation canals and roads, ancient cemeteries, tombs, graves, ancient burial constructions, dolmens, menhirs, cromlechs, stone figures, and such like, ancient drawings and inscriptions carved on rocks or cliffs, sites where bones of fossil animals (mammoth, rhinoceros, and so on) are found, and also ancient objects that are found'. 'Any change, alteration, transference, or destruction or building on reserved areas or cultural monuments is forbidden without permission in each case' ... 'In those exceptional circumstances when permission is given for the destruction or alteration of a monument the department concerned with protection according to the circumstances of the case must organize works for the completion of scientific investigation and treatment of the said monument (excavation, photography, measurement, survey, transference of finds to a museum, etc.) ... The expenses incurred in this are to be met by the body that received permission to destroy or alter the monument.' (In England the case is quite different and the party authorized to destroy a scheduled monument is under no obligation to pay anything towards the cost of excavation. Moreover in England only those monuments expressly placed on the list by the Minister of Works are protected. T.)

## EXCAVATION

Excavation of an archaeological site can be undertaken only by people with special scientific training and experience of archaeological excavations.

Fieldwork presupposes the most careful preparation. The archaeologist must acquaint himself with historical sources bearing on the site in hand and with the results of earlier workers, if any, on the same site, and with relevant museum collections. Only thorough preparation will lead to the right choice of position for trenches and right conduct of the work. Besides scientific preparation the archaeologist must furnish himself with the proper tools and equipment for the expedition.

Some people believe that the process of excavation consists in the removal of the earth and the exposure of the ancient site carried out by workmen while the archaeologist basks in the sun contemplating others working and waiting for the finds to be placed in his hands. This view is quite erroneous. 'Excavation is not a sport or a pastime; it is serious work, usually exacting and always responsible' said Spitsyn (*Archaeological Excavation*, 1910, p. 7). The responsibility arises from the fact that the investigator always destroys the cultural deposit that is being examined. The unsuccessful laboratory experiment can be repeated dozens or hundreds of times; the excavation cannot be repeated at all. Therefore it is essential to carry out the work so as to produce a detailed report from which the original form of the site can be reconstructed.

Soviet archaeologists consider it essential to make the most objective account possible, so that subsequent generations of students can use the record. This is especially important where the site is unique and further controlled excavations on this type of site are impossible. It is necessary to make a maximum of survey, drawings, and photography, for these form the most important documents from the site. Recently Soviet workers have adopted the use of cinematographic film for record. If the conditions of discovery of objects is not exactly fixed they lose half their scientific value.

The archaeologist tries to raise every object found with his own hands, for from its position in the earth and its relationship with neighbouring objects he has to draw many important conclusions. One of the most important is the stratigraphy, that is the sequence of layers deposited in antiquity. (The word 'stratigraphy' is derived from a Latin and a Greek word combined and means literally 'the description of layers'.) As a rule the later layers lie above the older. If the levels have not been disturbed by the digging of holes, the throwing up of a bank, or otherwise, then a section through the earth shows the sequence of layers. The distinction of layers is a difficult matter. The cultural level is as a rule of a darker shade than the material above and below, but within it distinct changes can be distinguished only by slight variations of shade. It is important to distinguish not only the layers but also their proper relationship, for the finds within them date the whole complex of finds. Sites may be either single or multi-layered, that is where the continuing life of the people through several periods left a corresponding number of layers. If life on the site was interrupted for a considerable time and later resumed, if occupation was intermittent, then there will be sterile layers between the archaeological layers. Stratigraphical observations constitute the most important method of dating a site and its various parts.

Stratigraphy usually allows the establishment of a relative chronology, that is the sequence of events in a given site. As for absolute chronology (that is the relating of this or that fact to a known time scale, either B.C. or A.D.), for this it is necessary to have objects from an undisturbed layer whose date of manufacture is known, for example, coins. The dates of the object and the layer are not identical, however, for a period of time must elapse between its manufacture and its later incorporation into the layer concerned, so that it gives only an approximate date. Generally speaking an archaeological site can rarely be dated with greater accuracy than to within between ten and twenty years, and then only if there is contemporary written evidence. The more remote the period the greater the degree of inaccuracy in dating. The earliest phases of human history are measured by geological periods extending over tens of thousands of years. For the dating of these phases stratigraphical observations are also necessary, although the margin of 'accuracy' is several thousands of years.

Sometimes stratigraphical observation can give a basis for a detailed chronological scheme. Thus in Novgorod the Great (the famous medieval Russian trading town about 160 km. south of Leningrad) excavations in one place revealed twenty-eight superimposed timber-surfaced roadways. This deposit was formed in 600 years from the middle of the tenth to the second half of the sixteenth centuries. So in Novgorod they made a new timber road at an average interval of twenty to twenty-two years. For the most part the roads are connected with structural complexes, like houses, storage buildings, and so on. The stratigraphy of the roads allows dwellings, with the things found in them, to be dated to within twenty years. It should be added that several of the roads are reasonably well dated independently, as coins or seals of Novgorod rulers or other official persons whose years of office are well known from the chronicles were found on them.

Plant remains found in excavations allow the study of climatic changes that took place in a given geological period. The sequence of climatic changes can also serve as the basis for chronological schemes.

For the archaeologist it is important to explore the site not only through vertical sections but also by making horizontal plans. These are especially important for the reconstruction of buildings. In multi-layered sites excavation proceeds layer by layer. Layers may not be flat all over and so in order to avoid inaccuracy the area being investigated is usually excavated in horizontal spits of 20 cm. depth, that is a spade's depth. As the layers are not usually horizontal these spits do not coincide normally with the layer divisions. Where the layers are very markedly inclined it is desirable to remove them one by one and not in spits.

For greater precision a contoured plan of the site is prepared, and the position of the various structures found in the cultural layers is compared with it. The level, theodolite, and plane table are the instruments most widely used for making this plan. The whole of the area to be explored is divided into squares 2 by 2 m. in size, and observations are made within these squares. Accuracy of recording requires division into the smallest possible units, but a real picture of the site can be obtained only from the uncovering of the largest possible area. Formerly Russian workers excavated in long narrow trenches or made small trial excavations. Such methods of excavation do not offer a picture of a site as a whole, with its complex of finds and buildings. Certainly they give stratigraphical information and at times some interesting finds, but at the same time the archaeologist adopting these methods of trench excavation is destroying the full structure and deposit to tear out a few finds from their proper context. Soviet archaeologists now excavate over a broad area in order to study settlements. Thanks to this, houses and industrial sites have been revealed that have given a fuller picture of social life in one or another archaeological site. It must be understood that the use of trenches is not excluded in the search for a cultural layer or for certain objects of interest to the investigator, but that this method of work is not suitable for basic research.

The ideal, unhappily seldom achieved, would be the total excavation of a settlement over its whole area. This is essential in the excavation of a grave or barrow. Soviet archaeologists dig the whole mound of a barrow. This is necessary because the methods of digging by a trench or a hole in the top were really those of treasure-seekers, and although ancient objects were often found it was impossible to study fully either the burial ritual or the construction of the mound. The stratigraphy in the body of the mound can be studied, so at the central point of the mound the archaeologist leaves a pillar of unexcavated mound in which the layers can be examined (the mound is normally 1–2 m. high). This central pillar is removed after the rest of the barrow has been dug. Large barrows are dug in sectors and in the central part two such pillars of undisturbed mound are left along a diameter.

It is the duty of the archaeologist to continue digging down to bed-rock, to the bottom of the cultural deposit, fully exploring the whole area of investigation. He must keep all material found in the excavation – sherds, bones, and the rest, things which from the layman's point of view might at times seem to have no interest. In some cases, it is true, they yield little information. Statistics of the finds, however, are necessary for a proper record. Concentration on the valuable finds and disinclination to turn attention to the ordinary 'dull' material can lead to serious error. In some excavations in the ancient towns of Syria and Iraq even today the system of 'bakshish' or payment for finds is practised. The workmen themselves select the valuable finds and at the end of the day give them up in return for cash. Objects of 'little value' are thrown away and naturally it is not possible to trace the position in which they were found. Only archaeologists paying full attention to the mass of finds and applying statistical methods can create an authentic and full picture of the life of an ancient society, and not just special aspects of it as is the case with workers who select only the valuable finds for study.

Excavations must not be hurried. Over-enthusiasm, striving to uncover new areas more quickly, is inadmissible. Sometimes, when an interesting discovery has just been made, the time has come to close the excavation to allow more objective study to be made at home. Patience and strength of will are now demanded, for the urge to find quickly the most interesting things is a temptation to continue the excavation.

The necessity for careful observation during excavation produces the curious situation that in this Machine Age the basic tool of archaeology remains the spade. Ideally an even smaller instrument such as a knife would be better, but this would make the work too slow. Once the cultural deposits are exposed by spades and we approach the archaeological layer, buildings, or graves, knives, tweezers, and brushes are taken up to continue the work. Excavators, bulldozers, and scrapers are not used in exposing the cultural level. They remove too much soil and make observation impossible. They may only be used if a sterile overburden has to be taken off the top first. Mechanization on excavations is possible only in the removing of spoil from the scene of operations (Pl. 1b). This laborious work can be made appreciably easier by the use of conveyors and other mechanical devices. The simple spade remains, and evidently will remain in the immediate future, unless there is some far-reaching invention in this field, the basic tool for archaeological excavation.

Architectural remains are preserved on the site but small objects are taken to a museum or to the laboratory of an archaeological institution.

However interesting in themselves the finds from antiquity may be, it must be remembered that they are not the purpose of the researches. 'Every new excavation must have as its purpose not the mechanical multiplication of antiquities but the solution of some scientific problem' (A. A. Spitsyn). So in archaeology the planning of excavation work is of immense importance to ensure that it is closely tied to the basic tasks confronting science.

In the Soviet Union excavations are conducted to a thoroughly organized plan, and they form the first most important stage of scientific research. Beyond the mass of finds and the thousands of detailed observations the scientist must see the whole picture of the social life in which the archaeological monument arose. In the graphic expression of an archaeologist: 'the ground is a book in which the objects are the text to be read.'

After the work of the archaeologist in the field comes the next stage, the sorting out of the material in the laboratory.

## WORK IN THE LABORATORY

Laboratory work is a most important part of scientific research. It is necessary above all to describe the objects and to study their form, purpose, place of manufacture, the material and technique used; and so finally to date them. This is difficult because few objects bear information about their date, and yet it is very important that this should be known. The method of dating objects in a layer by means of a single object of known date in that layer has already been described. But it is by no means always possible to establish the relationship of objects by their position in the ground, and in that case the archaeologist has to seek analogies elsewhere, comparing his objects with those whose date is known. This method of the study and comparison of types is called 'typology'. It serves as a means of classification for establishing a sequence of types and is an important aid in archaeology. . . .

Nowadays in archaeology descriptions of outward form are not sufficient. An attempt is made to study the object more deeply, to explain its history and so to throw light on the history of the society in which it was made. For this it is necessary to use the latest achievements of science: physics, chemistry, botany, statistics, and other sciences.

For example the method at present being worked out of measuring the loss of radioactive carbon, $C^{14}$ (an isotope of carbon with an atomic weight of 14), can have especial importance for dating. This carbon is present in the atmosphere as a result of the action of cosmic rays. Soon after its formation it is oxidized to carbon dioxide and assimilated by plants into their tissues, and of course into animals since they live on plants. The quantity of this isotope of carbon absorbed in one kilogram of organic material has remained constant during the last fifty thousand years. After the death of the plant or animal the $C^{14}$ content begins to diminish through disintegration, but this takes place at a constant speed. So if the investigator has samples of organic material from an archaeological site he can estimate their age with great precision. The life period of $C^{14}$ is sufficiently long (it has a half-life of 5,500–6,000 years) to allow this method of dating to be applied to material from one to ten or twelve thousand years.* [The method was devised by Professor Libby in Chicago and is now widely used in Europe. T.]

X-ray, spectographic, thermal, and chemical analyses reveal important historical facts. For example, metallurgical examination of ancient Russian objects has shown that already in the tenth century Russian smiths had mastered the technique of making steel and that a great number of iron objects found in early medieval towns were made in Russia. Not long before it had been assumed that these were imports from outside because it was thought that Russians had only learnt how to prepare iron in the seventeenth and steel in the nineteenth centuries.

Steel swords found in ninth-century warriors' barrows used to be considered as Norse imports. Spectrographic analysis established that swords found at Smolensk contained nickel which occurs also in the local ore and so these swords may well be of local manufacture and not imported.†

* A laboratory for dating objects by means of their radioactivity was founded at Leningrad in 1955.

† Special archaeological laboratories for spectral and structural analysis are attached to the History Faculty of Moscow University and the Leningrad section of I I M K.

The question as to the source of the material of which an object is made is therefore important for archaeology, especially for establishing connexions between ancient societies. The most obvious case is when an object is made of a material that does not occur naturally in the area where it was found. For example wooden combs of the tenth to fifteenth centuries were found at Novgorod made of boxwood, but the nearest point to Novgorod where box grows is the north Caucasus. Through five centuries then Novgorod merchants imported this material for their craftsmen to make into combs.

The matter is more complicated when the material of which an object is made occurs locally but its form is characteristic of another area. Then it must be decided whether it was made on the site to imitate a foreign form or whether it is a foreign import. Once the archaeologist has decided that objects in a site are foreign imports then there is posed the question as to how they came there, whether by barter, trade, as war booty, or by the physical transference of members of the tribe occupying the area where such objects were made.

X-ray examination allows study of not only the internal structure of animal bones found on sites but also the texture of objects, and, we may add, details of ornament on metal vessels almost undetected by the naked eye have been found. Thermal analysis establishes the firing temperature of pottery vessels, and explains the changes undergone by minerals in the clay as a result of raising the temperature.

For the study of geological periods especially important are petrographical analysis of the rocks concerned, granulometry, etc. [Granulometry is a technique developed in France for dividing levels in cave deposits, where no conspicuous change is noticeable, by changes in grain size. T.] To decide whether a rock is local or imported the facts of mineralogy must be used.

Tree pollen survives unusually well and lasts thousands of years. It is best preserved in bogs but also survives in soil. Systematic observations on the stratigraphy of bogs and the study of the pollen found there (pollen analysis) make it possible to follow the evolution of vegetation and with this the evolution of climate in a given area. The vegetation changes of course each time the climate changes. When the history of climate in an area is known we may assign the site being studied to a certain period of the climatic history. Wood and other archaeological remains are excellently preserved in bogs so there is an opportunity to correlate them with the pollen layers and thus establish the natural environment in which people of this or that culture lived.

It is established that a high phosphate content in the soil corresponds to an area of ancient settlement, so that phosphate analysis of the soil can help to define an inhabited area.

Soviet scientists have worked out a method of study of the functions of tools by the traces of work on the tool. Every tool of whatever material wears out in the course of use. The use in the laboratory of optical devices (binocular lenses and microscopes) to make microphotographs can lead to a decision about the tool's use by comparison with objects of known use. Thus some workers supposed that the fixing of an axe in a haft was a comparatively late invention of the Neolithic Age and that previously in the Old Stone Age axes were simply held in the hand without a haft. However, study of an axe from the palaeolithic site of Kostenki revealed on its working edge linear marks that occur only when an axe is hafted.

Analysis does not complete the work in the laboratory, for conservation and restoration are still necessary. In conservation various methods are used, again employing scientific discoveries, such as soaking wooden objects in various resinous solutions or the application of synthetic glue. Wooden objects that have been in humid conditions for centuries are very difficult to preserve. On coming into the air drying out deforms them; they crack and are destroyed. Slow drying out in plaster casts will partially save them from deformation.

The purpose of restoration work is to recapture the complete form of a partly destroyed object, as in the case of pottery it is to obtain the shape of the pot by sticking together the surviving sherds. Sometimes the task is enlarged when the intention is to reconstruct the whole object from a surviving part. This is called reconstruction rather than restoration.

Questions about restoration are finally settled in the laboratory, but the most important stages of the work are carried out in the field during excavation. Skilfully conducted excavations will afford the greatest opportunity for full reconstruction. For example, during the excavations on the Scythian town of Neapol in the Crimea in 1945–6 remains of the wooden coffin of a Scythian queen of the first century A.D. came to light. Its wooden parts had disappeared into dust, but in the clay that had accumulated around it were distinct impressions of engravings with traces of pink and blue colours and gilding. It was an extremely difficult task to recreate the appearance of the coffin from a few traces in the earth. A careful plan was made of the position of all the objects and the dust of the decayed wood was carefully cleaned out. Plaster was poured into the cleaned spaces. Thus casts were made of the planks, uprights, incised figures of animals, and other parts of the coffin, and so a reconstructed drawing of it could be made. It was rectangular, and carved figures of fantastic animals, sphinxes and griffins, formed feet on which it stood. The sides and the lid were made of planks, their faces decorated with incised garlands of conifer branches with fir cones, laurel twigs, fruit, and flowers, intertwined with ribbons. On the lining were figures of a lion and a sphinx. Thus a most complicated wooden object was reconstructed from the impressions it left on the earth. (This method is widely used all over the world and of especial interest are the casts made in the nineteenth century at Pompeii in the empty spaces left by the decay of the bodies of men and animals overwhelmed by matter from the volcanic eruption.)

In the USSR a solution has been found to the problem of the reconstruction of the outward appearance of fossil man from his skull alone. A number of reconstructions had been made but they were all schematic and for the most part represented the view of the worker about the type of skull he had dug up and not an example of a person who had actually lived. The archaeologist and anthropologist M. M. Gerasimov proved that special features of the skull and soft skin cover of the face are directly related to each other. Gerasimov's method has been tested and proved a number of times on skulls of contemporary people. Gerasimov has created a whole series of portrait reconstructions of excavated skulls including portraits of primeval people: Pithecanthropus, Sinanthropus, Neanderthal, Bronze-

Age people, Iron-Age Scythians, and portraits of historic personages. The work of Gerasimov constitutes an important example of reconstruction of archaeological material with the aid of another science, that of anthropology. In this case the archaeologist provides the material, but does not take part in the work of reconstruction.

Very important for the archaeologist are architectural reconstructions, and these demand his direct participation. Excavation reveals architectural remains only in a very fragmentary state and usually only the lower parts or even merely the foundations of the building. In central Asia, where forts and towns were buried by sand and excavation consists of clearing this away, upper floors may with luck survive. The weakness of the material of which the structure was built (sunbaked brick or mud) has meant that even here not a single building remains whole. The strength of the material gave no assurance, however, that it would be preserved, for other factors could lead to its destruction. For example, because of a lack of natural stone in the area the local inhabitants might rob the walls, even to their foundations, in which case the archaeologist's fate is to find only traces of the foundation trenches. From even these the plan of the ancient building can be restored, though the plan of the lower parts of a building is usually easier to reconstruct than that of its upper parts.

In some places wooden structures have entirely vanished. Ancient Russian huts in central Russia and the Ukraine contain only remains of clay stoves or holes below floor level. For reconstruction it is necessary to use comparisons from modern primitive peoples. Significant but scarcely noticeable details help to reveal certain parts of the building. For the reconstruction of the more complicated large buildings the architect and archaeologist must cooperate (Fig. 3). It is possible to adduce many accurate architectural reconstructions based on the archaeological data.

The work of the archaeologist in the field and laboratory is the heavy and exacting task of the collection of facts and their analysis, the basis of all scientific work. The collection of facts does not finish in the laboratory, for it is necessary to make comparisons with the results of other workers; it continues in

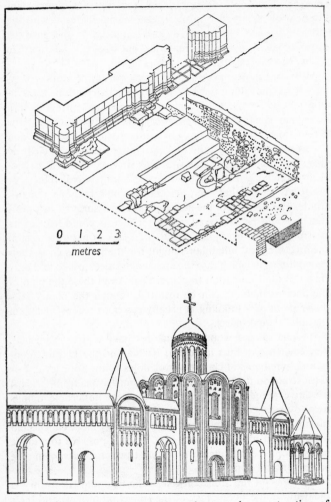

**3.** Bogolyubov. View of excavation, above, and reconstruction of twelfth-century palace, below.

libraries, scientific archives, and museums. Only after this may the worker undertake the final report including his conclusions and deductions. 'Facts – these are the air of the scientist, and without them you will never fly', as I. P. Pavlov said in a speech to Soviet youth.

The truth of acquired facts is the basis of all historical research. Only the accumulation of facts, the knowledge of concrete historical phenomena and events can serve the historian or archaeologist as a basis for scientific generalizations, for determining the particular or general regularity in the history of peoples.

## WORK IN THE STUDY

When the archaeologist works over his material in the laboratory he comes into contact with a whole group of sciences that help him to solve this or that problem. In completing his final work on the results he has again to rely on allied sciences. Such sciences are anthropology, ethnography, geology, palaeozoology, palaeobotany, linguistics, and history. With geology, the science dealing with the strata of the earth's crust, archaeology has close 'historical' links, for before archaeology had won itself an independent position it was regarded as a part of the natural sciences, part of geology in fact. Once freed from this status the links with geology have not been broken but strengthened. Firstly geological changes affecting substantial areas of ground are the best basis for chronology in the early phases of human history. Secondly the geological conditions in which objects of the past are found shed light on this past and allow it to be more fully understood. When archaeologists accumulated reliable knowledge about dating they were able to render a service to geology. So for example the dating of quaternary (last geological period) deposits rests on various data, some of them archaeological.

Since archaeologists began to collect objects found in excavations beyond those that have value only as museum exhibits, a great mass of bones of wild and domestic animals have appeared in collections. The study of these throws light on conditions of environment, the species hunted, development of stock-breeding, history of certain species, domestication, and changes in breeds.

The study of pollen, seeds and fruit, grain, and sometimes even flowers and leaves gives information not only about the environment but also about the history of cultivated plants as well as invaluable details for the history of agriculture. From grain or even from seeds of weeds that accompany agriculture there is a chance of determining the level of development of agriculture at various periods and even the system used, casual cropping, temporary cropping for a few seasons (slash and burn), settled subsistence farming, the three-field system, and so on.

The palaeozoologist and palaeobotanist thus have received basic material from the archaeologist for certain branches of their study, and this has formed a close bond between them. If the archaeologist gives these sciences source materials he receives in return information about the background conditions and results of man's activities as the context of the economic life of primitive society.

The establishment of the relation between social phenomena of the past and geographical factors is of great importance. Society develops not by laws of nature but by its own social laws. Consequently the geographical environment influences the development and form of society not directly but on the basis and through the system of its social forms of production. The geographical environment cannot decide and direct the development of a society, but the peculiarities of environment can slow down or speed up a society's development. This has constantly to be borne in mind. So it is very important to link the map of antiquities with the historical landscape in order to reconstruct the historical geography of the period that is being dealt with.

It is pertinent to observe that archaeological cartography is not only a graphic illustration to the text but above all a method of scientific research. Archaeological cartography is a graphic method of study and depiction of the historical process in space according to the archaeological evidence.

The creation of various archaeological maps and research with their help into the various problems of ancient history constitutes an important part of the work of archaeologists.

Palaeoanthropology is concerned with the remains of ancient man, with the physical types of past epochs, and the changes undergone due to the influence of certain social and natural conditions. Anthropology unrolls before us the long road covered by man in his development from ape-man to the modern rational man and allows us to assess the part played in this process by work, that is his influence and control over nature which has allowed man to change his own nature. Primeval history and archaeology would indeed be meaningless without the collaboration of anthropology.

With archaeology is closely connected ethnography, by which Soviet scientists mean that branch of historical science dealing with ethnic (racial) or national peculiarities of culture and life of a contemporary people in their historical development. When archaeologists study societies in a precapitalist condition they set themselves a broader task than the mere study of culture and consider their economy, techniques, and history, that is, all sides of their social life and existence.

Historical development of mankind in various parts of the world did not proceed at a uniform rate. When capitalism prevailed in Europe, many tribes in parts of Asia, Africa, Australia, and America were living in the primitive social stage. Ethnographic accounts of these tribes and of other precapitalist features which have survived into the life of contemporary peoples can offer a fuller understanding of various stages of social development in the past. For example, acquaintance with the manner of living of backward tribes using objects similar to those found on archaeological sites could explain the use and purpose of the latter. Knowledge of marriage ceremonies and other rites, of traditions in clothing, and of ornaments among contemporary peoples helps to explain many of the features of primitive ideology.

Changes take place in a people's life during the course of time but much survives from the old order of things. These ancient survivals constitute 'inexhaustible mines of historical knowledge', in the phrase of an ethnologist.

Important historical information can be extracted from local traditions preserved orally (folklore) and place names, whose study is a branch of philology that deals with the history of names of settlements, towns, rivers, lakes, and so on. As the archaeological material is often not adequate even for an understanding of the material culture and techniques of primitive peoples, it is even more necessary to make full use of comparative ethnographic material in order to understand their social life, art, and ideology.

In settling problems of the origin of different peoples ('ethnogeny') historians, archaeologists, ethnographers, and linguists must cooperate with each other.

One of the most important features of a people, clearly different from other features, is the language they speak. When we compare a linguistic with a cultural map of a certain period, then we are on the way to raising the question of who the respective peoples were that had a particular culture. But archaeology and philology are connected not only when problems of ethnogeny are being studied, for language preserves traces of its past. The change of meaning in words records their remote original meaning. Thus the contemporary word to 'shoot' (*strelyat*) derives from the 'arrow' (*strela*), that is it retains the meaning from a period when archers really shot arrows from bows. The history of words is closely connected with the history of things and their names.

Comparative philology by itself is powerless to give us even roughly trustworthy information about ancient culture. Linguistics can be of service to the history of culture only in close collaboration with archaeology. Attempts to link the history of words with the history of things, that is the history of language with the history of material culture, can be a valuable scientific procedure, for language is directly connected with the productive activity of man. If the philologist can help the archaeologist the assistance is repaid, for archaeologists and historians in their turn help the philologist to study the development of language in its connexions with the history of the people.

It must be remembered – as already mentioned above – that archaeologists discover not only 'ordinary' material things but also written sources, sources for the study not only of history but of language and literature.

It is not necessary to speak about the connexions of archaeo-

logy with history and the history of culture, for every archaeologist is at the same time a historian or historian of culture.
Knowledge of written sources is indispensable for the work of
an archaeologist, for he works in archives and libraries as much
as he does in his laboratory.

The final stage of the archaeologist's work takes place in the
study when, his material arranged, he writes his scientific report.
We saw the great variety of knowledge (arising from the close
interrelationship of contemporary sciences) that it was necessary to apply to even the smallest simple object, but the final
task of the archaeologist is a historical task and this above all
necessitates a knowledge of the true laws of the development of
society, that is historical materialism.

## RUSSIAN ARCHAEOLOGY UP TO 1917

Although still young, archaeological science already has its own
history. Soviet archaeology was not created on an empty site.
Significant achievements had already been made, a scientific
tradition of Russian archaeology already formed. . . .

If we are going to speak of archaeology as a science then it
follows that we must distinguish this from information provided by incidental excavation. Excavations not conducted by
archaeologists sometimes yield archaeological material and yet
cannot be called scientific research. For example, sixteenth-
century documents record curious facts about the resort to field
archaeology arising from everyday needs. In disputes about
ownership of real estate it was imperative to show traces of
manorial buildings. So in 1529 a special type of 'archaeological
expedition' set out to seek remains of stoves from the house or
barn as the result of litigation about ownership of some land.
The excavations of these judicial officials, although they show
that in sixteenth-century Russia it was known that the ground
contained remains of past life, are only a curiosity and have no
reference to science.

However, at this period one may already speak of the birth of
definite archaeological interests in Russia. This expressed itself
in the choice of material for the collection of the Moscow
Chamber of Weapons founded early in the sixteenth century.

c

Material remains, especially weapons and objects of decorative art, were systematically assembled here.

Peter the Great, the founder of a museum, in his *ukases* (legislative decrees) about the collection of rare things paid special attention to weapons, vessels and so on turned up in excavations. 'Whoever finds in the ground or under water any ancient objects, that is, unusual stones, human, animal, fish, or bird bones not as today but either exceptionally large or small, as well as inscriptions on stone, iron, or copper, or any unusual gun, weapon, and all other things old or unusual; they should be brought ... (to me)' (*Ukas*, 13 February 1718).

The eminent Russian historian V. N. Tatishchev in 1739 published his instructions for archaeological excavations, which are among the earliest extant. M. V. Lomonosov took an especial interest in archaeology. He not only used archaeological material in his historical works (above all in his *Ancient Russian History*) but with characteristic breadth of vision raised the question of the organization of planned archaeological researches on ancient towns in various districts of Russia. For this he had to create the first archaeological maps, on which were plotted ancient fortified sites, barrows, and other antiquities. At Lomonosov's suggestion the Academy of Sciences sent out questionnaires dealing with a series of points about archaeological matters. In 1763 more than 4,000 answers were received. ...

In the second half of the eighteenth century when the north coastal area of the Black Sea, an area rich in antiquities, was absorbed into the Russian state, a new interest in the ancient past developed in Russia. In 1763 the first large-scale excavations of a Scythian barrow took place. At the end of the eighteenth century excavation of the ancient Greek cities began.

At the beginning of the nineteenth century, apart from the Weapon Chamber, Kunstkammer (a German name given to the museum founded by Peter the Great in the first quarter of the eighteenth century), and the Hermitage (founded at the end of the eighteenth century), a series of local museums arose at Nikolaev in 1806, Theodosia in 1811, Odessa in 1825, Kerch in 1826, and others [mostly in the Black Sea area. T.]. Following the creation in Moscow University of the Society of Russian History and Antiquities local archaeological societies were formed in Odessa, St Petersburg, and the Baltic area. Archaeological work had wide scope. Ancient monuments became the subject of scientific descriptions and excavations, while care was taken in conservation and restoration.

In the 1830s systematic researches began on the ancient towns of the Crimean Bosporus (at the entry to the Sea of Azov north of the Black Sea). Excavations on barrows yielded important types of jewellery, and the most important nineteenth-century archaeologists made their appearance. One of the first of these was the President of the Academy of Arts, A. N. Olenin, who wrote many works showing accurate and scientific method, especially the monumental *Antiquities of the Russian State* (Moscow, 1849–53), produced under his direction.

In 1859 the time was ripe for the foundation of a governmental body controlling archaeology, and in that year was founded (within the Ministry of the Court) the Archaeological Commission, which was made responsible for excavation and research into antiquity. The Commission bore the imprint on its activity of its place in the Ministry of the Court, and a number of its regulations show the lack of scientific interests in the limited scope assigned to it. It was not concerned with the scientific value of the various finds but in what measure 'its acquisitions (from Chersonesus) will adorn the Hermitage of His Imperial Majesty'. (The Minister of the Court did however give instructions for the application of the methodical rules of archaeology.)

This approach to antiquity to some extent influenced the direction of work undertaken in pre-Revolutionary times, so that as the more impressive artistic objects were recovered from the graves and ancient cities, so those sites were excavated more than others. Prehistoric archaeology was neglected, and the excavation of settlements (which requires considerable expenditure) was not carried out. The most important aim of the Commission was not scientific observation, but the accumulation of objects. These were collected in vast quantities and published by the Commission which issued forty-six volumes of richly illustrated annual reports (*Otchety*), thirty-seven volumes of *Materials for the Archaeology of Russia*, sixty-six volumes of *News of the Archaeological Commission*, and so on.

Besides professional archaeologists a great number of local antiquaries – or lovers of old things – made investigations which in spite of the dilettante nature of the work produced important discoveries.

Various archaeological societies and district archive commissions played an important part in the archaeology of that period. Museums arose in several provincial capitals in which the societies had branches. In 1873 the Historical Museum was founded in Moscow in which collections of very broad scope were housed. The Russian Archaeological Society (in St Petersburg) had three sections: (a) Russian and Slav; (b) classical, Byzantine, and west European; (c) eastern. It issued a mass of publications: *Studies*, *Notes*, *News* (more than 110 large volumes). The activities of the Moscow Archaeological Society which was founded in 1867 were especially fruitful. As much as for numerous excavations and publications, this society was responsible for the initiative of holding the periodic all-Russian archaeological congresses. There were fifteen such sessions between 1869 and 1911.

This widening of activity in the field of archaeology in Russia led to impressive discoveries. Scholars emerged with a high scientific ability, and earned an outstanding place in Russian and world scholarship.

One of the founders of Russian archaeology was Count A. S. Uvarov (1828–84), who dedicated the whole of his life to its study. He was the founder of the Moscow Archaeological Society and one of the organizers of the Russian Archaeological Society, and undertook numerous excavations of various sites. Besides his undoubted services to science proper he incurred unhappy fame on account of his confused, unscientific excavations of 7,729 barrows in the Vladimir-Suzdal district (about 150 km. east of Moscow).

A remarkable self-taught Russian archaeologist was I. E. Zabolin (1820–1908) one of the founders of the Moscow Historical Museum, who used the collections of the Chamber of Weapons for a descriptive history of life in Muscovite Russia. He carried out excavations of large barrows and worked out a scientific method for their excavation. He was one of the first to denounce the prevailing opinion of that time that attributed Russian culture and art to influences from her eastern and western neighbours. . . . *

In 1888 V. A. Gorodtsov (1860–1945), the distinguished Russian and Soviet archaeologist, began work. He was one of the first Russian archaeologists to recognize the importance of archaeological sites as historical sources and to give first place to tools and their technique of production. He worked out methods of investigating houses of various cultures and periods, proved the existence of a Bronze Age in eastern Europe, and systematized the material from this period. As the result of prolonged and fruitful excavations and researches Gorodtsov produced a series of general works on the archaeology of Russia beginning with the palaeolithic and ending with the medieval period.

Other famous Tsarist archaeologists could be enumerated, but sufficient have been mentioned† to show that the successes of Soviet archaeology had been prepared for by the development of pre-Soviet archaeology through the activities of a whole constellation of remarkable Russian workers.

But advances in archaeology in Tsarist Russia were limited, in spite of the wealth, variety, and exceptional scientific significance of the surviving material remains and of gifted people devoted to science. For this the attitude towards science of the ruling classes was responsible. The 'object-seeking' motives prevailing in the official centre of archaeology, the Imperial Archaeological Commission have been mentioned above. . . . The most numerous archaeological researches were the private affair of a narrow circle of amateurs not making proper use of the state support they received, and all their activities bore the mark of amateurism and dilettantism, obscuring the achievements of the leading scholars. . . . No small obstacle was the law of private property on land. Remains of antiquity hidden below ground in pre-Revolutionary law were regarded as treasure: 'Treasure (concealed in the ground) belongs to the owner of the ground and without his permission neither private individuals

* Several paragraphs dealing with Tsarist archaeologists are omitted. T.
† See note above. T.

nor local authorities may search for it. . . .' (*Collection of Laws of the Russian Empire*, vol. x, 430.) The treasure-seeking of the more powerful landlords and lords of the manor, the rapacious looting of antiquities and trading in them, all this was a continuous obstacle to the advancement of science.

Russian scholars, however, were very conscious of their grave responsibility. Fifty years ago N. I. Veselovsky wrote:

The Russian state exercises control over important centres of ancient human culture. In Russia may be found antiquities of almost all periods and almost all peoples, from the primitive tools of the Stone Age to objects of unsurpassed elegance and technique of the classical world, from ancient cuneiform tablets of the Assyrian Empire to the rude scrawls on the rocks in Siberia. . . . On us lies the moral obligation to posterity and science to dispose correctly for general use the inheritance that we have acquired. It is to be expected that when favourable conditions arise Russian archaeology will occupy a pre-eminent position in the study of antiquity.

Such favourable conditions for the advancement of science were created by Soviet control.

## BIRTH AND DEVELOPMENT OF SOVIET ARCHAEOLOGY

The victory of the Great October Socialist Revolution opened a new era in world history. Soviet control created an unprecedented material basis for a great flowering of science. In the course of the great reconstruction of social relations, the interest of the masses in history grew. As early as 1919, during the conflict of civil war when the young Soviet state was maintaining a relentless struggle with its enemies, Lenin signed a decree creating the Russian (later State) Academy for the History of Material Culture (RAIMK, GAIMK). In 1937 this was absorbed into the body of the Academy of Sciences and transformed into the Institute for the History of Material Culture. . . .

Where formerly a variety of movements, conquests, and the influences of one tribe upon another tribe were recognized as the moving forces in archaeology, now such events were accorded their real place in relation to the basis of progress –

the development of a society's productive forces, with which is connected the change in form of the objects of material culture. Historical materialism, while it recognizes that in the last analysis economic conditions produce historical change, does not reduce all social life simply to this. It envisages two sides to life, the material and the idealistic or spiritual. The growth of the spiritual side of social life is governed by the conditions of the material life of the society, but itself has an inverted effect on these conditions. . . .

Not only methods but even the selection of objectives for research were changed, among which first place was taken by ancient inhabited settlements. These give a much fuller picture of life than graves. Excavations, formerly casual affairs undertaken by private individuals, now have been given a planned, purposeful character. The state supplies large resources for archaeological investigations, and for the first time in history these have been included in state plans together with important measures dealing with the people's economy. Planning of excavations was first undertaken within the learned foundations but a five-year plan for museum work in the RSFSR was brought to nothing by the war. In 1945 in an all-Union archaeological conference a five-year plan was drawn up for research and fieldwork on an all-Union scale. In subsequent five-year plans the planning of archaeological work has been organized in the academies of science of the republic centrally coordinated through the Academy of Sciences of the USSR.

Especially noteworthy is the enormous amount of work undertaken by archaeologists on sites of new construction projects. They investigate archaeological remains over huge areas where towns are to be developed, canals built, and hydroelectric and other schemes carried out. The impetuous advance of socialist construction in recent years is thus reflected in the volume of archaeological work carried out.

Thanks to the rapid advance of archaeology in our country specialization has become very strong, and various branches of the science have developed that formerly hardly existed [as has been the case in the West as well. T.]. Thus in Soviet times the Neolithic and Bronze Ages have developed as special divisions of archaeology. There has been great progress of archaeology in

higher education.* In Soviet universities and pedagogical institutes archaeological disciplines have become an organic part of
the syllabus of the historical faculties. A wide network of scientific research centres of archaeology is being developed: in the
academies of Science of the republics of the Union, special
archaeological institutes have arisen, while in the branches of
the Academy of Sciences of the Soviet Union and in the historical institutes in the majority of national *oblasts* (districts)
archaeological work is included in the plans. The growing network of museums plays an important part in the successes of
Soviet archaeology, for they not only preserve material sources
of history but also are centres of research work in the remotest
corners of our vast country (more than 500 museums in all
oblasts and republics have archaeological departments). Soviet
archaeological publications cover a wide range. . . .

The successes of Soviet archaeology were achieved as a result
of great and strenuous effort. The struggle against reactionary
traditions for the creation of Soviet archaeology demanded the
transformation of all scientific work. Individuals lacking science
and hostile to our social system tried to use this transformation
as a means of liquidating archaeology as a science. . . . Concrete
historical research was replaced by abstract sociological pro-
grammes divorced from factual material. This theorizing without reference to the facts is characteristic of the 'school of
Pokrovsky' in history, and in archaeology was carried on by
N. Y. Marr and his disciples. Such works were especially numerous in 1930–4. . . .

N. Y. Marr, the creator of the erroneous, non-Marxist 'new
science of language', directed GAIMK until 1934. . . . His
disciples, instead of drawing concrete, objective historical conclusions from archaeological material, spurned the data of material sources in favour of preconceived schemes. Works appeared
in which it was affirmed that at a certain stage of historical
development, in a flash and by a wonderful process of trans-

* The teaching of archaeologists is undertaken in archaeological departments or under a professor in the historical faculty in the Universities of
Moscow, Leningrad, Kiev, Tashkent, Tiflis, Baku, Erevan, Kazan, Saratov,
Perm, Sverdlovsk, Odessa, Kharkhov, Samarkand, and Tartu. In most
pre-Revolutionary universities archaeology was not taught. Since 1954 a
course of archaeology has been studied in the pedagogical institutes.

formation, one people would be converted into another: Cimmerians into Scythians, Scythians into Sarmatians. Sarmatians into Goths, and so on. Pretending to be struggling for the unity of the historical process, they insisted on disregarding concrete research in local ethnic peculiarities. The historical process was deprived of its colour and oversimplified. . . .

Vulgar sociology inevitably leads to the selection from the whole sum of data only those facts which fit into a preselected scheme; it leads unavoidably to the loss of the Marxist principle that history must not be improved or made worse but only the truth may be written. Although the majority of Soviet archaeologists were not Marr's disciples, yet his 'theory' did significant harm to the advance of science. . . .

Soviet archaeologists carry out their research in relation to the facts of world science. In the nineteenth century, the archaeology of western Europe achieved great successes. Progressive bourgeois scholars established the basic stages of primeval culture, and the vast quantities of material of all periods accumulated in museums and private collections were successfully classified and a sound chronology established. Great scholars appeared who laid the basis of the scientific approach to archaeological material and worked out methods of research. For instance, an important stage in the analysis of archaeological material was the geological approach. The Frenchman, G. Mortillet, established periods and epochs relating the history of humanity to periods of earth history. His classification of primeval antiquities was based on the theory of evolution.

With the change from assembling collections to the science of archaeology, based in significant measure on the study of things, it was important to systematize and date these objects, and in this a great part was played by the formal typological method, worked out by the Swedish archaeologist O. Montelius and his disciples. The nineteenth-century Evolutionary school in ethnography and archaeology by comparing the cultures of different peoples came near to understanding the unity of the laws of development of society. . . . In this century English archaeologists (Crawford, Fox, and others) have had considerable success in the application of the geographical method in archaeology. Recently several interesting pieces of research concerned with the social life and economy of ancient societies recon-structed on archaeological evidence have been carried out (by Childe, Clark, and others). . . . Does the opposition of Soviet and bourgeois archaeology mean that we would claim all in bourgeois scholarship is bad and all with us good? Naturally not. In bourgeois countries there have been significant suc-cesses, and with us as well as successes there have been deficien-cies, about which we shall speak in the relevant chapters. Soviet archaeologists try to have intercourse with progressive foreign scholars and are prepared to use everything important and interesting that bourgeois scholarship reveals.

We see many shortcomings in our science, and even in this book whose aim is to show the achievements of Soviet archaeo-logy we will not conceal these deficiencies but will speak about them frankly. When, however, we speak of the superiority of Soviet archaeology, we have in mind not separate achievements or successes (of which there are not a few among workers in bour-geois countries) but that real superiority of which we are pro-foundly convinced: the superiority of method of our work, based on Marxist philosophy, which ensures the most objective uncovering of the historical past.

Creatively mastering the great science of Marxism–Leninism, expanding and defining the methods of research, Soviet archaeologists will strive to reach that level of attainment in historical science at which 'the science of the history of society (in spite of the complexity of the phenomena of social life) can be just as exact a science as say biology, and provide laws of development of society for practical application' (*History of Communist Party, Short Course*, p. 109).

## Chapter 2

# THE MOST ANCIENT PAST,
# THE PALAEOLITHIC AND MESOLITHIC
# PERIODS

ONE of the most marked indications of the progressive speeding up of the tempo of economic life can be seen in the history of primeval society. In the beginning human culture developed very slowly. The Stone Age, that is, the period when man used stone tools, lasted hundreds of thousands of years, while the period since metals have been used has lasted only 5,000–7,000 years. The Stone Age itself is divided into two unequal parts: the Old Stone Age (Palaeolithic, from the Greek *palaeos*, old, and *lithos*, stone) and the New Stone Age (Neolithic). The Palaeolithic Period lasted several dozen times as long as the Neolithic. This very long archaeological period has been adequately studied in our homeland only in Soviet times.

In 1871 the Danish archaeologist Worsaae said in a lecture at the Royal Society of Northern Antiquaries at Copenhagen that almost the whole territory of Russia was uninhabitable during the Old Stone Age. In fact at that time no sites of that period were known in Russia. Worsaae's words had not yet appeared in print when the first palaeolithic site in Russia (Gontsovskaya) was discovered. In 1871 another palaeolithic site came to light on the site of the military hospital in the Irkutsk area. Further discoveries followed later. As only twelve palaeolithic sites were found in Russia in pre-Revolutionary times foreign scholars continued to maintain that Russia was at the extreme edge of the development of ancient culture and was in general occupied comparatively late.

This view has been proved quite wrong. Owing especially to the broad scope and rapid tempo of the excavation programme, a large number of palaeolithic discoveries have been made. In 1938 already 304 finds were registered, in 1953 there were 800. (Excluding casual finds the figures for actual sites were about 200 in 1941, and in 1953 more than 60 lower palaeolithic and over 300 upper palaeolithic sites were known (Fig. 4).)

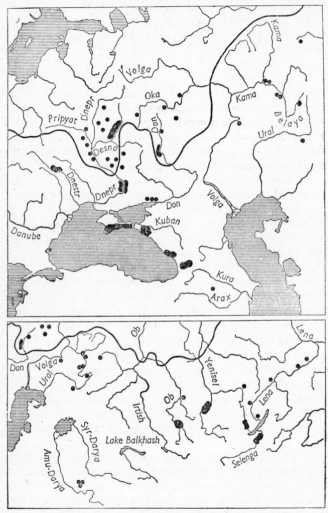

4. Distribution of palaeolithic remains in the U S S R.

*The black line shows the extreme southern limit of the icesheet*

Many areas that were white on the distribution map have been studied more or less thoroughly. Not only in the Ukraine, Crimea, and Caucasus, but also in the mountains of south Uzbekistan, central Asia, the rigorous *taiga* by the River Lena, in the Urals and Moldavia, on the great Russian river Volga, sites have been discovered, frequently of first-rate importance. Some of them have been subjected to detailed research. It has been established that in many parts of our country primitive human society passed through its initial stages of development. Moreover, at present it may be assumed that Transcaucasia lay within that broad zone where men first appeared. The grounds for this statement are the results of work undertaken by anthropologists and archaeologists in recent years.

The geological subdivision of the history of the earth is based on the evidence of palaeontology. The Cainozoic Period (the period of mammals) is divided into two unequal parts: the Tertiary (about 70 million years) and the Quaternary or Pleistocene (about one million years). In the Quaternary Period man first appears; the predecessors of man, man-like apes, turned into ape-men. In the process of transformation of ape to man a decisive role was played by work, for, in the words of Engels, 'work created man proper', so that the division between ape and man is defined by the use of tools for work. Thus where the archaeologist finds tools, even the most primitive, he can speak about the activity of man. Apes use sticks and stones found in nature in their quest for food but they do not make tools. 'No ape's hands have ever made even the most crude stone knife' (Engels, *The Role of Work in the Process of Transformation of Ape to Man*).

## THE LOWER PALAEOLITHIC PERIOD

### Early Man in Transcaucasia

Palaeontological, archaeological, as well as geological evidence allow the supposition that Transcaucasia (that is the area south of the Caucasus range proper) was one of the areas where the transformation of ape to man could have taken place. In 1939 in eastern Georgia, at a place called Udabno, remains of apes with human features were discovered. These apes had lived at the end of the Tertiary Period and are called scientifically from the place of discovery *Udabnopithecus*. . . .

In 1946–8 on the hill of Satani-Dar (about 150 km. southwest of Tiflis) situated near Mt Bogutlu in Armenia, rough obsidian tools of the oldest type came to light, belonging to the Chellean Period. These are the oldest tools so far found in the USSR. This is a firm link in the chain of evidence supporting the view that the southern areas of the USSR lay in the area where the complete emergence of man from animal existence took place. [Chellean or Abbevillian, Acheulian and Mousterian are the most important divisions of the Lower Palaeolithic Period according to the types of tool in use. The tools from Satani-Dar are regarded as early Acheulian by some Western archaeologists, many of whom would not entirely agree with the author's observations. T.]

The oldest late Chellean tools in Satani-Dar are rough, large, almond-shaped hand-axes [the characteristic tool of the earliest Palaeolithic Period. T.]; thick flakes, lightly chipped around the edge and at the end; lumps of obsidian shaped into rough chopping tools (Fig. 5). With the help of these tools the most ancient inhabitants of Armenia made wooden clubs and sticks and worked on the products of hunting and plant collection. 'By these means people first separated themselves from the animal kingdom (in the narrower sense of the word) and entered into history. Still half-animal, still savage and helpless before the forces of nature, they did not realize their own ability for they were poor like animals and not much above them in productivity' (Engels). Progress was so slow that thousands of years passed before people could even make such primitive tools as those from Satani-Dar. An extraordinarily low level of the productive forces is characteristic of human society on the threshold of history.

In 1946–7 a site with tools of a very archaic type was found at Luka-Vrublevetskaya on the left bank of the Dnestr (about 300 km. north-west of Odessa). The classification of these tools as Chellean is uncertain, for it depends merely on the appearance of the tools. The fact is that archaeologists generally do not find Chellean tools in an undisturbed site but only as loose objects. This is because the layer of earth in which Chellean

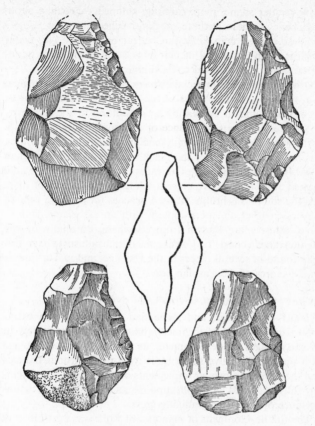

5. Satani-Dar. Obsidian axes.

tools were incorporated has been washed away by water, disturbed by movements of the earth's crust and other causes in the course of the hundreds of thousands of years that have elapsed since they were first discarded.

In Satani-Dar not only Chellean tools but also Acheulian tools of a later period were found. These bear witness to the long occupation of Armenia in the course of the Old Stone Age. Tools of the Acheulian Period were better finished, of more regular shape, more carefully chipped. Acheulian hand-axes have a more definite working edge than was usually achieved in the rough work on Chellean hand-axes. This better finish is often unnoticed at first glance and even seems unimportant, yet it demanded considerable labour and time.

Other lower palaeolithic sites have been found in Armenia, and on the Black Sea coast of the Caucasus. Here dozens of sites were found in 1934–6 by an expedition of the Academy of Sciences. The best studied site was Yashtukh (about 350 km. north-west of Tiflis). During Acheulian times when this area was occupied the level of the Black Sea was 60 m. higher than now. In Quaternary times terraces or raised beaches were formed 30–100 m. above present sea level and on one of these was the site of Yashtukh. [Raised beaches formed at a time of higher sea level and occasionally with an associated palaeolithic industry are known from elsewhere, especially by the Mediterranean coast. T.] Lower palaeolithic industries have also been found in several places in the Ukraine, and in Turkmenia on the shores of the Caspian Sea.

## Development of Man in Chellean and Acheulian Times

Tools of Chellean and Acheulian times show the extraordinarily low level of technical ability of primitive society in its early stages of development, its weakness in the struggle with nature. Primitive stone tools were used without handles and there were no proper implements of bone. Man was originally fully occupied with collecting plants and hunting. The importance of the latter gradually grew.

The full development of man and of work was possible only in collective, communal conditions. The early human community [Kollektiv in Soviet terminology. T.] is generally called 'the primitive human herd' in [Soviet] scientific literature. The low level of cultural development meant that in the first periods of history man could exist only in countries with a moderately warm climate.

There followed, however, the last glaciations. The climate became sharply colder: ice sheets and glaciers covered many millions of square kilometres and thrust forward even as far as the middle Dnepr and Don. Warmth-loving animals became extinct or migrated to the south. It seemed that man, too, must perish, for he was still ill-equipped in the struggle with nature. Man, however, did not perish but on the contrary transferred his activity to grappling with nature; he changed the whole form of his life, his techniques and his culture. He combined into great collective bands which were able to resist the formidable forces of nature encircling him.

So that they should not perish in conditions of extreme cold, people had to have fire, clothing, and dwellings. Already in earlier times man had learnt to use fire occurring naturally to warm himself; now he began to make it artificially. At all events in late Acheulian sites traces of fire are encountered everywhere. Man made primitive clothing out of skins, and perfected techniques for making tools. Not only did he not withdraw but he actually settled over a wider area than before, passing far beyond the limits of his primeval homeland.

This period of great movements in the history of humanity corresponds to the Mousterian Period in archaeological terminology, which lasted from 100,000 to 40,000 B.C. In the Soviet Union there are far more sites of this period than of the more ancient ones. The mousterian caves of the Crimea are widely known.

## The Crimea

The most remarkable site of the Palaeolithic Period in the Crimea is the cave of Kiik-Koba which has universal importance. It lies 25 km. to the east of Simferopol, and was discovered in 1924. It opens southwards and is formed by a shallow rock overhang warmed beneath by the sun's rays; there is a spring close by. A cave in such a situation attracted the attention of lower palaeolithic people. It was originally occupied at the end of Acheulian times, and the lower layer from that period contained charcoal, split bones, and flints. The bones belonged to wolf, giant deer, saiga antelope, wild horse, wild ass, and hare. The flint tools were irregular, roughly chipped along the edge, or sharp flakes, suitable for cutting. After the disappearance of the Acheulians the cave remained unoccupied for a long time, but was reoccupied in mousterian times. By this time there had been significant progress in the hunting economy. In the upper layer belonging to this period the majority of the bones belonged to mammoth, woolly rhinoceros, aurochs, wild horse, giant and red deer, cave hyena, and other animals. [The cold-loving animals, mammoth and woolly rhinoceros, indicate colder conditions. T.]

People had learnt to hunt not only small but also large and powerful animals. For this evidently large-scale beating of cover was used so that the exhausted animals could be driven into some natural trap such as a bog, or over a cliff.

The flint tools found in the lower layer of Kiik-Koba were rough, primitive, and very varied. Humanity had not yet worked out the best shapes adapted to the work. In the upper layer quite definite forms and types predominate. Bone points were also present and used for fine flaking of flint and simple working of bone. Flint tools were made by a new method of flint-working, by the removal of a flake from a disc-shaped core, which gave a thin sharp cutting edge to the finished tool. The working edge of the flake was retouched, that is, defined by a row of fine scars left by the removal of chips to make the edge sharper.

In Kiik-Koba burials in grave trenches of an adult and a child were found. Although the adult's grave had been badly damaged (only a small part of the bone was preserved) it yielded valuable material for the study of the physical structure of man of the Old Stone Age.

*Neanderthal Man in Uzbekistan*

At the end of the Acheulian and in the Mousterian Periods essential changes took place in the physical structure of man. The most ancient ape-man (Pithecanthropus, whose bones have been found in Java and China) gradually changed into a type of man whose physical structure was closer to that of contemporary people. The mousterian people of short stature (155–6 cm.), thick-set build, slightly stooping and clumsy in gait, have been called Neanderthalers (from the site of the well-known find at Neanderthal, near Düsseldorf in Germany). They had large heads of elongated form with low receding forehead and projecting eyebrow ridge, set on a thick short neck which was so constructed that it seemed to form one piece with the nape.

Neanderthalers had a wide nose, and a chin that receded like an ape's and did not project as does contemporary man's. The excavator studied in detail the hand of the Neanderthaler from Kiik-Koba. It was very powerful, rough, and clumsy with wide stumpy fingers. The muscle formations indicate strength of grasping and hitting, but not the flexibility or mobility of a modern hand. The Neanderthaler could not master finer work demanding skill and dexterity.

A second interesting find of fossil man was the discovery at Teshik-Tash (about 150 km. south of Samarkand) of the grave of a Neanderthal boy of 8–9 years. Teshik-Tash is a deep cave 20 m. broad and 21 m. deep which was occupied for a fairly long period. Five times people came to the cave on a prolonged visit and then left the shelter of its roof, each time leaving there remains of ashes, bones, and traces of the manufacture and use of stone tools.

The basis of life of the cave inhabitants was the hunting of mountain goats (most of the bones found in the cave belonged to this animal). Besides this, the bones of wild boar, horse, deer, leopard, and birds were found. All the stone tools were made of siliceous limestone. The working waste from making stone tools, and bones used as 'fabricators' for stone tools, were found.

Animal bones, working waste, and stone tools were scattered thickly in places around the hearths. Fires gave light and warmth and so played a central part in domestic life in caves. The occupation at Teshik-Tash was especially closely connected with them. Here the game taken in hunting was cooked and eaten; rough clothing was prepared from skin, and tools and weapons made from stone and wood. The body of the boy whose bones were found at Teshik-Tash was buried deliberately, as the circumstances of the find make clear. Around the human bones in the boy's grave lay several pairs of large goats' horns (in the opinion of some workers these represented some detail or other of the funeral rite, while others think that no such rite yet existed). . . .

Care for the corpses of the departed is the result of the formation of new, clearly human, mental characteristics. It is doubtful whether at that time burials were already connected with religious beliefs about the soul and the world beyond the grave.

Perhaps they covered the body because they were afraid of it or wished to protect it from wild beasts, but at all events they did it with some care, and to this care we owe the finding of a skeleton of a primitive boy from the cave Teshik-Tash. The skull and other bones of the boy were well preserved, at least well preserved in an archaeological sense since the pieces were capable of restoration. The skull was massive with a low crown, sloping forehead, no chin, and large teeth. M. M. Gerasimov made a portrait reconstruction from the restored skull, which shows the physical appearance of the Neanderthal boy from Teshik-Tash (Pl. 2).

The excavation at Teshik-Tash has considerable scientific significance. In the first place it increases the small list of reliable material of fossil man which contemporary science possesses. In the second place this is the first palaeolithic site in central Asia excavated over a large area with due attention to stratigraphy, as a result of which it has been possible to reconstruct the type of economy, form of life, and even the broad outlines of ideology of mousterian times. The cave's position in central Asia is important, for hitherto there had been no finds of Neanderthal man or his culture in this region.

One of the most complicated problems connected with the origin of man is the relationship of contemporary man to fossil Neanderthal man. Were Neanderthalers direct predecessors of contemporary man? Anthropologists consider that in the process of transformation from ape to man humanity passed through distinct phases preceding the appearance of contemporary man. To the last of these phases the Neanderthalers may be referred. Some foreign anthropologists hold the view that contemporary man is more ancient than and unconnected with Neanderthal man. . . . The finding of bones of Neanderthalers in many parts of Europe, Asia, and Africa shows that they were not a local group occupying only Europe in the Lower Palaeolithic Period, but were widespread over a significant part of the Old World. [A widely-held view in the West is that some Neanderthalers, such as those in France, were too specialized to have evolved into modern man but that some less specialized groups especially in the Middle East did evolve to become contemporary man. T.]

Teshik-Tash is a site of special importance, but it is not the only palaeolithic site in Uzbekistan. Other caves with cultural deposits were found close by. Another new discovery of outstanding importance was made in 1953 in the cave of Starosele (in the Crimea). The grave of a child aged 1–2 years came to light in a mousterian deposit. In close proximity to the corpse a little stone hand-axe, a point, and scrapers were found, together with bones of wild ass, ox, and bear. Study of the skeleton by anthropologists established that it had belonged to a man of modern type, but with a number of features that are closer to Neanderthal man; powerful teeth, thickening of the malar projection of the frontal bone, and so on. The skeleton from Starosele is one of a number of finds of remains of similar representatives of ancient man who occupy an intermediate position between Neanderthal and modern man.

## Other Mousterian Sites

Among numerous mousterian sites on the Black Sea coast of the Caucasus especial interest attaches to the caves of Akhshtyrskaya and Navalishinskaya excavated in 1936–8. The former cave is on a river that flows into the Black Sea. It was occupied by many different peoples over an exceptionally long time from the Lower Palaeolithic to the Middle Ages (with interruptions of course). The basic game the inhabitants hunted was cave bear in the mountains. Hunting this large and powerful beast (the cave bear was bigger than the brown bear of today) was hazardous and difficult. The second cave was not continuously occupied, but was used as a dwelling during periods of seasonal hunting of the cave bear.

An extremely important discovery of the last few years is that of the mousterian sites on the river Volga. While studying the geological conditions and fossil material of the Volga region scientists concluded that palaeolithic man would have enjoyed favourable conditions there. Systematic search was made, especially during the expedition in 1951–2, and was crowned with success, for palaeolithic sites came to light on the banks of the river. Lower palaeolithic remains were found at Krasnaya Glinka (about 200 km. north-west of Kuibyshev). A mousterian settlement has been found at Stalingrad, remarkable not only for the surprising state of preservation of the cultural deposit but also because of the unique geological conditions, for it had been covered over by a thick deposit laid down in a transgression of the Caspian Sea. (When the sea intrudes on to an area of dry land this is known as a transgression. In this case the level of the Caspian was 50 m. higher than previously, and as the transgression can be correlated with other geological events of the Ice Age, the deposits left by it can be roughly dated. The Caspian is an inland sea, so that movements of sea level along its shores were not the same as on coastlines by the open sea.)

The finds on the Volga have pushed far to the north the limits formerly known to us of Neanderthal settlement. Not only the Crimea but even the great Russian plain was occupied at that period. Thus an important fact for history has been established: the early settlement of the centre of the European part of the USSR.

In mousterian sites remains of a particular animal usually predominate, representing the main object of hunting. In the caves of the Crimea this is wild horse, elsewhere deer, in Teshik-Tash mountain goat, in Akhshtyrskaya cave bear, at the site of Ilskaya aurochs. Ilskaya is 43 km. south-west of Krasnodar on the road to Novorossiisk. It is an open site and was investigated in 1925–8 and 1936–7. It covered an area of 10,000 sq. m., but so far only a part of this has been examined. The extent of the site and depth of the cultural layer indicate that people had lived there a long time. Sixty per cent of the bones found at Ilskaya belonged to aurochs [large wild ox now extinct. T.]. The inhabitants of the site killed in all not less than 2,400 individual animals of this species. Besides this they hunted mammoth, wild horse, wild ass, and red deer. In the cultural layer at Ilskaya there were areas containing flaked and partly worked flints. These were working floors. The industry belongs to the time of transition to the Upper Palaeolithic Period. (Mousterian sites have also been found on the north Donets near Voroshilovgrad, on the right bank of Dnepr near Dnepropetrovsk, and in the basins of the Dnestr and Prut.)

The relationship of archaeological to geological periods in the Quaternary Period is a subject that has given rise to controversy. In this period there were four separate glaciations or four advances of the ice sheets and formation of large glaciers. The four periods of glaciation were each separated by warm Interglacial periods. The four glaciations are called Günz, Mindel, Riss, and Wurm after four Alpine villages where they were first distinguished. Of these glaciations the Riss was most severe. (In Russia the southern limits of the expanding Scandinavian ice sheet reached the river Oka in Mindel times, the middle Dnepr and Don in Riss times, and as far as the Valdai Hills in Wurm times.) [The sites where hand-axes have been found are considerably south of the main sheet, but belong probably to the Mindel-Riss Interglacial. The mousterian and other flake industries belong to the Riss–Wurm Interglacial and to the earlier part of the last Wurm glaciation. These are mainly found in caves in the extreme south. The upper palaeolithic sites are found in these caves, but also on the loess areas of the Ukraine. Loess is a fine wind-blown material found over large areas to the south of the glaciated area, as its deposition probably took place during the glaciation. Some of the upper palaeolithic sites are overlaid by deposits of loess of the final stages of the Wurm glaciation. T.]

## THE UPPER PALAEOLITHIC PERIOD

The Upper Palaeolithic Period lasted from 40,000 to 12,000 years ago. This is the so-called Late Glacial Period when the severity of climate was most extreme. In much larger areas of Europe and northern Asia than formerly, a landscape of tundra or cold steppe with islands of northern forest obtained.

### Development of Primitive Man

The change to the Upper Palaeolithic Age was expressed in important changes in the way of life of primitive man. New techniques and forms of economy appeared and even the physical appearance of man underwent changes. Men made their appearance without the animal characteristics conspicuous in Neanderthal man; upright carriage was fully developed, as was the hand, to its modern form, allowing an exact command of movements. As a whole upper palaeolithic people hardly differed at all from modern people. The working of flint reached a high level. In the Mousterian Period triangular flakes were struck from disc-shaped cores, but now cores were conical and elongated thin flakes called *blades* were struck off from one end (Fig. 6). Tools were made not only of flint but also of bone, deer antler, and mammoth tusk. Wood was widely used. Wooden tools have not survived but the form of a number of stone and bone objects indicates that they are the working part of an implement set in a wooden handle. The change to composite tools and weapons was an important advance in technique. Hunting tools appear as a distinct type as a result of the hunt becoming the basic form of economic activity of upper palaeolithic man. The high stage of development of the productive forces allowed him to adopt settled life. Permanent durable dwellings make their first appearance, as well as art and some religious manifestations.

## Upper Palaeolithic Sites

The Upper Palaeolithic Period in the USSR is well studied. Systematic and planned researches have led to the discovery of a great number of sites of different dates, in some cases in the same area, which has allowed study of the peculiarities of development of palaeolithic culture in a particular region. Soviet archaeologists have discovered the most northern palaeolithic sites in the world, such as Talitskaya near Perm (named after the archaeologist who first dug the site and was killed in the Second World War) and a series of sites on the river Lena in the Yakut SSR. As a result of many years' work by several expeditions, compact groups of sites have been found and studied. Thus at Voronezh, on the Don, in a length of 30 km. along the riverside no fewer than twenty palaeolithic stations of different periods have been found. The Kostenki-Borshevo region on the Don contains one of the most important concentrations of upper palaeolithic sites in the world. On the banks of the Desna near Novgorod-Seversk some seventeen sites are known.

These groups of sites are generally situated in the valleys of large rivers, and they testify to an appreciable growth in the primitive population, especially in favourably situated areas. In the European part of the USSR sites are known from an

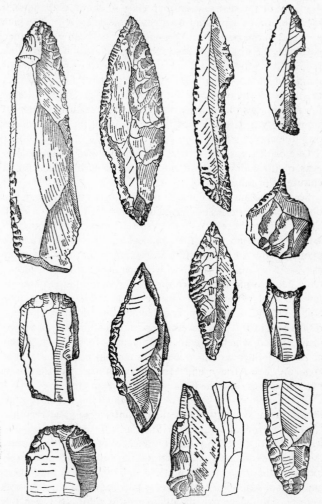

6. Flint tools from Russian upper palaeolithic sites (Kostenki I,
Telmanskaya, Mezin).

extensive area, from south White Russia to West Georgia. A glance at the distribution map (Fig. 4) shows that the sites fall into groups separated by areas, sometimes large, in which no traces of this period have been found. These can be explained partly by the absence of research in these areas but partly by physical circumstances of the time. There was only a limited number of inhabitants, who lived in small isolated groups in the areas most favourable for settlement. Therefore although the possibilities of further discoveries are great it must not be supposed that it will be possible to fill in all the blank spaces on the map.

One of the most interesting problems studied by archaeologists of the Palaeolithic Period relates to local variations in culture of primitive society.

Soviet scholars have come to the conclusion that none of the observable differences of culture in primitive society is original. These differences are due to historical causes. Throughout lower palaeolithic times the technical equipment of primitive man was so weak, the culture so backward that the latter was expressed in similar forms in widely separated parts of the globe. Only because of dependence on varying natural environments several local variations of culture made themselves felt. The higher cultural level of upper palaeolithic man led to different results and in this case several important cultural areas can be distinguished which owe their differences to prolonged geographical influences experienced by man in each area. These areas are: the African and Mediterranean area, the European periglacial area, and the Chinese and Siberian area. . . .

In the opinion of Soviet scholars the Upper Palaeolithic Period in our country can be divided into three great regions: (1) east European plain; (2) Siberia; (3) southern regions, which did not experience direct influences of glaciation, that is, the Crimea, Caucasus, and central Asia. In each of these some local peculiarities of technique, economy, and culture were manifested. Although both the east European plain and Siberia were partially glaciated, the differences in culture between the two areas are fairly significant. Evidently this was due to the fact that Siberia was isolated from Europe by the southward movement of the ice sheet and the northward transgression of the Caspian Sea, which produced a difference of culture on either side of the barrier. The inhabitants of the third area enjoyed an environment in which warmth-loving animals and plants also lived, so that here gathering of plants was carried out to a greater extent than in the north, while fishing and the use of the bow and arrow were started earlier. Each area was occupied by a large number of small primitive clan communities separated by extensive unoccupied areas.

## Upper Palaeolithic Dwellings

A substantial number of palaeolithic dwellings have been discovered and investigated in the USSR. . . . Formerly, with rare exceptions, archaeologists were interested only in layers and finds, and almost always cut vertical sections. Their methods of excavation did not permit opening of the whole site and so did not allow a full understanding of it or of the remains revealed. A new contribution to archaeological research allowed full exposure of palaeolithic houses. It was necessary during excavation to adopt the practice of making not only a vertical section but also a horizontal plan and so by uncovering a large area to study the changes in character of the settlement and its houses as a whole. [Most of the west European sites are caves whose deposits are encumbered by stalagmite and boulders: the palaeolithic houses found on open sites in east Europe are often in loess or in a subsoil not far below the surface, which has greatly facilitated this method of work. T.]

The first palaeolithic dwelling found in the Soviet Union was discovered in 1927 at Gagarino on the Upper Don (about 200 km. north of Voronezh). It consisted of a shallow scooped-out hole, oval in plan, measuring 5·5 by 4·5 m. The floor was paved with limestone slabs. The roof was probably conical and supported on poles covered by branches or animal skins. A similar hut was found in 1937 during excavations at Telmanskaya near Voronezh. Evidently an upper palaeolithic settlement consisted of a whole group of such earth-houses [*zemlyanka* in Russian, dwelling partly below ground level. T.]. Thus five earth-houses and several dug-out storage pits were found at Timonovka on the right bank of the Desna (about 400 km. south-west of Moscow). . . . Sometimes an earth-house of large dimensions served as shelter for a substantial group of people. Such a one was found at Pushkari I near Novgorod-Seversk (about 200 km. north-east of Kiev), which had three hearths spaced at equal intervals along the long axis (Fig. 7). It measured 12 by 4 m. and was only slightly dug into the ground (roughly 0·3 m.), so that most of the original hut was above ground. It is assumed that it was covered by skins supported by inside posts and was shaped like three conjoint cones. The hut at Pushkari I consists of the same type of earth-house as those at Gagarino and Telmanskaya, but in this case it housed a larger community, and as the technique of house construction was still insufficiently developed to allow the construction of a large communal house, the accretion of three ordinary huts had to make do.

At Pushkari the settlement was occupied continuously through the full cycle of the seasons. Besides the winter house described above traces were found next to it of places where man had lived in the open air preparing food and tools by the camp-fire.

An involved complex of domestic structures was found at Kostenki I (near Voronezh). It consisted of an oval area (35 by 16 m.) with a row of hearths along the long axis placed at two-metre intervals. In the hearths was a great quantity of bone ash – the large bones of animals serving as fuel because of the shortage of wood. By the side of the hearths were a row of holes for cooking food and also three small earth-houses. Such a settlement was occupied by one large community who had a communal domestic economy.

In the same Kostenki-Borshevo district (on the Don below Voronezh), famous for its palaeolithic sites, was found the settlement known as Kostenki IV. Here amongst others were found two long and spacious earth-houses (the area of one of them was 190 sq. m.) subdivided into three sections with a series of hearths in each part. Parts were evidently added as the community, which must have numbered several dozen individuals, grew.

An extensive domestic complex analogous to Kostenki I was discovered in the site of Mezin (near Pushkari), inhabited for a long time by upper palaeolithic hunters of mammoths, wild horse, and reindeer.

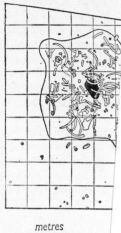

7. Pushkari I. Upp... ...thic earth-house, plan above, and ...ction, below.

In Siberia earth... ...ave been discovered at Malta, 80 km. north-west ... ..., and at Buret, 50 km. north of the former site. He... ... at Eliseevichi (near Timonovka) and in Gontsi (abo... ... east of Kiev) and on other sites bone was widely u... ... construction of dwellings, mammoth femurs servi... ...ts and struts, and mammoth and rhinoceros skulls as the base of the walls. For the framework of the roof reindeer antlers were used.

In Eliseevichi remains of some kind of structure were found (possibly a ritual area) in the form of an area demarcated by mammoth skulls. Flakes of mammoth tusk bearing drawings of fish and other sketches and the figure of a woman carved out of the same material were also found here. A long shallow dug-out corridor led from this area and was marked out on either side by mammoth pelvises and scapulae.

In connexion with the study of upper palaeolithic dwellings it is necessary to explain the use of some of the tools found in settlements of that period. Thus in the construction of dwellings robust flint chopping-tools probably served as axes, while for excavating the ground bone mattocks were probably employed.

### Early Art

With the advance from the Lower to the Upper Palaeolithic important changes in the manifestation of thought and beliefs took place; art appeared. [It is to the Upper Palaeolithic Period that the cave paintings and engravings in France and Spain belong. T.] Geometrical ornament made its appearance, as well as numerous sculptured, engraved, and coloured drawings of animals and women. Palaeolithic statuettes representing women have been found in various countries (Fig. 8). Over 100 are known in Europe and Asia, of which more than two-thirds were found in the Soviet Union. In Kostenki there were forty-three, in Gagarino six, in Malta twenty, in Buret five, in Avdeevo (about 250 km. east of Kiev) four, in Eliseevichi one. [They have also been found in Austria, France, and Italy and are a very important means of correlating the Russian open sites which have only one or two layers with the late aurignacian or gravettian layers in stratified cave deposits in the west. T.]

Some scholars have linked the widespread representations of women in the Upper Palaeolithic Period with the change to clan society, to matriarchy in which women controlled affairs. . . . [See remarks on Engels's scheme in Translator's Foreword. T.] Although the statuettes had ritual significance, they are realistic and generally speaking the best examples of primitive art. They do not represent deities but real women, sometimes in dress of

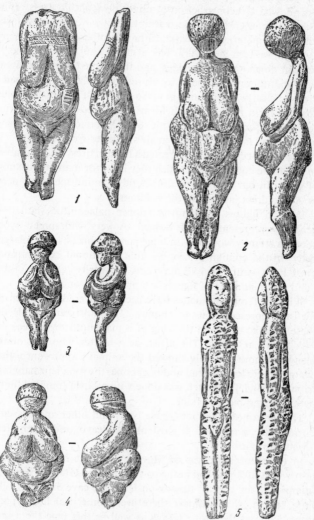

8. Upper palaeolithic female statuettes.

the period. An analysis of the statuette from Buret (Fig. 8, *5*) has allowed a reconstruction of upper palaeolithic dress. This example shows a small figure sculptured from mammoth tusk [the usual material in Russia, although other materials were used on western sites. T.]. The arms of the figure are held straight down against the sides, and the whole body is covered with half-moon ornament to represent clothing. The head-dress is clearly shown and is made of fur; it passes over the head to form a hood which forms one piece with the warm costume of fur covering the body. Such a hooded costume may be indicated in some of the female statuettes from Malta.

The ancient craftswomen created a form of dress fully suitable to the arctic conditions in which they lived for many thousands of years. In our own day the fur hood is an indispensable part of Arctic dress [as among the Eskimos. T.].

Dressed figures are a rarity: upper palaeolithic statuettes generally represent naked women. A very widespread type shows a stumpy woman with huge pendant breasts and a large belly. In the opinion of scholars this intentional exaggeration must have symbolized fertility and prosperity. On the other hand a fair number of figures are properly proportioned.

With the female statuettes have been discovered a number of realistic representations of animals. The most remarkable of these was the engraved drawing of a mammoth on a piece of tusk found at Malta. The artist, as a hunter who had often seen mammoth, skilfully showed the animal's appearance, the characteristic line of head and backbone, the long hair hanging from its belly. The sketch was done with a burin (pointed flint) on a polished piece of bone.

The figures of mammoth, cave bear, and other animals cut out of soft stone found at Kostenki, Avdeevo, and other sites are interesting.

In the Georgian caves of Mgvimevi (about 200 km. west-north-west of Tiflis) and in the so-called Stone Grave at Terpen (about 300 km. west of Rostov-on-Don) are cave drawings still little known. At Mgvimevi there are geometrical linear patterns, while at the Stone Grave as well as this type there are sketches of animals, apparently done with stone tools. These are not accurately dated but it is likely that some belong to the end of the Palaeolithic Period and that others are later. Scholars suppose that both the geometrical drawings and some of the sketches of animals like the figure of a horse on the roof of the Stone Grave rock shelter are palaeolithic. Primitive engravings filled in with colouring are known from a site in Uzbekistan and are evidently partly upper palaeolithic in date. In the valley of the river Lena at Shishkino (west of L. Baikal, north of Irkutsk) there are rock drawings which extend for three kilometres. Among hundreds of drawings of elk, bovids, camels, riders on animals, birds, and horses, two animals – the wild horse and aurochs – belong to the animal world of the end of the Ice Age. These late palaeolithic drawings are the oldest artistic monuments in northern Asia. However it must be noted that in all three cases the palaeolithic dating is controversial. Extensive research on these sites is needed and, it is hoped, will finally resolve the problem of when the drawings were made.

## Primitive Beliefs and Ritual

These examples of palaeolithic art raise the question of the beliefs of primitive man. Such discoveries as the grave of a child under a palaeolithic dwelling at Malta testify to a sophisticated outlook on the world, to the development of a cult of the dead, for the body was sprinkled with red colouring and with it were placed a necklace and buckle and also figures of birds, and weapons. [It has been suggested that the figures of 'birds' are a final stage in the degeneration of the female statuettes discussed above. T.] A small cairn of stones was placed above the grave.

In 1952 at Kostenki XV (called Gorodtsov's site) the first upper palaeolithic burial on the Don came to light, similar to the one at Malta. The skeleton of a child aged four to five years was found in a small burial trench, the bottom of which had red ochre scattered over it. In the grave there had been placed a little spade with a handle, cut from the side of the long bone of a mammoth, a polisher, a bone needle with eye, a heap of flints including several scrapers, and about 150 fox teeth perforated through the root forming part of a head ornament. The skeleton was covered over with the large fragment of a mammoth scapula.

D

In the excavations at Kostenki II in 1953 together with a dwelling was discovered an annex beside it in the form of an oval (4 by 1·5 m.) carefully demarcated by mammoth skulls and extremity bones. This annex was a regular tomb in the centre of which was the crouched body of a man (aged about fifty). In the 'Pokrovsky' ravine in the village of Kostenki beyond the limits of the palaeolithic settlement the upper palaeolithic grave of a child aged about eleven was found in 1953. The skeleton was covered over with a construction of mammoth bones.

In the Upper Palaeolithic Period a proper burial ritual was in use, connected with the formation of primitive religion and expressing a belief in life after death.

It is very probable that the mass of bones at Amvrosievskaya (west of Rostov-on-Don) situated near a site of this period was a ritual place. It consisted of a shallow natural hollow filled up with a great accumulation of bones belonging to 950–1,000 wild oxen. The nature of the finds, their position in relation to the site, and other factors allow the conclusion that the inhabitants deposited here all the bones of the wild oxen they killed while hunting, in the belief that in this way they would make the living animals fertile and that this would lead to good hunting in the future. In the ritual of hunting magic the bones of the wild oxen personified the animals themselves. Spears were thrust into the skulls and bones of the dead animals in the belief that in this way successful hunting would be granted.

## EXTENT OF PALAEOLITHIC REMAINS IN THE USSR

As was said above, upper palaeolithic sites are very widely spread in the European part of the USSR. This is not the place to list all or even the most important of them. It is desirable only to remark that in other Soviet republics outside the RSFSR [which includes Siberia. T.] research is carried out on palaeolithic sites. In the Ukraine a large group of scientists is at work; in White Russia (Belorussia, north of Ukraine) work is also carried on; while mention has been made above of researches in Armenia. In 1926 an aurignacian deposit was discovered in the cave of Devis-Khvreli (in west Georgia), when the existence of palaeolithic remains in Georgia was first proved. In 1936 an upper palaeolithic cave site was excavated at Sakazhia (about 200 km. west-north-west of Tiflis) and other sites have since been excavated. In 1951-3 archaeologists of the area carried out excavations at the cave of Sagvarjile. This contained numerous layers from the lower palaeolithic to the first centuries A.D. In the upper palaeolithic levels, together with obsidian and flint tools were also found bone darts and awls. One awl made from a long bone was in the form of a fish, whose tail was decorated with herring-bone ornament. There were pendants of plaster decorated in the same way, a bone pin, and a necklace of nineteen perforated shells from southern seas was also found. The search for palaeolithic remains in Georgia continues.

Extensive searches for palaeolithic remains are being made in central Asia. Outside Uzbekistan, which was mentioned above, palaeolithic remains have been found in Tajikistan, Kirgizia, Turkmenia, and Kazakhistan. As the result of work in 1938-53 the following parts of central Asia and Kazakhistan yielded evidence of occupation in the Old Stone Age: the western part of Turkmenia along the shores of the Caspian Sea, the district of Baisun-Tau, the lower parts of the rivers Vakhsh and Kapirnigan, the central part of Tien-Shan, the valley of the Irtysh between Lake Zaisan and Samipalatinsk.

## TRANSITION TO THE MESOLITHIC PERIOD

At the end of the Upper Palaeolithic Period great changes took place in the economy and way of life on the east European plain. The Ice Age drew to a close, the climate became warmer. Hitherto the characteristic large settlements with dwellings had as their basis the hunting of mammoth; now at the end of the Palaeolithic Period mammoth and woolly rhinoceros were encountered less frequently and the smaller animals were hunted instead. For hunting large animals like mammoth none of the lower palaeolithic implements had been effective. In upper palaeolithic times more accomplished implements appeared, capable of piercing the thick skin of a mammoth, but the basic method of hunting remained the battue, whereby the hunted beasts were driven into a vulnerable position. An illustration of such hunting is provided by the conditions on the site found at Afontova Mountain near Krasnoyarsk. Mammoths were driven to a precipice over which they fell and broke their limbs. Success in the hunting of small animals on the other hand depended to a significant degree upon the refinement of the hunting weapon. Flint arrowheads were improved and bone began to be used also. Together with hunting, fishing became important.

The large settlements with permanent winter dwellings disappeared, and occupation became less fixed, or even migratory. The picture of such changes became clear from observations on the cultural layers at the site of Gontsi in the Ukraine on the right bank of the river Udai. In the lower layers remains of permanent settlement came to light including winter earthhouses, burnt material, and great piles of mammoth bones. The upper cultural layer was thin and contained remains of only a light hut and material burnt in the open fire.

## THE MESOLITHIC PERIOD

In the post-glacial period a gradual transformation to a new historical epoch took place, the so-called Neolithic Period (New Stone Age). This transitional stage constitutes a separate period which is called the Mesolithic Period (from the Greek words *mesos* middle, and *lithos* stone), or Middle Stone Age (called epipalaeolithic by those who regard it as the final phase of the Palaeolithic Period. This period covers the time between 10,000 and 5,000 B.C.). In the Mesolithic Period there is a significant movement of people northwards to the areas formerly occupied by ice sheets. In eastern Europe people pushed forward in a comparatively short time to the shores of the Baltic, the upper reaches of the Dnepr and Volga, and farther north.

The most important change in technique in the Mesolithic Period was the general adoption of the bow and arrow, raising immeasurably the productivity of hunting economy. There is evidence that the dog was now first domesticated by people living mainly by hunting and fishing. Together with hunting an important part was again played by gathering. Man ate edible molluscs, fruit, and berries in great quantities in the more favourable natural conditions of post-glacial times.

The Mesolithic Period is less well studied throughout the world than the Old Stone Age [except in Scandinavia and the British Isles. T.]. This is because hunters and gatherers of the Mesolithic Period lived a semi-nomadic life, and the cultural deposits they have left contain few remains. Many settlements or temporary camps were set on sand dunes where the cultural deposit is subject to wind and is easily eroded. Sites of longer occupation are often in caves.

In the USSR remains of the Mesolithic Period are well known in the Crimean caves of Shan-Koba and Murzak-Koba, in Georgia, on the river Oka and the upper Volga, and elsewhere.

*

Soviet archaeologists have not only advanced the study of the Palaeolithic Period by their discoveries, but have brought about a transformation in the study of the social development, economy, and ideology of the period. The general works of Soviet archaeologists have not only solved problems of the Palaeolithic Period in the Soviet Union but have put these problems in their world setting. . . .

Problems of the most ancient history of Europe cannot be settled without study of its eastern parts, above all of the European part of the USSR. In order to resolve many problems of world history in its initial stages Soviet and foreign scholars will have to collaborate. . . .

Soviet archaeologists have traced out the earliest history of the USSR beginning with the first appearance of man on its territory, and the undoubted fact is established that the culture of the most ancient population of the country did not fall below the level of culture of any other areas occupied in the Old Stone Age.

## Chapter 3

# THE NEOLITHIC AND COPPER AGES

THE Neolithic or New Stone Age took its name from the technique of making stone tools by means of rubbing or polishing, drilling, and perforating stones, a new technique in relation to the preceding period. There was a time when the Neolithic Period was called the age of polished stone, but numerous later discoveries have established that this was not the most important indication of the new period. The majority of stone tools of the period are not polished, and as in the preceding period are simply flaked. Very important in the field of technical progress was the manufacture of clay vessels, pottery or ceramics (Greek *keramos* means clay). In the beginning of the Neolithic Period people discovered that by baking it was possible to convert soft moist clay into a permanently hard impermeable substance. The appearance of pottery is considered by some archaeologists so important a sign of the Neolithic Period that they even speak instead of a 'pottery age'. In this period, together with hunting and fishing, agriculture and stock-breeding began. After pottery, the most important form of manufacture to appear was textiles. Neolithic communities were acquainted with spinning and weaving, with the spindle and the weaving loom of the simplest type. Barter developed between tribes – especially in such materials as stone for the preparation of tools, and amber for personal ornament. Primitive trade led to the spread of various cultural achievements from one area to another.

In Tsarist Russia a substantial amount of neolithic material was collected, but all the same this period was poorly studied. Neolithic sites were excavated but the results were not always published, and except for some of the works of Gorodtsov there was no attempt to systematize or introduce order into the accumulated material, so that really the study of the neolithic cultures of the USSR began only in Soviet times. Naturally there has not yet been opportunity for study of the whole boundless extent of our country, and the period is still little known in several districts of the USSR. Thus the north of the European part of the Union is much better studied than the south.

Neolithic remains are much more widespread than palaeolithic ones. Improvements in material productivity led to a growth in population. More ample forms of economy required large areas for the feeding of the expanded population, and so demanded further settlement, the occupation of substantial new territory. This is why neolithic remains are so widespread. If there are areas where still none have been found this should not be attributed at once to absence of inhabitants in the period but to inadequate archaeological survey of that part of the USSR. Work on the south of the European part of the USSR has been slight.

## THE SOUTH

At the end of the fourth and during the third millennium B.C. the steppe expanses were occupied by hunters and fishers. A great number of sites of these tribes have been found in the rapids zone of the Dnepr and the north part of the area near the Sea of Azov, but few have been dug. Light huts were used as dwellings, and pottery (partly decorated with comb impressions) has been found on the sites. Numerous tools of bone and flint indicate a hunter-fisher economy.

In 1930 during construction work an important neolithic cemetery was found at Mariupol near Zhdanov on the left bank of the river Kalmius near its entry into the Sea of Azov. It consisted of 122 graves, some of them belonging to children. In one grave a woman's skeleton was found with a baby in her arms. All the skeletons lay on their backs and above was sprinkled a layer of red ochreous clay, which is not found near the cemetery and so had been brought from elsewhere. The clay was covered over with black earth. In the graves were found a number of objects, for the most part of bone or stone, as well as animal teeth and shells. In the majority of the graves there was no sign of metal, but a few of them contained copper objects belonging to a later period. For the most part objects in the graves were for adornment. On the skeletons a whole array of bone plaques originally sewn to the clothing survived, as well as boars' teeth, perforated shells, and so on. Sometimes a man's costume had been so decorated from head to foot. Among the especially interesting ornaments were the figures of animals cut out of bone, evidently representing pigs and oxen. A piece of rock crystal was found which does not occur naturally nearer than the river Ural or the Caucasus. The tribe who left the cemetery at Mariupol had intercourse with those remote parts. Flint knives, scrapers, arrowheads, and even polished stone axes and maces were found in the cemetery. Although the objects recovered in the cemetery threw little light on economic conditions yet it is possible to make some assumptions as to the occupations of the population. They still did not know agriculture but to judge by the figures of pigs and oxen they kept animals; hunting and fishing remained the basis of their economy. There were no property distinctions, no rich or poor amongst them and, although the mace appears as a symbol of authority, yet this was the authority of the head of a clan or tribe not owing his position to property.

In the north Caucasus at Nalchik (about 200 km. north-north-west of Tiflis) a cemetery has been excavated which was formed by a low hill due to the joining up of the material heaped up over each grave. One hundred and twenty-one burials were found there, for the most part consisting of contracted skeletons on their side and sprinkled with a red mummy-coloured dye. The few objects in the graves were flint knives, scrapers, awls, and arrowheads. There were bracelets made out of a soft stone, rings cut from limb bones of animals, and pendants of teeth of wild boar, bear, deer, fox, and so on. The finds are generally similar to those from Mariupol. A few copper objects were also found. One and a half kilometres to the north-west an older settlement was excavated. No dwellings were found, but there were numerous flint knives, scrapers, and arrowheads, some stone axes and chisels, and undecorated pottery. The inhabitants of the settlement had a primitive hunting and gathering economy.

These three sites are roughly dated to the third millennium B.C.

Neolithic settlements have been found on the shores of the Black Sea, but with the exception of the Akhshtyrskaya cave mentioned above (p. 85) are not excavated. Here flat polished axes, made mainly of shale, were found together with small flint tools, oddments of bone, sherds of pottery, and animal bones. Not far from the site was a working site where axes and picks of slate were made.

Similar finds were made at the open site of Tetramits (west Georgia). Here there was definite evidence of agriculture in the form of querns for grinding grain, small-toothed flakes of flint which were set in a wooden haft to make the blade of a sickle, and stone hoes.

There is also evidence for the Neolithic Period in Trans-caucasia. One site had two layers, a mesolithic level below, and a neolithic level above containing implements for hunting as well as hoes, querns, and pounders used in agricultural operations. No traces of stock-rearing have been found in Transcaucasia.

In central Asia on the lower Amu-Darya (Oxus) an important neolithic site is Janbas-Kala IV (south of the Aral Sea). It consisted of one large communal house set on a sand dune. It was approximately oval in plan covering an area of about 290 sq. m. The excavator supposed that the dwelling above ground consisted of a wooden framework of posts and beams covered by a roof of reeds. In the centre was set a large hearth. In other parts of the house there were remains of small fires used for cooking food, each of which could have been used by a separate family. One hundred to one hundred and twenty-five people probably occupied this vast dwelling. Domestic finds occurring for the most part near the fires consisted of a large number of flint knives, scrapers, spokeshaves, and arrowheads. Polished axes were rare. Pottery vessels had a pointed base and were covered with incised decoration, often roughly coloured with red mat-ter. The inhabitants were mainly occupied in hunting and fish-ing. The site is dated to the late fourth or early third millennium B.C. Remains of this culture are found in Chorasmia and West Kazakhistan.

## SIBERIA

Occupation of the limitless expanses of Siberia had already begun in the Old Stone Age; in the Neolithic Period early settlement was completed. On the lower Lena neolithic sites are found within the Arctic Circle, and similar sites occur far to the east in the valley of the river Kolyma. Deep into the Chukotsk peninsula and in Kamchatka objects belonging to neolithic hunters have been found. Everywhere archaeologists find traces of the activity of neolithic man, from the shores of the Arctic Ocean to the Mongolian People's Republic, from the Urals to the Pacific, in the treeless tundra and in the wooded taiga, and in the steppes beyond Lake Baikal.

However far-flung may be neolithic remains in Siberia, only in one place has research been carried sufficiently far to serve as a basis for historical divisions of neolithic tribes in this region. This is the region around Lake Baikal. Within a radius of 500 km. to the north, east, and west of the lake are situated a mass of known neolithic sites which have provided material for close study. The first typical burials found here have provided the names of the stages of development of the Neolithic Period of the Baikal area.

The first stage, the Khinsky, in the fifth millennium B.C., takes its name from a burial at that place. It is marked by the appearance of the bow and arrow.

In the second stage, the Isakovsky, of the fourth millennium B.C., polished tools and pottery made their appearance. There were still very few inhabitants. No settlements are known, but burials have been found.

There was significant progress in technique in the third stage, the Serovsky (third millennium B.C.). Metal was still unknown, but the working of bone and stone reached a very high level. The semi-precious stone, nephrite, was used in the making of stone tools. Evidently wood and bone tools were made with the polished stone knives, but the wood has, of course, perished. In the graves stone arrowheads and bows are often found, and weapons occur both in men's and in women's graves. The bows are very skilfully constructed of wood with bone outer facing and their length was almost equal to a man's height. Besides hunting, fishing was important, fish being caught in nets, harpooned, or even shot with arrows. Later a fish hook was invented. Especially characteristic of the Siberian Neolithic are stones carved to represent fish (Pl. 3c). Formerly it was supposed that these stone fish were used in ritual magic; they would have been put into the water to give luck in fishing. Now it is established that they served as fish lures. Remains of this period are very numerous.

The fourth stage was the Kitoisky, in the third and early part of the second millennia B.C. Fishing now became the most important branch of the economy. The supply of nephrite was important as it was the predominant material used for stone axes. Nephrite objects and lumps of it still unworked occur over a wide area and were used for trade between tribes. The first evidence of rich burials indicates the birth of inequality within the clan.

In north-east Asia the neighbours of the Baikal people were the tribes of settled lake-fishers and wandering hunters occupying the modern Yakut area. In neolithic times the whole northern taiga and forest tundra was settled, and traces of ancient sites are found within the Arctic Circle.

An important task for Soviet archaeologists is the study of the tribes of the Far East. On the coast neolithic tribes are known from shell middens, heaps of shells of edible shellfish. These middens are usually up to 1 m. high and between 10 and 25 m. in diameter. Besides marine shells, fish and animal bones, stone tools, arrow- and spearheads, knives and daggers are found in them. Around the river Amur neolithic fishermen led a settled life and their settlements consist of numerous winter earth-houses set close together. These sites sometimes reach 100 m. in circumference and 3-4 m. in depth.

## THE FOREST ZONE OF THE EUROPEAN PART OF THE USSR

Neolithic remains have been studied better in the forest zone of the European part of the USSR than in other areas. Not long ago all these cultures were lumped together under the title 'pit-comb ware'. Actually over a great period of time in the Neolithic and Bronze Ages, in a vast area from Karelia to the east side of the rivers Ural and Volga, pots were decorated with ornament consisting of little pits and comb impressions, but this is hardly the most significant feature of the cultures. At all events this feature was so marked that no one was able to look beyond it to the other characteristics that, far from uniting the whole area, on the contrary, divided it up. In the last few years not only has a whole series of cultures been distinguished by characteristic types of objects, but also an attempt has been made to give a connected history of the tribes living in each area. The study and systemization of a mass of facts was an immense task undertaken by A. Bryusov.

There is one general feature characteristic of neolithic sites of the forest areas; all are situated by water. Either they are near a lake, now turned into a peat bog, or on a sand dune or hill by the side of a river. This close connexion with water is explained by the fact that in the economy fishing and catching water-birds took prime place. Tribal territories more often than not spread out around the lake and river basins and within these were grouped the smaller clan settlements. The more archaic remains are found in the basin of the Oka and Klyazma and also in the north. Some mention of the tribes of the Oka has already been made (see p. 44). In the north there were further groups of tribes. One group is united under the general term of central Ural group, another under the title of south Baltic group.

It is difficult to assess their relationships with neolithic tribes of the south, for these are so little studied, as explained above, that it has not been possible to subdivide them. We will not enter into the distinctions between the tribes and their history, but will only describe some of the more prominent remains of the neolithic cultures discovered by Soviet archaeologists.

Lyalovskaya is a site on the river Klyazma 40 km. to the north of Moscow. It belongs to the third millennium B.C. The inhabitants lived on a platform of boughs on the edge of a lake that has now become a peat bog. Amongst the stone tools predominated large roughly flaked tools which were used for digging. Polished tools were entirely absent. The pots had pointed bases and were ornamented with circular incisions and comb impressions.

On many sites in the Oka valley circular or rectangular earth-houses have been discovered which had elongated entries and were joined to each other by corridors. Settlements here are comparatively large and approximately 100–150 people lived in each one.

The settlements of Karelia are not very large. Sunskaya I, situated on a creek on Lake Onega (about 300 km. north-east of Leningrad), occupied an area of about 100 by 7–10 m. There were no more than three huts. One of them was quadrilateral in plan, measuring about 3 m. along one side, and was slightly dug into the ground. Its floor was made of branches, and at one of the hut's angles was a short entry-passage. The middle of the hut was occupied by hearths constructed of several large stones. The site can be referred to the end of the third millennium B.C.

Such sites of moderate size with twenty-five to thirty inhabitants are characteristic of the hunter–fisher economy of the north.

Some neolithic sites in the north are referred to a later period, 1500–1000 B.C. In the settlement at Voi-Navolok remains of winter huts and store-rooms were found. The huts consisted of moderate-sized circular earth-houses with one steep and one gently inclined wall beneath a conical roof of wood and skin sprinkled over with sand. The stone hearth was on the same side as the entry, while the southern higher part of the hut served as sleeping quarters. In the northern part was a passage. The area of the hut was 5 sq. m. Such a hut would be occupied by a single family.

Near Kargopol on the river Kinem close to where it debouches into a lake a site with two layers has been discovered, Upper and Lower Vereta (about 400 km. east of Leningrad). These sites are situated one on top of the other in an alder marsh on an island that formerly existed here. From the banks discarded objects fell into the sand; by degrees through growth of reeds and silting the area turned into soft wet ground, and with the growth of peat the sites were buried. Although the peat with cultural remains of the lower layer is only 10–15 cm. below that of the upper layer they are separated in time by hundreds of years. The former is dated to about 2500–2300 B.C. and the latter to 1500–500 B.C. Between the two periods of occupation the site was deserted.

On these sites no traces of earth-houses survive but hearths are preserved in good condition. The greatest interest attaches to the numerous finds of various objects and animal and bird bones. The ancient fauna is distinctive; elk and beaver predominated, and amongst the birds loon (*gagara*), wild duck, goose, and swan occurred. Pine, fir, and birch trees grew there in great numbers. Hunting and fishing gear constituted a large part of the finds: arrowheads predominantly of bone, harpoons, fish hooks, and a fairly large quantity of flint implements. In the lower site no pottery was found, but the upper level was distinguished by large quantities of pottery and a special form of bone tool.

The construction of huts on piles is a fairly widespread occurrence in primitive society found in various countries. The first pile settlement excavated and studied in our country was on the river Modlon at Charozero (about 500 km. east of Leningrad). The settlement extended along a long, narrow promontory between this and another river. Excavation revealed two rows of houses constructed on the marshy bank and raised slightly above the surface of the ground. They stood on piles driven into the ground. All the houses were of irregular square shape about 3·5–4 m. in length, and had walls made of plaited twigs, a timber platform at an entry on the south side, and a gabled roof covered with birch-bark. The huts were connected to the bank and to each other by pairs of logs resting on the ground or supported by piles. Amongst the huts were found great heaps of fish scales and bones, large, flattened and rotten plaited fish snares, and masses of other objects. Amongst these were: flint implements including numerous leaf-shaped arrowheads, bone harpoons, and wooden objects – parts of paddles and part of a distaff. The latter, together with the grains of cultivated flax found allows us to assume that the inhabitants were familiar with the rudiments of agriculture. This site may be referred to the beginning of the second millennium B.C.

Research has extended to the extreme north of the European part of the USSR and sites have been discovered there. On the coast of the Barents Sea temporary fishermen's sites have been found without any trace whatever of permanent houses, but the tribes who left these sites had regular winter settlements of small size on inland lakes. Small earth-houses were used here.

Amongst neolithic sites excavated recently in the Baltic area we will mention a peat site on the shores of Lake Tamul in south-east Estonia. Several seasons' work has been carried out on the site since 1938. Seven graves were found in the cultural layer. The majority of the finds indicate a hunter–fisher economy at Tamul. Figures of people and birds and animals made of bone (or in one case of clay) were found here. This site is assigned to the second millennium B.C.

Among sites of the central Ural area a most interesting discovery was made at the Gorbunovo peat-bog (150 km. north-west of Sverdlovsk). It was discovered in 1908 during the cutting of peat but only excavated in 1926–39. The site belongs to both the Neolithic and Bronze Ages. The settlement was not large and was constructed of wood. On its edge broken up one-runner sleighs were found, of a type pulled by the hunter himself. A carved wooden duck of natural size came to light. This duck would be used by the hunters as a decoy for birds. Flint, bone, and wooden arrowheads, fish hooks, net weights and plummets, and a great number of animal and bird bones were found. The latter show that the inhabitants of the central Ural area retained a hunter–fisher economy in the third millennium B.C. to which the site is assigned. Agriculture may have appeared here early, for twenty-five antler mattocks or hoes were found on the site, the greater part of which bore traces of strong wear or breaks during use. Such a number of earth-digging tools may be a sign of the practice of agriculture.

Although other sites of the Gorbunovo peat-bog belong to the Bronze Age (metal objects were found in them) we will speak of them here in the neolithic section. This does not conflict with the system of periods, for archaeologists themselves have not yet decided how to define the boundary between the Neolithic and Bronze Ages. The fact is that bronze implements could not wholly replace stone ones. Everywhere they are found together. Thus some archaeologists refer a site to the Bronze Age if only a single metal object is found in it. Others consider that if metal was not used widely and there was no metal-working then the site can be considered as belonging to the Neolithic Period.

The Gorbunovo settlements were not large and consisted of light structures set on floors of chopped planks coated with clay.

The inhabitants were engaged in hunting and fishing, and also partly in primitive agriculture. Another proof of this apart from digging-tools mentioned above was a press for squeezing oil, possibly from the seeds of cultivated plants. The most unusual objects found were paddles, bows, boomerangs, and parts of decorated birch-bark objects.

The Gorbunovo sites gave some wonderful examples of the ancient art of wood-carving in the shape of large anthropomorphic idols of rough work, beautifully made ladles with birds' heads (Pl. 3b), figures of elk, and drawings of snakes. Some of these objects were undoubtedly of ritual significance, but they were not all idols. Such clearly was not the case with the elk with its extraordinarily realistic head. Its legs were simple pegs which could be stuck into the ground, and on its back was a hollow place where the meat, fat, or blood of the killed animal could be poured. Idols and other objects relating to rituals were found close to a pile dwelling which some scholars suppose served for sacrifices and magical ceremonies. These Bronze-Age sites and other contemporary sites of the middle Ural area belong for the most part to the middle of the second millennium B.C.

To the period of transition from the Neolithic to the Bronze Ages (1500–1000 B.C.) belongs the peat site at Sarnat in north-west Latvia. It showed great similarity with the Gorbunovo settlement although the two sites are separated by 2,300 km. Here also were found wooden ladles with ducks' heads as handles, as well as paddles and hoe handles. Amongst interesting wooden objects found were spears, skis, implements for cracking hazel and water nuts, and amber ornaments. At the entry to one of the houses were found parts of a dug-out boat, paddles, and a fish basket of plaited twigs. The houses were large. In one case the remains of a polygonal structure with an area of 35 sq. m. were found; in another the structure was square. The walls consisted of posts driven into the peat supporting intertwined branches and twigs filled in with grass. Outside the walls were faced with tree-bark. The construction of the hearths was unusual. Under each, logs were placed in crisscross fashion. On this, birch-bark was laid out and on top of this was sprinkled a layer of sand 10–12 cm. thick on which the

fire was lit. This prevented the underlying peat from being set
on fire. Some hearths had been renewed as many as six times.
The excavations at Sarnat give a very fine picture of the conditions of life of ancient tribes in the Baltic area.

Artistic productions and ritual connected with burials throw
much light on the beliefs of the Neolithic Period. Besides frequently occurring sculptures of bone, wood, and stone, a peculiarity of neolithic art is the miniature sculptures of stone found
everywhere from the shores of the White Sea to the middle
Volga area. These are representations of birds, reptiles, fish,
various animals, and human beings. They had some kind of
ritual significance, as did the remarkable rock drawings of
Karelia. The petroglyphs (rock drawings) of Karelia occur on
the eastern shore of Lake Onega and in the coastal area of the
White Sea. More than a thousand drawings survive, chipped
out by neolithic people on the granite rocks. Sketches of animals (elk, deer, bear, and so on) and birds (swans, geese, ducks)
predominate. The human figures shown are usually hunters,
and there are also signs evidently connected with a cult of the
sun and moon. On the Besov Nos ('Nose of the Demons') is
shown a large figure of the 'demon', the deity of the locality.
Some of the petroglyphs have the appearance of a rough
composition as if they dealt with stories of a mythological content. Some sketches were made with magical aims, for example
a scene of driving deer is carved in order that the actual driving
of deer by neolithic hunters might be successful. Such a group
was that discovered at Zalavruga, which is of almost natural
size and shows elks running from three sides towards one point
and chased from behind by a figure with a bow and arrow (Fig.
9). The drawings are interesting not only as monuments reveal-
ing the religious beliefs of the population but also because they
render it possible to distinguish certain features of the material
culture of the ancient hunters of Karelia. There are pictures
here of long and narrow lake craft, catching game, hunting with
harpoons, the spear, and bows and arrows, and the use of the
dog in hunting. Evidently the areas around the drawings were
tribal or clan sanctuaries where periodically ceremonies took
place. Excavations near them have revealed stone hearths,
various tools, pot sherds, or in other words traces of temporary

9. Zalavruga. Rock carvings.

visits. Although not all the drawings belong to one period a significant number may be assigned to the first half of the second millennium B.C.

Rock drawings are known not only from Karelia, for there are also many in Siberia, the Urals, and central Asia. In the majority of cases, however, either they are not dated or they belong to a later period, to the Bronze or Iron Age in fact.

Among numerous rock drawings of Tajikistan and Uzbekistan a part may probably be referred to the Neolithic Period. To this period and the Bronze Age belong some of the drawings at Zaraut-Sai already referred to during discussion of the remains of palaeolithic art. On rocks, in rock shelters and niches, nearly 200 paintings survive, painted in red colouring by primitive man. [Spain is probably the only European country that has as many rock paintings as the Soviet Union, and in both countries the date of the drawings is very uncertain. T.]

The paintings at Zaraut-Sai were discovered in 1940 by one of those important agents of Soviet archaeology who do not write large scientific works and so remain unknown, but who carry the study of archaeology forward by their activity and devotion to science. Hunter–guide I. F. Lamaev (now a Fellow of the Surkhan-Darinsky Museum of Local Studies) found an important series of archaeological remains in the places where his work took him. To him we are indebted for the discovery of the palaeolithic cave of Amir-Temir, the paintings of Zaraut-Sai, and many other monuments of antiquity.

The most interesting drawing at Zaraut-Sai is a scene showing the hunting of wild oxen. The hunters are armed with bows, arrows, spears, and boomerangs. Some of the people are dressed in something like skin cloaks, their heads concealed under hoods. An ox is beautifully drawn. A javelin is plunged into its ear, an arrow is directed into its chest, a stone from a sling flies into its back. The whole picture is 60 by 100 cm. in size. The drawings at this site form a remarkable monument of primitive art.

The neolithic cemetery on Olen Ostrov (Deer Island) in the

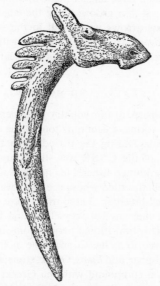

10. Olen Ostrov. Neolithic carving of
an elk's head.

north-west part of Lake Onega has great interest. More than 170 graves were excavated here in 1936–8. The site was evidently a cemetery for the lakeside population. The dead were brought here in boats or on rafts and interred in shallow trenches, bright red colouring matter being thickly sprinkled over the corpse. Objects were placed with the corpse in the grave and these included stone and bone implements, and ornaments. In the men's graves were found stone arrow- and lance-heads, bone daggers and harpoons, slate axes and knives, and necklaces and pendants of teeth of wild animals (most frequently elk incisors or bear canines). On the women's skeletons objects of adornment made of animal teeth and stone knives were also found. A number of bone figures of people and wild animals came to light (Fig. 10). Especially interesting were burials of women with unweaned babies, lying beside them or between their legs. There were some burials in which a skeleton was set upright in a deep vertical hole. In one such burial, on the chest of the dead person was found a large dagger made of bone with a blade of thin flint flakes set in a groove along the edge. A quiver containing numerous arrows was found in the same grave. The corpse was adorned from head to foot with animal teeth, incisors of beaver and elk, and canines of bear.

## UKRAINE AND MOLDAVIA

In the southern parts of our country the emergence and development of new forms of economy took place more intensively than in the north. During the period when the north of the European parts of the USSR was still occupied by neolithic tribes leading a hunter–fisher life, in the south-west, in the Ukraine, tribes had settled whose economy was based on agriculture and stock-breeding. These tribes were acquainted with metal, although they used it very little and their basic tools were of stone. This transitional period from stone to bronze is sometimes referred to as the Copper Age or Eneolithic Period (*aeneus*, Latin, copper, and *lithos*, Greek, stone, meaning copperage; sometimes a compound with the Greek, *chalcos*, copper is used, 'Chalcolithic'). Bronze was not yet employed, the metal objects were of copper.

*The Tripole Culture*

The first sites of the early agricultural tribes in the Ukraine were discovered sixty years ago by the archaeologist V. V. Khvoika near the village of Tripole (pronounced 'Tripolye', below Kiev on the Dnepr). From this first find the whole culture has been called the Tripole culture. Although a fairly large number of sites were discovered in pre-Revolutionary times (since the Revolution the growth in the number of sites has been very great; more than 300 settlements were found in Moldavia and the Ukraine between 1934 and 1954 alone), the basic problems of this culture remained unsettled. Above all there was the riddle of the chief sites – the 'clay areas'. Controversy raged around these. Some considered them as ritual grave constructions, others as the remains of houses, yet others as pottery manufacturing sites.

The dispute was settled by Soviet archaeologists only after the complete uncovering of these structures by excavation over a large area. Thus at one Tripole site, Kolomiishchina I, on the Dnepr near Kiev, an area of 15,000 sq. m. was uncovered (Fig. 11). This allowed study of the whole tribal settlement with sufficient evidence to establish the social life of the Tripolyans. Researches on ancient Tripole sites have clarified the history and shown the characteristics of the way of life of the most ancient agricultural tribes who from *c.* 3000 to *c.* 1500 B.C. occupied large parts of the basins of the Dnepr, southern Bug, and Dnestr from near the tributaries of the Pripyat in the north to the northern shores of the Black Sea in the south.

The Tripolyans generally settled on the higher parts of the Black Earth plateau [the rich soil of the south Ukraine is called the Black Earth. T.] near springs or along the small rivers that flow here. One of the more interesting sites is Vladimirovka (about 200 km. south of Kiev) on a tributary of the southern Bug. More than 200 Tripole houses were found here which were set out in five concentric circles. This circular arrangement of houses is characteristic of Tripole settlements. Within the closed circle of buildings there was a fold for animals, the most important property of the community. The settlement was occupied by one clan, and large families lived communally in each of the houses.

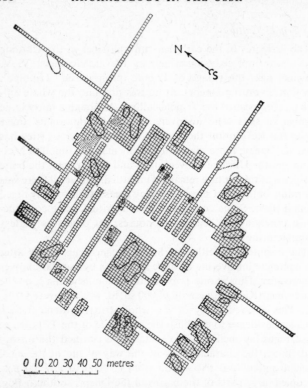

0 10 20 30 40 50 metres

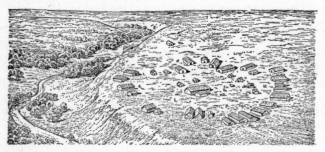

11. **Tripole** site of Kolomiishchina. Plan of site from excavations, above, and reconstruction of settlement, below.

The Tripolyans lived in beaten clay or earth-houses. The large house was divided by lateral partitions into several living compartments. In each of these was a clay oven and all the necessary domestic equipment; vessels for storing provisions and for cooking food, agricultural tools, and querns (for grinding corn). The houses at Vladimirovka were constructed of thick stakes joined by wickerwork coated with clay. They scorched the latter after the construction of the house and sometimes they painted it. The houses are usually rectangular, from 5 to 30 m. long and 5–7 m. wide. The floors, the ovens and their stands, the benches, and the ritual altars were all made of clay. After the destruction of the house thick layers of clay remained, the so-called 'clay areas'. The general appearance of a Tripole house has been established for us by the Tripolyans themselves, for they made models of baked clay of their own houses for an uncertain but probably ritual purpose.

At Kolomiishchina (site II) a large house 27 m. long and 6–7 m. broad containing several hearths was excavated. It was divided by four internal lateral partitions and by pairs of posts in them into five compartments. In one were two ovens, in another a circular altar decorated with red colouring. Careful observation of each part of the house and the good state of preservation of the remains made it possible to establish several alterations and additions to the building. The ancient builders extended their house to keep pace with the growing size of the communal family occupying it.

Besides beaten clay houses an earth-house was also dug at Vladimirovka. Its walls were lined with twigs plastered with clay. That Tripolyan settlements had not only beaten clay houses is brought out by the excavations on the settlement at Luka-Vrublevetskaya (about 300 km. south-west of Kiev) on the left bank of the Dnestr. This is the earliest of all Tripole sites. Here long semi-subterranean houses for winter use were found containing a number of hearths. One house for example was a three-roomed building with eleven hearths arranged along its long axis.

Soviet archaeologists have given special attention to problems of the Tripole economy. The archaeological evidence does not allow an exact definition of the time when agriculture was first practised or a full reconstruction of its course of development. Evidently it developed directly out of plant-gathering but it was not born at one spot on the earth's surface but in different places independently. In the initial stages the earth was loosened with a hoe usually formed of an ordinary branch or stick with a 'blade' of stone, bone, or wood fixed to it. This form of agriculture is usually known after the tool used as 'hoe cultivation'.

The evidence about the economy of the Tripolyans has come from numerous excavated sites. For example, the clay coating of the Tripole houses contains traces of burnt grain and chaff, of flax seeds (*zhmykhy*), wheat, barley and millet grains, and natural seeds of cereals. Querns, sickles of bone or flint with a wooden handle, and hoes, also show that the inhabitants were farmers. Finds of the bones of cows, pigs, and sheep bear witness to stock-breeding. The importance of this gradually grew, for in the earliest sites it was less important than in the later ones. Luka-Vrublevetskaya is an early site showing the transition from hunting to stock-breeding, for here the proportions of domestic and wild animals are similar but with a slight preponderance of wild.

Most of the tools found on Tripole sites are made of stone, copper being very rare and bronze non-existent. From copper were made needles of quadrangular section, fish hooks, small rings, and small flat splayed axes, similar in form to polished stone axes. Numerous objects of bone and antler are found on the sites.

Tripole pottery is especially interesting (Pl. 3a). It shows a high standard of technique in preparing the paste, in modelling, and in firing, with a wealth of shapes and elegant and varied decoration. The designs are usually painted in white, black, or red, which has given rise to the term 'painted pottery'. In this respect the Tripole culture has been compared to similar agricultural cultures with painted pottery found from China to the Balkans. Applied and incised decoration is also found. The normal patterns are spirals, circles, and ribbons of double lines. Sometimes symbolical drawings of the sun or figures of animals are found. This pottery with its fine painting was for display and was at the same time serviceable and decorative in the house; rough primitive pots were made for general use and for cooking.

Clay statuettes (usually broken) portraying women are found in enormous quantities on almost all the sites. The figures are conventionally schematized, while statues of men are much rarer. The female statuettes are connected with the cult of fertility, regenerating nature, symbolized in the female form of the mother. In the clay of the figures are incorporated wheat grains, which would symbolize the fertility of the soil. The female form is also connected with the cult of ancestors, protectors of the domestic hearth, and women leaders of the clan. Tripole statuettes are usually found on the clay ritual altars or near the hearth.

Study of the remains of the Tripole culture has shown that the historical development of the most ancient agricultural tribes of the Dnepr area followed a complex course. Soviet archaeologists have the material to study this course, but in spite of much success in the study of the culture, several matters remain unexplained.

Above all there is still no solution to the question as to the origin of the Tripole culture. [Some favour entirely autochthonous development, others see the whole culture as an intrusion from Asia Minor or the east Mediterranean area, and between these extremes are views emphasizing one side or the other. T.] Bibikov considers that the Tripole culture between the Dnepr and Dnestr rivers was produced by the intermixture of two components: local hunting tribes and intrusive agriculturalists from Asia Minor. The former would have been assimilated by the latter.

The causes of the disappearance of the Tripole culture are still unsettled. It has been supposed that with the development of the economy and of new social relationships the culture degenerated. The change to stock-breeding as the basis of the economy destroyed the equal rights of men and women and gave control to the men, so that a patriarchal society was established. [The author refers to the Engels scheme. T.]

Stock-rearing required pastures and so primitive tribes had to occupy the flood meadows of river valleys. Driving cattle from place to place people halted on sand dunes where we find temporary sites of this period. Agriculture did not vanish, indeed it continued to develop, but the whole appearance of the material culture changed owing to the increasing part played by stock-rearing.

Gradually the typical large family houses disappear and are replaced by comparatively modest structures, semi-subterranean earth-houses and more deeply dug earth-houses with beaten clay hearths. The finds testify to a significant increase in stock-rearing. Unpainted pottery becomes typical, while copper tools become common. A time is reached (c. 2000–1500 B.C.) when on the sites of former Tripole sites appear settlements and graves lacking typical features of the past culture. The best site excavated from the following period is at Gorodska (about 100 km. north-west of Kiev). Here were found small beaten clay and semi-subterranean huts. Bones of domestic animals were more numerous there than on Tripole sites. The domestic horse is believed to appear for the first time now. Other similar sites are known.

The settlement and barrow cemetery near Usatovo, near Odessa, are especially interesting. Here were found stone houses constructed of limestone which is very common in this area. Together with painted wares there was pottery decorated with cord impressions. The inhabitants were farmers but stock-rearing played a greater part than arable farming in their life. Hunting and fishing were important also. There were numerous finds of fish bones, stone net weights, and bone fish hooks.

The contemporary barrows are mounds up to 40 m. in diameter and revetted at the base with limestone blocks. The skeletons are usually found in the centre of the barrows in a pit with the knees drawn up. Sometimes the burials are in pairs, a man and woman in one pit. Later burials have been put into the body of the mound. In the opinion of the investigators the chief was put in the centre, his followers in the body of the mound. The skeletons were sprinkled with red ochre and on them were found necklaces of animal teeth, copper diadems, flat daggers, flanged axes, and short hoes. The inhabitants received metal and finished metal tools from the shores of the Aegean Sea [i.e. tools of similar design are found in the two areas. T.]. In the graves as in the settlement besides pots decorated with cord impressions painted pots were also found. In some barrows special pits with offerings have been discovered, in one case clay female statuettes, in another a stone sculpture of an ox's head. Among the limestone flags surrounding some of the barrows was found a flat stone (1 m. high) bearing an engraving in deep lines of a man and four animals, horses and a deer. The settlement and barrows in Usatovo are not the only ones in the Black Sea area: similar sites have been found at other points.

The short description of the sites at Gorodska and Usatovo show that although they retain many features of the Tripole culture (painted pottery, beaten clay huts) on the whole they are clearly different, and it is rather difficult to explain all the changes simply as being the results of economic changes. Therefore a second view has gained credence: that the Tripole tribes were conquered and subjected by other intrusive tribes who brought a new culture with them. The question is still, however, an open one, as also is the ethnic position of the Tripole people [i.e. with which later group known from written sources they should be identified. T.]. Other problems about them also remain. Soviet scholars continue work on the study of this culture in order to settle the whole intricate problem of the history of agricultural tribes between the Dnepr and the Danube. Miss T. C. Passek's many years' work on the Tripole culture has been embodied in a book entitled *The Periodization of Tripole Settlements*.

## THE CAUCASUS

Remains of farmers of the Copper Age are not only known in the Ukraine and Moldavia, but have also been discovered in central Asia in Turkmenia, in Transcaucasia, and in the north Caucasus. The fullest picture of farmers' settlements of the third millennium B.C. is obtained from Transcaucasia from the excavations at Shengavit near Erevan. This ancient settlement is situated on a raised promontory on the left bank of the river Zanga. Even before excavation large circles about 7 m. in diameter were clearly visible on the surface, especially after rain. It appears that these are the remains of circular central rooms of houses which were adjoined by rectangular rooms. The walls were built of large sun-dried bricks set on a stone foundation. The floor of the central room was laid with pebbles arranged in concentric circles. In the centre was a large stone on which a post rested to support a conical roof of struts and wickerwork. Near this stone was placed a shallow circular clay hearth about a metre in diameter, decorated with relief ornament on its edge. Querns and large pots containing wheat and barley grain were found by the hearth. Besides arable farming the inhabitants also reared cows and sheep. Stone and clay figures of animals, a schematic and very stylized female statuette, and a miniature model of a hearth were found in the houses.

The pottery was black or occasionally red with its surface polished to a shine and bore grooved and applied geometrical decoration. There were numerous flint and polished stone tools, bone pins, arrowheads, and beads, and also certain copper tools.

Eneolithic settlements in the Caucasus generally similar to Shengavit are known from a number of sites, as well as in Armenia and Georgia. In the north-east Caucasus a similar site belonging to the second half of the third millennium B.C. was excavated at Kayakent (about 250 km. north-east of Tiflis) but it was fortified. The houses were constructed of stones and wickerwork, plastered with clay. Agriculture was the basis of the economy. The stone querns, pestles, and sickle flints, and the finds of bread cereals in the baked clay of an oven and in the clay of the pot sherds testify to this. Stock-rearing played an important part in the economy, above all sheep-breeding.

In the north Caucasus, especially in the Kuban valley, a series of important Copper-Age barrows were excavated in pre-Revolutionary times, among them the famous Maikop barrow of the middle of the third millennium B.C. [These include a number of rich finds. The Maikop barrow contained silver vessels decorated with animals and a series of copper tools, especially shaft-hole axes and adzes similar to tools from Mesopotamia. This is important for dating in south Russia. T.]

Soviet archaeologists have made a thorough study of the results of the excavations of the so-called 'great barrows of the Kuban', their date, and so on. The barrows may be referred to the second half of the third millennium B.C. and are graves of tribal chiefs. No settlement of this period was known until recently. At Dolinsk (about 200 km. north of Tiflis) the results of the excavation of a Copper-Age settlement threw light on the everyday life of this period. The site is situated on a high river terrace and extends for 1,500 m. It was made up of separate groups of huts, large wickerwork cabins with walls plastered on both faces with clay, a beaten clay floor, hearths in deep holes, and storage pits. The economy was agricultural; hoes, querns, and sickle flints were found. The ground adjoining the huts was cultivated.

The older steppe cultures of the Lower Don, Dnepr, Volga, and southern Siberia belong to the Copper Age. These will be dealt with in the next chapter. [These barrow cultures are in part contemporary with the cultures described in this chapter. T.]

### THE EXTREME NORTH-EAST

As a result of the unequal rate of development the whole area of our country did not experience the Neolithic and Copper Ages simultaneously. When metal was widespread in the south, in the remoter regions of the north neolithic cultures continued. Some measure of such a late neolithic 'survival' can be obtained from archaeological sites studied by Soviet archaeologists on the uttermost margin of human settlement on the shores of the Bering Sea in the Chukotsk peninsula. The most ancient remains are referred to the end of the second and beginning of the first millennia B.C., others to a later time when already over the greater part of our country iron had become the basic material for making tools. Here on the Arctic coast of Asia neolithic cultures still existed, and iron objects are only found as rare imported objects. (The dating of the sites is controversial, and some workers would date them to the beginning of the Christian era.)

Close to the contemporary settlement of Uellen (near the Bering Straits) a very ancient settlement of hunters of coastal animals has been studied, the predecessors of the Eskimos. The huts had been on the surface without any excavation into the ground, so survive badly for the archaeologist. The cultural deposit was only recognizable by the stronger growth of grass above it. Hunting of sea animals [such as seals. T.] and of reindeer and polar bear, as well as the catching of birds and fish, were the inhabitants' means of existence. They had numerous items of highly-developed hunting equipment: bows and arrows with stone arrowheads, harpoons of complicated construction [that is proper toggle heads like the Eskimos', not simple barbed heads. T.], and special implements for cutting holes through the ice. Stone tools were made also exclusively by the oldest means of strike or pressure flaking and polished objects were rare.

The descendants of the people of Uellen were more advanced. They lived in small rectangular earth-houses with a paved stone floor and long walls. The hunting of sea animals was carried on in the open sea in skilfully constructed skin boats. Clay pots and lamps were used everywhere, as well as vessels of bone and of whale fin with wooden stiffeners. This peculiar and interesting culture passed through a number of stages before the adoption of iron, instead of stone, tools. Its study has shown how, under very difficult conditions in the midst of the ice of the Arctic seas, man triumphed in his struggle against the forces of nature, even if the trying geographical conditions somewhat arrested his cultural development.

*

We have lingered on the remains of the neolithic survivals in this chapter on the Neolithic Period only because they have outward resemblances to true neolithic cultures; but in chronological terms another age had already started, the age of metal.

In spite of the substantial successes of Soviet archaeologists in the field of Neolithic- and Copper-Age studies, many unfinished tasks remain. . . .

## Chapter 4

# THE BRONZE AGE

THE first metal objects were hammered out of natural copper. Metallurgy was born later when people grasped that copper can melt, that by applying strong heat it becomes a liquid, and that in this state it can be given a desired form in which it will harden on cooling. This outstanding discovery, although an important advance in the development of the productive forces, produced no radical changes in technique. Pure copper, soft and pliable, could not replace stone tools. Tools cast from bronze, an alloy of tin and copper, were much more reliable than copper ones, so finally bronze took the place of copper as an industrial metal. The adoption of bronze could not lead to the complete rejection of stone for tools. This only happened with the discovery of iron-working.

In the Bronze Age stock-rearing became a wholly independent branch of the economy. While the central and northern forest zones of the USSR were still occupied by tribes of hunters and fishers in the steppe and wooded steppe and in the Caucasus and central Asia hunting had become unimportant and stock-rearing had become the main source of meat. A subdivision into pastoral tribes took place. This important social division of work led to the development of barter between tribes. Successes in the sphere of material production and the development of social division of labour and barter led to changes in the social relationship between peoples. The old matriarchal clan with its equality of the fields was transformed into a new patriarchal clan. The man became head of the family. Accumulated riches were a stimulus to robbery or warlike raids of one tribe upon another. At the end of the third millennium B.C. pastoralists of the southern steppes began to use metal tools. In the forest areas they were not acquainted with metallurgy until somewhat later.

Pre-Revolutionary Russian archaeology accumulated a substantial amount of Bronze-Age material but study of the Bronze Age developed very unevenly. In many areas nothing was known about it. In the early years of this century V. A. Gorodtsov worked out a scheme for the southern steppes and later for the whole area of the USSR.

## THE CAUCASUS

In the Bronze Age of the USSR an outsanding part was played by the tribes and peoples of the Caucasus.

Remains of the Bronze Age of Transcaucasia have been comparatively well-known for some time. Objects of high quality of the Late Bronze Age have long adorned museums. Yet as little as twenty years ago nobody knew anything of the earlier stages of the development of metallurgy in the Caucasus, and it was even supposed that metallurgy was brought into the Caucasus from outside: from the west or east by a wave of Late-Bronze-Age invaders.

Soviet archaeologists have found the first links in the chain of general development of metallurgy in the Caucasus and proved that this process was here ancient and indigenous. The Caucasus contained not only copper ore but also the necessary ores to make alloys: antimony, found within the Caucasus itself, and tin, found in neighbouring Transcaucasia. The wealth of the Caucasus in natural ores is one of the basic causes of the creation here of a powerful centre influencing the development of the Bronze Age in the whole of eastern Europe.

It has been established that during the Caucasian Bronze Age there was a series of important local metallurgical centres which were using the local ore and making metal objects which at times were carried far beyond the boundaries of the area. It is necessary to remark that in the third millennium B.C. the Caucasian tribes knew not only copper and bronze, but also gold and silver, generally used to make ornaments and vessels.

Some of the oldest grave remains of the Caucasian Bronze Age are the dolmens of the western Caucasus, especially those at Abkhazi excavated in 1934–7. Dolmens are constructions of rough stone slabs intended for collective burial, and the same dolmen was used for later burials over a long period of time. The oldest burials in dolmens at Abkhazi belong to the beginning of the Copper–Bronze Age, but they were in use until the Late Bronze Age.

Dolmens fall into the group of structures called by archaeologists 'megalithic' (Greek *megas*, big and *lithos*, stone). 'Menhirs', free-standing stones, and the so-called 'cyclopean' walling, built of large roughly dressed stones (up to 2 m. high) laid without mortar, are also called megalithic constructions. Cyclopean walling is so called because in antiquity there was a legend about building by the one-eyed giants, the Cyclops. From the middle of the second millennium B.C. warlike collisions between tribes and separate communities became more violent. Therefore settlements were constructed on high inaccessible hills and surrounded by walls of cyclopean construction behind which the population and cattle could be protected. Cyclopean constructions are known in several parts of the USSR; in Transcaucasia they are found in Azerbaijan, Georgia, and Armenia (best studied in the latter area). Not only the excavations of these remains in the Caucasus but also their inter-relationship and description have great scientific importance.

Especially outstanding remains of the Caucasian Bronze Age are the barrows in one of the oldest cultural areas of Georgia, Trialeti (about 110 km. south-west of Tiflis), excavated in 1936–40 and in 1947. These are burials of chieftains of a rich pastoral tribe living in 1800–1700 B.C. Under the barrows burial shafts 7–9 m. deep were found, sometimes faced with stones. In the centre of such a grave chamber were placed the ashes of the burnt corpse, sometimes on a massive wooden four-wheeled cart. Around the cart lay remains of large- and small-horned cattle and also a large quantity of richly decorated clay pots. In one barrow twenty-four pots were found, red and yellow in colour painted in black or brown, and also black pots with incised decoration filled with red colouring. Most of the tools were made of bronze but some silver daggers were also found. Arrowheads were made of flint as usual. The graves were very rich and much gold and silver was found in them; indeed the objects of precious metals from this site are especially remarkable. Amongst these the massive gold goblet decorated with inset red stones of agate and turquoise and with

E

fine filigree ornament is especially remarkable (Pl. 4). With the goblet in the same grave was found a little silver bucket with a gold handle and decorated with drawings of a scene showing the hunting of animals in a forest. The most interesting find of all was a silver goblet standing on a small foot with a chased design in two horizontal bands. In the lower band is shown a file of deer, and in the upper a procession of twenty-three figures bearing blocks (*kubki*) in their hands. These are strange beings with human bodies and animal heads and tails. The procession is going towards a figure seated on a throne near a sacred tree close to which there are two altars and animals for sacrifice.

Not one of the very large barrows at Trialeti (more than forty were excavated in all) contained any trace of human sacrifices, such as are found in the later Scythian burials of the Iron Age. Besides the rich graves like Trialeti there are other poor cemeteries of the same period.

The Trialeti barrows are not unique, for in Transcaucasia there are other similar sites. An even older burial was dug at Kirovakan (about 200 km. south of Tiflis). The grave consisted of a great trench covering 30 sq. m. and more than 3 m. deep. At the bottom of this pots were placed similar to those from Trialeti, and also a gold cup engraved with three pairs of lions (Pl. 5a), and four silver vessels. The ashes of the dead man had been poured into a wooden bier decorated with bronze nails plated with silver, and with him were placed his rich necklace of carnelian and gold beads. In the same barrow a bronze axe-adze, a flat axe, three daggers, and a spearhead were found.

Bronze-Age settlements in Transcaucasia are still inadequately studied but the numerous cemeteries excavated in various areas have proved extraordinarily varied. The most interesting monument in central Georgia is the ancient cemetery at the monastery of Samtavro (see p. 221). Excavations were begun in 1871 but systematic planned study was not made until 1938 which allowed the site to be assigned its proper place in the series of monuments. The study was undertaken by a section of an expedition of the Georgian Academy of Sciences. One thousand eight hundred graves were investigated dating from 1000 B.C. to A.D. 800. Bronze-Age graves were found containing a great quantity of pottery vessels and bronze objects: axes, daggers, flat belt clasps, and so on. Especially deserving mention are the beautiful examples of small sculpture, cast figures of aurochs and leopard.

One of the oldest centres of mining activity and metallurgy in the Caucasus was found near Gebi (in Georgia) in 1948. Galleries for mining antimony and furnaces for reducing the ore were found here. A great quantity of metal objects of hammered or cast antimony bronze [copper with antimony added instead of tin. T.] have been found. At the cemetery of Brila 9 km. away such objects were especially numerous. The lower layer of the cemetery is referred to about 1500 or 1000 B.C., the date being controversial. Cemeteries of this period discovered in the other mountainous areas of Transcaucasia belonged to pastoral tribes, living close to the source of raw materials for metallurgy, as a result of which metal-working skill developed rapidly. Objects attesting a highly-developed metallurgy and metal-working based on local ores are found in the graves.

In Armenia a most interesting complex of Bronze-Age sites was examined in 1951–2 on the dried-up area of Lake Sevan (the sites had evidently been under water for a long period when the level of Lake Sevan was higher than now). These were burial fields, in the majority of cases of stone cists containing one, two, or occasionally three bodies in a contracted or sitting position. Each burial was accompanied by 3–5 jugs, bronze ornaments, daggers, carnelian beads, and so on. Further burials from the end of the Late Bronze Age (eighth century B.C.) were found in pits at Astkhodzor (Armenia). In one of these a man was found lying on his side with two bronze belts, one worn across the shoulder. Together with these were bronze daggers, bracelets, beads, and other ornaments. Eleven skeletons of people buried in a sitting position were found in this same grave. Evidently this was the grave of a chieftain buried with his slaves and can be referred to the time of the birth of class society.

In 1935 large stone cists were excavated at Kirovakan, some of which contained collective burials. Thus in one grave three skeletons of adults and one of a child, all in a flexed position, were found, together with the complete skeleton of an ox. There were twenty-three pots above the skeletons. This cemetery may be referred to the ninth to eighth centuries B.C.

Even in pre-Soviet times a good deal was known of the painted pottery from Kizil-vank (in Azerbaijan), and in 1926 two expeditions worked here. Stone cists were excavated containing skeletons lying on the right side with the knees drawn up. Together with copper and bronze objects black polished pots and painted pots were found in the graves. This Kizil-vank culture characterized by pottery decorated with geometric ornament and spouted vessels, like tea-pots, covers the whole of the Nakhichevan A S S R (south of Erevan near the frontier). The cemeteries belong to the fourteenth to eleventh centuries B.C. The cemetery at Shakhtakht belongs to the very end of this period. In one grave amongst thirty different pots there was one painted in different colours showing animals and birds. This site belongs to the end of the second millennium B.C., the period of the development of semi-migratory pastoralism.

The two villages of Kedabek and Khojal in Azerbaijan have given their names to a culture characteristic of this area from the tenth to the seventh centuries B.C. Similar sites are spread over the greater part of central Trancaucasia. The characteristics of the culture are stone cist burials, earthern barrows of varying sizes, stone cairns, cromlechs, and menhirs. Grave goods consist of pots decorated with incised ornament, sometimes filled with gypsum, and a great number of bronze objects. To this period belong also the forts built of cyclopean masonry.

The excavations on Bronze-Age sites around Khanlar (about 200 km. south-east of Tiflis) were especially valuable. The houses were semi-subterranean and rectangular in shape, with walls faced with stone, divided internally by partitions into four rooms with a hearth in each. The houses examined gave material indicative of the economy of this ancient period. Besides the stones of wild fruits, stones of peach were also found testifying to the existence of orchards. . . .

At the end of the Bronze Age and beginning of the Iron Age, that is about 1000 B.C. in this area, bronze objects distinctive of the Koban culture are found over a wide area of the Caucasus. This culture takes its name from the village of Koban (about 200 km. north of Tiflis). This culture has been studied both before and since the Revolution. . . .

The Koban culture extended over the foothills and mountains in the central part of the northern Caucasus and existed up to the seventh century B.C. Characteristic of this culture are special bronze axes, long, narrow, and curved, as well as copper vessels and varied ornaments such as copper pins, wide plated belts, fibulae (safety-pin brooches), bracelets, and so on. Burials were placed in stone cists, sometimes surrounded by stone circles, while burials in a wooden framework are also known. Simple pots, usually with incised geometrical decoration and varied ornaments, headgear, beads, and copper bracelets were placed in the graves. That mourning ceremonies took place for the dead is shown by ritual hearths and holes in the graves. The graves were set out in rows. Women's and children's burials were put next to a stone circle surrounding a man's grave.

The basis of the economy of the Koban tribes was pastoralism. Previously all Bronze-Age remains in the Caucasus similar to the Koban remains were referred to this culture, but now similar local cultures are distinguished by a number of features. [The author then mentions several local variations of this culture in the area of the Caucasus. T.]

## THE WESTERN STEPPES

On the steppes on the lower reaches of the Volga, Don, and Dnepr are numerous barrows of various periods, the oldest of which can be referred to the Copper and Bronze Ages. The characteristic feature of the Bronze-Age barrows is that the skeletons in the graves are usually in a contracted position (their knees drawn up) and the greater part are painted with red colouring. (The corpse was smeared with red colour, ochre or red lead, which according to ancient belief had the cleansing effect of fire. As the flesh disappeared the colouring remained on the skeleton.) V. A. Gorodtsov already at the beginning of this century classified the primitive barrows of the steppes according to variations of the burial beneath the barrow into three consecutive periods: Old Pit, Catacomb, and Timber-Frame (*Srubnaya*) cultures. New excavations in the Ukraine, Don, and Volga areas have confirmed this basis of classification. Soviet archaeologists have not only dug new sites and explained a number of local variants of this culture, but also defined the forms of economy of the different periods of the Bronze Age and the various tribes. The Old Pit barrows belong to the Copper Age, barrows with burials in catacombs (meaning here a special form of tomb construction below a barrow in which the burial chamber lies on one side of the burial shaft and is entered by a hole through its wall) and in timber-framed trenches belong to the Bronze Age (Fig. 12). Between the Old Pit and Catacomb cultures no sharp interruption exists and many archaeologists regard one as the direct continuation of the other, but the Catacomb and Timber-Frame cultures are

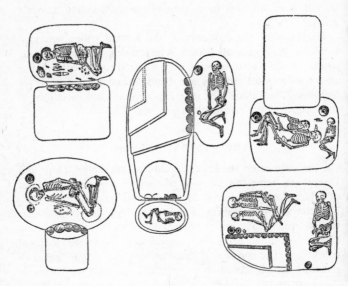

Катакомбные погребения. Таблица составлена В. А. Городцовым.

12. Catacomb burials from south Russia.

not consecutive stages of development of the same community but remains of separate ethnic groups.

Barrows of the Old Pit culture usually had a small mound about a metre high under which was a shallow pit containing the burial. The bottom of the pit and the corpse above were sprinkled with red colouring matter. Flint knives, scrapers, arrowheads, bone tools, and copper objects like awls and knives are found in the graves. Pots are egg-shaped. Old Pit culture barrows are found between the Dnepr and Lower Volga.

An interesting barrow of the Old Pit culture is *Storozhevaya Mogila* (the Sentry or Look-out Barrow) on the right bank of the Dnepr (18 km. south of Dnepropetrovsk). The barrow was 7 m. high and excavation in 1949 revealed three burials, a primary at the centre and two later secondary burials in the mound. All the skeletons were contracted and sprinkled with red colouring. Above the pits was a ceiling of logs, in some cases covered by rushes. On a ledge around one of the graves were found the remains of a two-wheeled cart (*arba*). The wheels were made of solid blocks of wood split lengthwise with bulbous hubs containing apertures for the axle. This barrow belongs to the second half of the third millennium B.C. and is the oldest evidence for wheeled transport drawn by a team of beasts in east Europe. [If, as is quite likely, the dating is reliable this applies to all Europe north of the Mediterranean area as well. The find is of great interest. T.]

In recent years numerous Bronze-Age sites have been excavated in the Lower Volga area. Thousands of barrows have been excavated and several hundred Bronze-Age settlements recorded in this area. The Stalingrad expedition of 1952 alone dug about 400 burials. Excavation of barrows has made it possible to establish not only the changes in the way of life taking place among the pastoral tribes of the steppes but also the changes in social relationships. The development of patriarchal society can be observed in the following fact. The basic burial in the Old Pit culture was of a man, the head of the family. Above this the mound was thrown up, and in this were placed the female relatives, as women were still held in esteem. Some secondary burials of women have fairly rich grave goods and the mound was enlarged over them. In barrows of the

Catacomb culture pairs of burials are often found in which the woman was killed and placed beside her husband, as she had to accompany him in his journey into the next world. The burials of the Timber-Frame culture were often accompanied by ritual murder. Especially prominent are burials of well-armed warriors, evidently chieftains.

In the barrows of the Catacomb culture the dead were buried in tombs with a deep niche. The bodies were placed in a flexed position on the right side. Beside the body are found pots with flat bottoms and remains of food, bones of domestic animals, sometimes millet grains, and also various tools and ornaments, perforated stone axes, arrow- and lance-heads, bronze knives, pins, and so on.

Finds in the Old Pit culture barrows show that the basis of the economy of the tribes in this area was hunting and fishing while stock-rearing, which in the long run became the chief branch of the economy of the steppe tribes, had only just begun. In the Catacomb barrows there is widespread evidence for pastoralism and agriculture among the inhabitants of the steppe.

As was said above in the chapter on the Neolithic Period, Soviet archaeologists have devoted much attention to defining local variants within the great archaeological cultures and to connecting these local variants to various tribal groupings. Thus, so far six local variants of the Catacomb culture have been defined. One of these showed the first instances of artificial deformation of the skull, later widely practised among the Sarmatians, Alans, Huns, and other tribes. Excavations continue uninterruptedly and are yielding interesting new results.

In the middle of the second millennium B.C. tribes of the Timber-Frame (*Srubnaya*) culture began to move westwards to the Don, Donets, and Dnepr.

The Kuibyshev and Stalingrad expeditions discovered and investigated a series of Bronze-Age remains, settlements and barrows, whose study has significantly broadened our knowledge of this area.

We will give a description of a barrow of the Timber-Frame culture excavated by one of the sections of the Kuibyshev expedition. The barrow is at the village of Yagodnoe in the north of the Kuibyshev district. Thirty burials were discovered arranged in two penannular concentric settings. In the barrow the original primary burial was in a pit covered with two layers of logs. On the bottom of the pit lay the skeleton of a man beside whom pots were laid, under one of which lay two knives in criss-cross fashion. There was no burial at the centre of the barrow, but the remains of a great fire over 4 m. in diameter. In the ashes were found the skeleton of a cow and numerous bones of other domestic animals. Sacrifices were evidently made here in honour of the dead chief of the community. Subsequently for one or two generations the barrow was used as a cemetery for the patriarchal family whose head had been buried at the time of the original construction of the barrow.

At the end of the second millennium B.C. metal-working developed locally among the steppe tribes (formerly metal objects had apparently been imported). On the settlements copper slag and pieces of crucibles and moulds are found.

In one of the barrows of the Timber-Frame culture excavated in 1952 at Kalinovka (near Stalingrad) a man's skeleton was found with a stone pestle at his head and at his feet a collection of a metal-worker's tools: two bivalve moulds for casting bronze axes, a clay double mould for casting flat axes, chisels, funnels, and so on (Fig. 13). This burial is referred to the period 1200–400 B.C., and has contributed extraordinarily important evidence for the study of ancient metal-casting.

Large barrows were thrown up over the graves of warrior chiefs in the Middle Bronze Age. The burial itself was carried out with magnificent ceremony in tombs constructed of wood or stone.

An example of such a burial of the Middle Bronze Age is found at the 'Three Brothers' barrows (about 300 km. south-east of Rostov-on-Don) and in other barrows of the steppes near the Caspian Sea. The social position of the dead in these barrows is defined not only by the magnificent ritual and great size of the barrow, but also by accompanying burials of subordinates, women, and slaves. Barrow No. 9 was 7 m. high and 60 m. in diameter. The remains of a great fire were found on its summit below which (1 m. beneath the surface) was the sacrificial place. There were animal bones here under a stone slab,

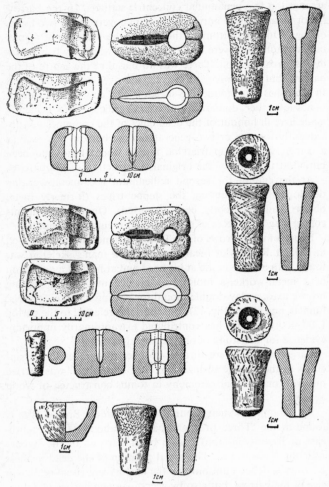

13. Kalinovka. Bronze-worker's kit from barrow burial.

as well as pots and the clay model of a two-wheeled cart (*arba*). Below the sacrifices at a depth of 7 m. from the top of the barrow the original grave was found. It consisted of a large square shaft, the bottom of which was laid with boards, soft stuff, and grass. The dead man was placed in a sitting position, and the skeleton was covered with red colouring. Beside it were a bronze knife, two small awls, and wooden and clay cups and pots. The grave was covered with thin planks and logs which in turn were covered by a rug and mat. Around the edge of the tomb was a setting of stones, and at each corner of the burial shaft was placed a cart-wheel (made of solid wood, without spokes). Evidently pieces of three two-wheeled carts were placed in the barrow.

Thanks to the work of Soviet archaeologists, in the steppe area of the European parts of the USSR numerous Bronze-Age settlements are known. Settlements of the Timber-Frame Bronze-Age culture have been especially well studied. One of these settlements was excavated at Lyapichev Farm (south-west of Stalingrad near the Don). This ancient site consisted of ten rectangular earth-houses, measuring 12–15 by 7–9 m.

The earth-houses were roofed by a pyramidal framework with a flat top. This framework was made from unsawn branches selected for suitable length and these were not joined at the top. The roof frame was capped with grass and the whole covered over with a layer of packed earth. There was a hole in the roof to allow smoke to escape. Thus the earth-houses looked like an earth-knoll on the outside, while within there was a spacious room, in the southern half of which the cattle were kept. The cattle had a separate entry on the south side down a sloping ramp cut out of the ground. In the long, dark, and damp but warm subterranean house there probably lived two or three families with their livestock. This site provides evidence of settled as opposed to migrant pastoralism. Stone and bone tools were found on the site, as well as many pots and animal bones, mostly of large-horned cattle.

Such settlements with large semi-subterranean houses have been excavated beyond the Volga on the river Irgiz, on the lower Volga near Stalingrad, and elsewhere.

Bronze-Age settlements in the basin of the Irgiz are of

modest size, 60 to 100 m. in length and of about the same breadth. Within this area there are three to six earth-house huts. Elsewhere settlements are significantly larger and had more inhabitants. The earth-houses are similar but differ in details of construction from those at Lyapichev. Many had a plank bedding below the house and the walls and floor were sometimes faced with wooden blocks. On one site there were five hearths on the floor, one large and four small, belonging perhaps to separate families. Study of the settlements of the Timber-Frame culture has allowed the conclusion that the basic economic activity of the bearers of this culture was stock-breeding together with agriculture.

As was said above, in spite of a wide measure of uniformity of material culture it has been found possible to distinguish six local groups of tribes of the Catacomb culture. Such work ought to be carried out on all Bronze-Age cultures, but the start already made shows the total inadequacy of stadial schemes and confirms the correctness of the method now employed by Soviet archaeologists. This is the study of concrete archaeological cultures as expressions of ethnic entities and not just as stages of development. Study of the history of tribes does not exclude but in fact demands in the first instance a study of their economy and social relationships in their development and changes. . . . [In an omitted paragraph the author criticizes a book which had applied the Engels scheme too rigidly. T.]

During the period when tribes of the Catacomb culture were settled on the southern open steppe, cultures related to the Tripole culture were spread over the wooded steppe on the west side of the Dnepr as far as the Dnestr. Bronze-Age cultures were studied here by Polish archaeologists and after the reunification of the Ukraine in 1939 important work has been carried out by a number of Soviet workers.

An extraordinarily interesting site is the cemetery of the first quarter of the second millennium B.C. excavated in 1948 at the village of Sofievka (near Kiev). The 145 burials excavated consisted of burnt human bones, sometimes placed in urns. The grave goods comprised stone battle-axes, polished flint axes, arrowheads, sickles, and so on. A flat axe, knives, awls, and ornaments of copper were found. The pots were decorated in relief, or with cord impressions, stamps, or little pits, or painted. This site is similar to other cemeteries which are closely related to late Tripole sites.

Later on, Bronze-Age agricultural and pastoral tribes appear in the wooded steppe zone in the basin of the Dnestr as far east as the Dnepr.

## THE FOREST ZONE

We will now turn to the forest zone of eastern Europe.

In the second millennium B.C. agriculture, stock-rearing, and the use of metals began to spread into the forest zone of the European parts of the USSR amongst the hunter–fisher tribes discussed in the earlier part of the last chapter. Originally these features penetrated here from the south; only later did metal-working begin in the Kama and Ural areas. In some regions, around the upper parts of the Volga and Dnepr, the neolithic way of life survived up to the first millennium B.C., and in the extreme north even up to the first millennium A.D. However at the end of the third millennium B.C. there appeared one tribe or another with a Bronze-Age culture in the midst of tribes whose outward form of culture was still completely neolithic. The settlements of such tribes are still almost unknown. We know a great number of burials which from the site first excavated in 1875 at the village of that name are called Fatyanovo burials (Fatyanovo is about 300 km. north-east of Moscow). The culture was first defined in pre-Soviet times but the material was not fully classified. Since the 1920s twenty-six Fatyanovo graves have been examined and studied by Soviet archaeologists. This has permitted accurate demarcation of the area of distribution of this culture and split it up into three groups: one around Moscow, another around Yaroslav, and a third in Chuvashia (the Chuvash ASSR is in the bend of the Volga). Judging by the finds it can be assumed that these groups represent three consecutive chronological stages in the development of the Fatyanovo culture during its eastward movement. Thus in graves of the Moscow group there is still no metal. In the Yaroslav group, metal is common, but all the same poorer than in the Chuvash group where there are many bronze ornaments and very varied stone objects.

The Fatyanovo burials are generally found on high places but at the same time have no external indications [no barrow on top. T.]. The dead man was placed in a deep shaft on his side with his knees drawn up. The most typical implement of this culture is a perforated stone battle-axe, which is finely polished and is of distinctive form, sometimes resembling a bronze axe. Especially characteristic of the graves are the elegant, elongated, so-called boat-shaped axes. Metal implements are found side by side with stone ones, and the shaft-hole bronze axe of a special type with the so-called drooping butt is distinctive. Besides axes, globular pots with cord impressions or varied geometrical decoration are peculiar to the culture (Pl. 5b). Amongst the discoveries of Soviet archaeologists the finds in Fatyanovo graves of domestic animals, cows, sheep, pigs, and horses have special importance. In this way the existence of stock-rearing in the forest zone of east Europe was established at this early period. Besides stock-rearing hunting, fishing, and gathering still had some importance. The Fatyanovo cemetery richest in the variety of its tools and weapons and by the quantity of its bronze objects was that found at the village of Balanovo (about 600 km. east of Moscow). The skeletons found here lay in a flexed position on their sides. Collective burials were not uncommon. With the skeletons were found round-bottomed pots, bronze implements such as an axe, spearhead, awls, diadems, perforated stone axes, and polished stone chisels, small clay copies of axes specially made for placing with the dead, little clay wheels from miniature carts, and flint arrowheads.

A distinct feature of the economy is the absence from the sites of any traces of connexion with the surrounding neolithic tribes. The absence of any sites showing the local development of the Fatyanovo tribes favours the supposition that they came there from outside. Additional evidence in support of this view is that to judge from anthropological evidence the Fatyanovo tribes were sharply distinguished in appearance from the local population.

In recent time possible roads of entry for the Fatyanovo

tribes into the area from the middle Dnepr where the cultures are similar have been suggested. The Fatyanovo and Bronze-Age tribes of central Europe are linked by a number of common features, and the whole lot are grouped together under the title of 'corded-ware' peoples, as their pots are usually decorated with cord impressions. These pastoral tribes which were formed on the south Russian steppes in the third millennium B.C. appeared in central Europe in the second millennium B.C. In the USSR they occupied Podolia and Volynia (west Ukraine) the Dnestr and middle Dnepr, the south-eastern coastal area of the Baltic, and the upper and middle Volga area (roughly the area south-eastwards from the southern Baltic to the Volga).

Some German racialist–archaeologists maintained that bearers of the 'corded-ware' culture were pre-German warriors who invaded eastern Europe and colonized the areas as far as the upper Volga. . . . [The author refers to the famous controversy over the original home of the Indo-Europeans, speakers of the hypothetical language from which most modern European languages are believed to be derived. This was a special preoccupation of German linguists and was used by Nazi propagandists. The 'corded-ware' or 'battle-axe' cultures are found over wide areas of northern and eastern Europe, and some German scholars believed that from an original home in north Germany they spread eastwards. They assumed that the bearers of these cultures were speakers of the original Indo-European language. Others have reversed the direction maintaining that they started from south Russia and moved north-westwards. While probably most Western scholars believe that there is a connexion between the spread of Indo-European languages and these cultures, this is probably about as far as they feel it wise to go. T.]

In the middle and second half of the second millennium B.C. there spread over the wooded steppe of the Volga area and beyond in the direction of the river Ural the so-called Abashevo culture. Unlike the Fatyanovo burials the Abashevo burials occur under burial mounds or barrows. In 1925 the first barrows of this culture were excavated at the village of Abashevo (about 600 km. east of Moscow). Since then a number of these sites have been discovered and their area of distribution marked out: the Volga area, particularly modern Chuvashia, and beyond the Volga in the basin of the river Belaya.

The Abashevo tribes were occupied mainly with stock-rearing and agriculture, and to them belong the numerous copper and bronze implements found in the middle Volga area. The Abashevo barrows are moderate-sized mounds with a shallow burial shaft beneath. The bottom of the shaft is lined with birch-bark, and covered over with logs or planks. The corpse was placed in the hole with knees bent up, lying on its back, not on its side, fully clothed, with grave goods and well supplied with food in the shape of part of an animal carcass. Remains of permanent settlements have been found which supposedly belong to the Abashevo culture. The bronze tools come from the Urals. Similar tools are found widespread on the east side of the Ural range (on the south and eastern slopes of the central Urals).

The most important site of the Bronze Age in the river Ural region excavated in the Soviet period is the Gorbunovo peat-bog described above (p. 111).

The settlements situated on the higher slopes of the river banks in the Ural area also belong to the Bronze Age. An example of such a settlement beyond the Ural river is the site at Kalmatsky ford (near Sverdlovsk). The area covered by the settlement was fairly extensive. Evidently there were ten to twelve earth-houses here, each of which would hold between fifteen and twenty people. The three large earth-houses excavated were circular, measuring about 7·5 m. in diameter. Around the circle were placed fairly large stones intended to receive the ends of the poles forming the framework of the conical roof of the house which was covered over above with animal skins. Hearths were found near the centre of the house. Around the hearths numerous sherds of pottery were found, and various other objects including large flat stones used to polish stone implements.

Remains of huts have survived on other sites of the eastern Ural area. A very interesting Bronze-Age site is the cemetery at the village of Turbino near Perm (about 250 km. north-west of Sverdlovsk). The bodies had been placed only just below the surface and so the skeletons barely survived. The bronze objects from Turbino are remarkable for their richness and variety of forms. Bronze axes with rhomboid and circular decoration, bronze knives, flint lances, and arrowheads were found. Amongst the bronze objects was found a special form of knife with curved back. One of these has a handle decorated with open-work depicting three figures of rams. Similar knives have been found near Gorky and near Irkutsk. They reproduce the form of Chinese knives of the period of Yin (fifteenth to twelfth centuries B.C.). Tanged spearheads and curved knives with cut-out handles are general types of implements found over a widespread area from Finland to the Yenisei and from the north Ural area to Bessarabia and it is possible that they were made from the rich ores of the Urals. Bronze tools and weapons made in the Ural area were of such fine quality that they continued to be made even in the Early Iron Age.

## SIBERIA

Archaeological researches in Siberia before the Revolution were conducted by local amateurs of folklore, who dug many important sites but did not go beyond excavations and descriptions. Marshalling the results of archaeological research in Siberia and the creation of a history of the tribes living there in antiquity has been one of the special merits of Soviet archaeologists.

Just as the Neolithic Period in Siberia is best studied near Lake Baikal, so the Bronze Age of the same area is best studied on the central Yenisei, in the Minusinsk depression, and in the Altai. Soviet archaeologists have systematized the remains of the Bronze and Iron Ages in the Minusinsk depression and distinguished a series of archaeological periods illustrating the development of the ancient tribes of southern Siberia.

The Eneolithic and Bronze Ages of southern Siberia are divided into three consecutive archaeological cultures: Afanasevskaya, Andronovo, and Karasuk.

### The Afanasevskaya Culture

The first culture is an eneolithic one found on the upper

Yenisei and the Altai Mountains and belongs to the third and beginning of the second millennia B.C. It takes its name from Afanasevskaya Mountain (south-west of Krasnoyarsk) where a cemetery was found.

There were traces of occupation on the river bank evidently temporary and belonging to an ordinary community of hunter–pastoralists. Only the eighty graves were well studied. At the beginning there were flat graves marked on the surface by circles of stone slabs, symbol of the sun god. Later barrows were made, also surrounded by stone circles. The dead were interred in a flexed position. The presence of collective burials in which up to seven persons were encountered is evidence of the existence of large families. Burials of men and women were found together in the same grave.

As the researches showed, the forms of economy gradually changed and the transformation to settled pastoralism was completed. This is especially shown by the changed forms of pottery. The early Afanasevskaya culture is characterized by egg-shaped pots with pointed bases and decorated with herring-bone pattern. With the appearance of permanent houses with flat hearths the pots became spherical and finally small, jar-shaped, and flat-bottomed. With the Afanasevskaya culture is connected the beginning of metallurgy but stone and bone objects predominate over copper ones.

The physical features of this people were curious and unexpected. They were of a European not Mongoloid type. So while the *taiga* belt of Siberia was occupied by Mongoloids similar to the modern Tungus the southern steppe zone was inhabited in ancient times by people of European type. The forest areas of Siberia were still occupied by descendants of the neolithic peoples of this area.

## The Andronovo Culture

The Andronovo culture belongs to the second and beginning of the first millennia B.C. It takes its name from the village of Andronovo (north-west of Krasnoyarsk). Afterwards similar sites were discovered not only on the Yenisei but also in the whole of western Siberia and Kazakhistan up to the river Ural. In recent years remains of this culture have been found in

14. Types of object found on sites of the Andronovo culture.

Kirgizia and even as far as the southern slopes of Pamir (see Fig. 14).

The tomb constructions consist, as in the case of the previous culture, of stone circles; barrows are less frequent. Burial shafts have a timber frame or lining of thick stone flags. Sacrificial places are found near the cemeteries. Settlements are distributed along rivers whose valleys were suitable for hoe cultivation and the flood meadows for pasturing stock.

The most important site of the Andronovo culture is the Alekseevskoe settlement and cemetery (about 600 km. south of Sverdlovsk). The settlement existed a long time. Permanent houses were discovered here in the form of spacious (up to 250 sq. m.) rectangular earth-houses. The roof was supported on dozens of log props. In the house besides a central hearth (intended evidently for heating) were found a number of other hearths (for cooking). Enclosures for cattle adjoined the inhabited earth-house. Bones of sheep, cows, and horses were found on the site. The importance of pastoralism in the economy had grown, while the significance of hunting had diminished, for there were hardly any bones of wild animals on the site. The finding of querns and stone hoes is evidence of agriculture. These objects were found in the five completely excavated houses. Together with the settlement a sacrificial site on a hill was excavated where pots had been put in specially excavated holes, in some of which were found scorched bones of domestic animals, and stalks and ears of wheat. A cemetery was also excavated. Numerous bronze objects were found in the huts in the settlement. Copper was worked here on the site; pounders for beating up the ore were found and shallow cup-shaped holes where the ore was melted.

The development of metallurgy required an extension of mining. The Andronovo tribes used deep subterranean workings for obtaining copper, tin, and gold.

In the western Altai an expedition in 1935–7 examined ancient tin workings dating from the fourteenth to the third centuries B.C. Full-scale working began in this area in the time of the Andronovo culture. Ancient copper mines are found on the steppes around Minusinsk, in the western Altai, and at many points in Kazakhistan. Andronovo tribes of the south part of the area near the river Ural supplied metal to the Volga area with which there was communication along the steppe routes.

Comparative study of the Andronovo culture with contemporary cultures situated to the west, north-west, and south makes it possible to say that during the Bronze Age the cultures of the tribes in the USSR began to be more closely connected, giving rise to a number of common traits in this area.

## The Karasuk Culture

While the Andronovo culture was continuing in the west, farther east on the Yenisei and upper Ob it was replaced by a new culture, the Karasuk culture (1200–700 B.C.). Stock-rearing took the leading part in its economy, more especially sheep breeding, and so the permanent settled Andronovo sites with thick deposits are replaced by sites with very thin cultural layers. Study of the new culture is based on the cemeteries, and nearly 250 graves have been examined.

Cemeteries of the Karasuk culture sometimes contain more than a hundred burials. The number of cemeteries is substantially greater than that of the preceding culture, and there is evidence of a strong increase in population in the Minusinsk depression caused not only by natural increase but evidently also through an incursion of some tribes from northern China. This is shown both by anthropological evidence, the appearance of Mongol traits in the population (the Andronovo skeletons are of European type), and also by similarities of bronze implements between those from this area and contemporary examples from north China.

The Karasuk graves are distinguished on the surface by rectangular enclosures of stone slabs set on edge. The sides of the grave shaft were faced with flat sandstone flags, while among the grave goods a very typical object is a bronze elbow-shaped knife. Of especial interest among the monuments left by these people are stone sculptures in the form of pillars crowned with rams' heads or representations of human figures, or carved stylized animals.

In northern Siberia researches in the Bronze Age in recent years have yielded so much new information that our views about the cultural development of the tribes inhabiting this area have completely changed. Ever since Krasheninnokov published his book *Description of the Land of Kamchatka*, after a visit in the first half of the eighteenth century, it had been known that the inhabitants of Kamchatka retained a surviving neolithic culture until the arrival of the Russians. This information, while completely accurate for Kamchatka and the other areas of the extreme north-eastern part of Asia, was quite misleading when extended to the whole of Siberia, and gave rise to a deeply rooted legend that up to a very late period large parts of Siberia were occupied by surviving neolithic cultures. At present this legend is being destroyed by work in the Yakut area which has shown that in the second millennium B.C. bronze-using cultures extended northwards along the Lena and its tributaries up to the Arctic Circle, while other work is confirming the same facts in the *taiga* zone of west Siberia.

## CENTRAL ASIA

In central Asia the Bronze Age has been little studied, but a culture has been defined in Chorasmia.

In Turkmenia (which adjoins Iran) there were excavations at two tells at Anau near Ashkhabad (close to the Persian frontier) early in this century [by the American Pumpelly. T.]. The tells had grown up through the accretion of cultural remains accumulated over centuries. One of these layers belongs to the Bronze Age (Anau III). Soviet archaeologists have established that tells like Anau are distributed over a wide area in the northern foothills of central Asia, especially in the south-west. Recent excavations have revealed an important monument similar to Anau III, a settlement of a clan community at Mamazga-Tepe [*Tepe* is the Persian word for hill. This site is also near Ashkhabad. T.]. The impressive tells of the ancient settlement of Mamazga-Tepe extend for almost a kilometre along a north–south axis. The general area of the settlement covers 50 hectares (145 acres). Twenty-seven rooms of a large family house have been excavated, which was built of sun-dried brick. Beaten clay or adobe brick hearths served for heating and cooking. The rooms underwent several alterations and repairs. This building is dated to the second half of the third and first half of the second millennia B.C. The remains of six layers of buildings were found below this building following consecutively one after another [showing a sequence similar to the Anau tells. T.].

The main occupation of the inhabitants was agriculture although stock-breeding was well developed. The implements were mainly of stone; bronze objects were rare. The pottery was painted, sometimes with pictures of animals and plants. Terracotta figures, especially of human beings, were numerous, some of them schematized. Statuettes of dogs and sheep were found as well as the clay model of a house. The skeletons of ten unweaned infants were found under the floor and walls. Burials within houses are known from other settlements of early agricultural peoples.

*

The Bronze Age in the history of the peoples of the USSR is a time of significant social alterations, a time of consolidation of the tribes and the birth of large linguistic entities. Research on Bronze-Age antiquities of the USSR proves that even in that remote period the ancient tribes occupying our country had reached a high level of development.

By the end of the Bronze Age even in the northern areas metallurgy, agriculture, and stock-rearing were known. In this period there is evidence for important cultural connexions of the inhabitants. Although the Bronze Age in the USSR followed its own line of development, yet there were links with the contemporary world outside and use was made of the important achievements of the leading civilizations of the Ancient East.

## Chapter 5

# THE EARLY IRON AGE

THE discovery of iron is the beginning of the greatest technical transformation in the history of humanity. Iron ores are found almost everywhere, and yet this metal, the most widespread throughout the world, was not used by man until a very late period. This is because it is difficult to work; it easily becomes oxidized or rusts; and it is generally found combined with other elements. It is more difficult to extract than copper. Without the application of a strong draught requiring mechanical contrivances iron will not melt, and without a special furnace with apertures for inserting bellows not even small quantities of iron could be obtained. Moreover the melting of iron, turning it into a liquid, was not possible for ancient metallurgists since this required the very high temperature of 1530° C. So the metal was not extracted as a liquid (as copper had been) but in a soft state and objects were not cast but hammered from it. So long as iron was rare only ornaments were made from it but from the beginning of the first millennium B.C. it was widely used for making weapons and working tools. [The Hittites are believed to have discovered a process for working iron 500 years before, but it was not widely used. T.]

The softness of copper and brittleness of bronze prevented them from entirely superseding stone as a material for tools. Only iron rendered these tools finally unnecessary and greatly extended men's control over nature. 'Iron permitted the cultivation of large areas, the clearance for fields of broad forest expanses; it gave the artisan tools of such hardness and sharpness that no stone or metal then known could compete with them' (Engels, *Origin of the Family*).

The technical transformation brought about by the use of iron led in the course of time to the reorganization of the whole of social life. Owing to the growth of productivity surplus products came into existence which were the basis of the exploitation of man by man. Slavery developed in the Iron Age. One of the sources of the accumulation of valuables and the growth of property inequalities was the developing trade of the Iron Age. The possibility of enrichment by means of exploitation gave rise to war with the aim of robbery and enslavement. [This of course is a pivotal tenet of classical Marxism. T.]

Soviet archaeologists studying the remains of the Early Iron Age deal with the period up to the formation of class society and the state, together with which appear writing and consequently history, based not only on archaeological but also on written sources.

However in Mesopotamia, Egypt, India, Greece, and China, ancient slave-holding civilizations had been born long before, which reached a high level of development in the Eneolithic and Bronze Ages and mastered the art of extracting and working iron earlier than elsewhere. An Iron-Age division is generally not included in the history or history of culture of these countries. The use of the expression is limited to the cultures of the primitive tribes of Europe and Asia living to the north of the areas of ancient civilization. In this period these tribes lived in the stage of the break-up of the primitive social system and stood on the verge of the formation of class society and the state.

The Early Iron Age is very short in comparison with the preceding periods.

In the USSR iron first appears in significant quantities in Transcaucasia at the beginning of the first millennium B.C. The metallurgy of iron spread rapidly amongst the tribes of Transcaucasia, into the southern steppes of the European part of the USSR, and into central Asia, where it became one of the fundamental causes of the formation of the most ancient states in the USSR (see Chapter 8).


## THE SCYTHIANS

The spread of the use of iron in the steppe zone of the European part of the USSR is closely connected with the history of the Scythians, a people about whom classical Greek authors wrote much and enthusiastically, and modern historians also have written thick volumes. However the history of the Scythians is so complicated and forms such a tangled skein of varied problems that, in spite of abundant sources for its study, the 'Scythian problem' remains an intransigent subject that is still far from settled.

Interest in the Scythians was aroused in Russian historiography a long time ago. The Smolensk priest Andrei Lyzlov wrote a *History of the Scythians* in 1692. Much attention was paid to the Scythians in the eighteenth and nineteenth centuries, owing to the assumption that they were the proper and direct ancestors of the Slavs and so ancestors of the Russian people. The first excavations of Scythian barrows that were important scientifically took place in the 1760s. From then on the attention of Russian archaeologists was firmly concentrated on their barrows as well as the finds of outstanding artistic and historical importance that they yielded. [There is a large literature in English, French, and German on the Scythians of which the most valuable is the monumental volume of the late Sir Ellis Minns, *Greeks and Scythians*, 1913. T.]

In the rich 'royal' barrows excavated in the nineteenth century fine weapons, rich vessels, slaughtered male and female slaves, and quite commonly dozens of sacrificed horses were found. The latter had been sacrificed at the time of burial and placed around the tomb and in the body of the barrow mound. The remarkable objects of jewellery, hundreds of gold objects, sometimes made by Greek craftsmen, are very interesting not only from the artistic point of view but also as historical evidence. The silver vases from the barrow at Chertomlyk (near Nikopol in the south Ukraine), the gold vase from the barrow at Kul-Oba (near Kerch in the Crimea), and the gold comb from the barrow at Solokha (near Nikopol), with their numerous representations of Scythian life, have achieved special fame. [These famous objects are now at the Hermitage in Leningrad. There are many published pictures of them. T.]

Soviet archaeologists have received a vast scientific inheritance from the preceding period of Scythian studies. The richest single collections in the world are gathered in the museums [mostly at the Hermitage in Leningrad. The collection there is of astonishing richness. T.]. . . .

The Imperial Archaeological Commission did not lack the means for the excavation of the Scythian royal barrows, excavations which made it possible to fill the museums with luxurious collections, but in the pursuit of 'royal' remains it completely lost sight of the importance of other archaeological remains. As a result, no attention was paid to areas very important for solving the 'Scythian problem', while Scythian settlements were hardly dug at all. . . . Besides these matters Soviet archaeologists have also set themselves the task of solving the problems of pre-Scythian times.

According to the story of the ancient Greek historian, Herodotus, who wrote in the fifth century B.C., the Scythians replaced the Cimmerians who at one time had controlled the south Russian steppes. The Cimmerian culture is referred to the Late Bronze Age, but so far it has been little studied. Gorodtsov lumped together under the name of Cimmerian archaeological material found north of the Black Sea in hoards or as chance finds, but not all this is specifically Cimmerian. To distinguish in this material what is Cimmerian is difficult, for Cimmerian graves too are still not defined. Many flexed burials found in the lower layers of Scythian barrows and in the cemeteries of Greek town colonies and also burials in stone cists found between the Dnepr and Kuban area may probably be regarded as Cimmerian. At the same time the question has been raised in scientific circles but not settled as to a possible genetic relationship between the Cimmerians and the bearers of the Catacomb culture. [The identification of tribes named by classical authors with known archaeological remains is always difficult and often baffling in both England and Russia. T.]

Settlements of the Cimmerian period are hardly known. A pre-Scythian settlement of the beginning of the first millennium B.C., that is the final Bronze Age, has been excavated on the shore of the White Lake estuary. The houses discovered here are reminiscent of the semi-subterranean buildings of the Andronovo culture.

A Bronze-Age settlement at the ancient Greek town of Cimmericum on the shores of the Black Sea (on the straits leading into the Sea of Azov) can also be referred to the Cimmerians. Greek writers connected the name Cimmericum with the Cimmerians who had once lived there. [It is possible that the word Crimea has a similar derivation. T.]

On the right bank of the Dnepr in the basin of the river Tyasmin a series of remains of the Cimmerian period has come to light. Amongst these are a group of small earthworks of the eighth to the first half of the seventh centuries B.C. consisting of tribal fortifications abandoned in the seventh century B.C. Then there was a change to newly-constructed large hill-forts. One of these from late Cimmerian times was investigated on the right bank of the little river Chernolesk (300 km. south-east of Kiev). It was surrounded by three concentric banks and ditches. In the area between the second and third bank was a barrow cemetery containing 250 barrows which was later than the hill-fort. In this hill-fort (unlike other similar sites) occupation did not cease in Scythian times.

The discoveries at Chernolesk and similar sites have special historical significance, for they provide an explanation of the origin of culture of the Scythian period on the wooded steppe. It has been established that this culture had its roots in the Bronze Age. The local agricultural and pastoral population that had lived for centuries on the wooded steppe did not vanish when the Scythians appeared.

Although the ancient authors preserved legends about Cimmerians being driven out by Scythians, it is doubtful whether the invasion of the Scythians was accompanied by extermination of the local population. Traces of culture of the preceding period continued into early Scythian times.

Sites referred to the Cimmerians contain few iron objects. Iron swords and daggers become widespread with the arrival of the Scythians in the north coastal area of the Black Sea. The first reference to Scythians in written sources is from the end of the eighth century B.C., but the material culture of this time differs little from that of the Late Bronze Age in the same area. Only in the seventh century does there appear a culture which may be properly called Scythian. Iron wholly replaced bronze only with the complete development of the culture. With the establishment of Scythian control in the Black Sea area at the end of the seventh and beginning of the sixth centuries B.C., the Iron Age came into full bloom. Whence they came into this area is unknown. As was said above, there is a hypothesis that they were descendants of tribes of the Timber-Frame (*Srubnaya*) culture. With the change from settled pastoralism to nomadic life they would have thrust forward westwards from the lower Volga area into territory occupied at the end of the Bronze Age by Cimmerians between the southern Bug and the Sea of Azov. Probably they then became known to ancient authors under the title of Scythians.

Some similarity of culture over a fairly broad area has led some archaeologists to use the term 'Scythians' incorrectly. Ancient Greek authors were also guilty of this. Together with the geographical term Scythia, applied to a definite area where the Scythians lived, they used the word in an ethnographic sense, applying it to peoples living beyond the limits of Scythia proper, so long as their customs and way of life resembled those of the Scythians. Following some Greek authors, pre-Revolutionary historians and archaeologists attempted to unite into one cultural and ethnic entity the various tribes of the period. . . .

In the Black Sea area there were three basic cultural areas in Scythian times: (1) An especially Scythian steppe culture on the lower Bug, the lower Dnepr, and in the Crimean and Azov Sea steppes. Here there was a union of related, partly agricultural and partly nomadic tribes, with the nomadic 'royal' Scythians at their head. Their language was evidently one of the north Iranian group of languages. They were united by language, war customs, and so on. (2) The culture of a series of agricultural and pastoral tribes of different origin found in the wooded steppes [i.e. west of (1) T.]. Very probably part of this population were predecessors of the Slavs. (3) The culture of the Sindi and Meotae on the north side of the river Kuban and to the east of the Sea of Azov [i.e. east of (1). T.].

All the three cultures enumerated have features in common in peculiarities of weapons, horse ornament, and the so-called animal style in their art. This unity is explained by the cultural and trade connexions between the steppe tribes who were the chief transmitters of Scythian cultural elements. These elements were created not only by the Scythians themselves but also by the various tribes in the southern part of eastern Europe. Scythian influence was felt outside their area on the west side of the Urals, in Siberia, central Asia, and the Caucasus.

Such is the answer at the present time to the question of the distribution of the Scythians. Another important matter in the history of the Scythians is their degree of social development. . . . Scythian chiefs gradually turned from tribal chieftains into kings of slave-holding states. Evidently such a state was the kingdom created in the fourth century B.C. by Atei. . . .

Soviet archaeologists have made a great contribution in the field to the study of Scythian settlements. Hill-forts of the period have been excavated in many areas.

The most important monument from Scythian times is the Kamenskoe (Stone) hill-fort on the Dnepr (about 130 km. south-west of Dnepropetrovsk). It was evidently the centre of the state created by Atei, but a settlement first developed here at the end of the fifth century B.C. and lasted up to the beginning of the second century B.C. The site consists of a vast fortified settlement with an area of 12 sq. km. It was a town chosen by Scythian metallurgists, founders, and blacksmiths. Everywhere on the site iron and copper slag, and remains of furnaces and crucibles were found and many places yielded traces of the craftsmen's workshops. Ore was obtained from a site 60 km. to the west. The inhabitants of Kamenskoe hill-fort were not only craftsmen, for in the citadel there were fine houses. The citadel comprised one-thirtieth of the total area of the site. The houses consisted of structures with walls of vertical logs set in the ground. Sometimes under the floors of the houses there were semi-subterranean basements with beaten clay hearths. Houses and basements were usually subdivided by log walls into three or four rooms with an area of 15–20 sq. m.

The top of the defensive bank was defended by a wall of sun-dried brick. Near the hill-fort were undefended Scythian villages also with traces left by ancient smiths. Here, evidently, there was an area of ancient Scythia specializing in metal-working, a permanent settlement of craftsmen-smiths in this country of nomads.

There is an interesting hill-fort at Varvarovka (200 km. north-east of Odessa) on the right bank of the Bug. Large bell-shaped pits were found here evidently intended for storing grain although they contained hearths and chimneys. It must be supposed that they were used as grain pits for a short time and later more or less accidentally as dwellings. This hill-fort came into existence in the fourth century B.C. and went out of use about 200 B.C.

The settlement of the Scythian period at Shirokaya Balka (Wide Gorge) on the banks of the Bug estuary 1·5 km. south of the Greek colony at Olbia has especial interest. The living quarters consisted of rectangular earth-houses, their sides faced with stone flags set in a clay mortar. A well-equipped corn store was found *in situ* here and also a special place with an oven of complicated construction for drying the grain. Evidently this settlement preceded the founding of Olbia and ceased to exist in the middle of the fifth century B.C. It was swallowed up by Olbia, behind whose walls the inhabitants of the settlement could find protection.

The excavations at the hill-fort at Sharpov yielded material throwing light on life of the time. The banks of the hill-fort were of complicated construction, for a layer of burnt wood was found in them. Adjoining the bank is a deep dry ditch with smooth slippery sides. The entry was reinforced by posts on either side.

At the impressive Nemirov hill-fort (250 km. south-west of Kiev) in south Podolia, excavations carried out over many years have explored the ramparts and huts within. Settlement started here in the seventh century B.C. and continued for 150 years. The formidable banks were only thrown up in the sixth century B.C. The foundation of the bank consisted of large stones and thick branches covered over with clay. Huts consisted of circular earth-houses 4·5–7 m. in diameter with vertical walls about 1·5 m. high. In the centre of each hut was a thick post on which the conical roof rested. The earth walls were faced with branches set vertically. The clay beaten hearth was situated on a flat floor near the centre of the hut. The earth-houses were laid out at an appreciable distance from each other. Numerous grain and refuse pits of bell-shaped form were found in the intervening areas. [Similar bell-shaped pits are very characteristic also of Iron-Age sites in the chalk areas of southern England. T.]

The last two hill-forts lie on the edge of the Scythian area proper, in the region where Herodotus placed various agricultural tribes. These tribes resembled the farmer Scythians culturally, but were evidently distinguished from them by a more primitive level of economy and of social relationships.

Excavations at Bolshaya Sakharna (the Big Sugar-loaf) hillfort in Moldavia yielded interesting material for the study of defensive constructions. In the course of five construction periods the height of the bank was raised from one to four metres. In front of the wall proper were found additional defensive works in the form of outworks projecting 35–120 m. The purpose of these was to prevent direct assault on the ditches and walls.

Scythian barrows yield a vast quantity of archaeological material, because of the burial rites then practised. The large 'royal' barrows were mostly excavated in pre-Soviet times. Soviet workers have concentrated attention on the excavation of small groups of burials. Such Scythian and Sarmatian barrows have been excavated in the Ukraine, while a great number of fresh excavations have been undertaken in the lower Volga area, the west side of the Ural river, and on the burials without barrows of the Meotae and Sarmatians north of the Kuban river.

We will describe the Scythian barrows near Nikopol (120 km. south-west of Dnepropetrovsk). They are not of impressive size, but do in fact repeat the spectacular burial constructions of the 'royal' barrows; instead of being 15–20 m. high, they scarcely reach 1 m. In place of grandiose shafts with an underground chamber, they hold narrow pits from one side of which opened a fairly large chamber, a catacomb, partitioned off from the entry shaft by vertical stakes, wickerwork, or occasionally by stone flags. The skeletons, one or several, lay on their backs, head to the west. In the body of the barrows there were sherds of wine *amphorae* left from the funeral feast. [Wine and wine *amphorae* were one of the most important imports from the classical world. T.]

The Scythian men were warriors, mounted archers. Short iron swords (*akinakes*) and six-foot lances with large iron points are found in their graves. Their main weapon, however, was the bow and arrow, so that in the men's graves lie bronze or less

a. Barrows in the Poltava region.

b. Novgorod, 1952. Electrically operated equipment at work on a medieval corrugated timber road.

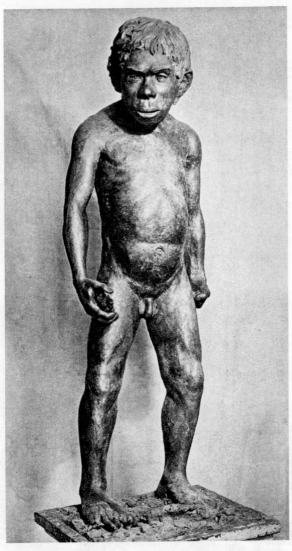

Teshik-Tash (Uzbekistan). Gerasimov's portrait reconstruction of the Neanderthal boy whose skeleton was found in the cave.

2

a. Zhury (Moldavia). Painted Tripole pot.

b. Gorbunovo peat-bog. Spoon with bird's head.

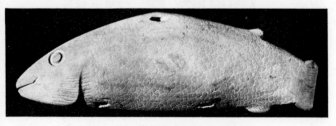

c. Siberia. Neolithic stone carving of fish.

Trialeti (Georgia). Bronze Age gold goblet decorated with filigree and inset jewels.

a. Kirovakan (Armenia). Bronze Age gold bowl ornamented with animals.

b. Pot from grave of Fatyanovo culture.

b. Pazyryk. Barrow 2. Carving in wood of deer's head in the beak of a griffin.

a. Pazyryk. Barrow 5. Pile carpet.

6

Bash-Adar. Decorated tree-trunk coffin.

7

Pazyryk. Carved wooden plates used as harness ornaments, found in barrows.

a. Copper plaque of griffins from Barrow 2 at Pazyryk.

b. Panticapaeum. Attic black-figure krater,
late sixth century B.C.

9

b. Nymphaeum. Terracotta relief showing dancing girl.

a. Tiritace. Cimmerian stone statue of a woman.

a. Panticapaeum, third or second century B.C. Terracotta head of an actor.

b. Phanagoria, third century B.C. Terracotta head of a satyr.

11

Karmir-Blur (Armenia). Urartian wine store.

a. Dvin. Vessel, end of twelfth century.

b. Armazi (Georgia). Silver bowl with relief of goddess carrying horn of plenty, from Tomb 6 of the tombs of the *eristavi*.

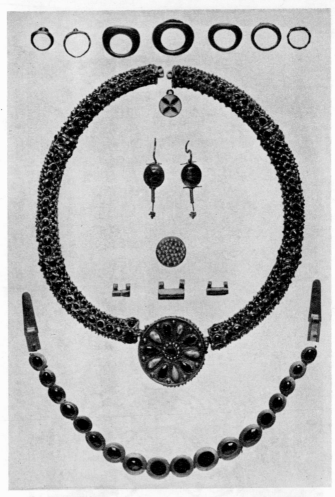

Armazi. Jewellery from Tomb 6 of the tombs of the *eristavi*.

Figure of a man in clay, found near Koi-Krylgan-Kala.

a. Teshik-Kala.

b. Aerial photograph showing partially uncovered fort.

a. Afrasiab. Clay statuette of
Anakhita, cast from a mould.
Found in a pottery workshop.

b. Varakhsha. Statue of a ram.

a. Sculptured frieze in stone from Airtam.

b. Mug Mountain (Tajikistan). Wooden shield lined with leather painted with a rider.

18

Pyanjikent (Tajikistan). Wall painting showing a banquet.

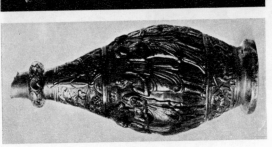

a. Silver vessel with reliefs of the nine muses, found in a fifth-century burial in the Kursk region. b. Old Nisa (Turkmenia). Ivory rhyton with metal embellishment. c. Kopeny (South Siberia). Barrow 2. Decorated gold jug.

20

Borshevo (on River Don). Wooden burial chamber in a barrow.

21

a. Borshevo. Circle of stumps of posts around burial chamber beneath a barrow.

b. Novgorod. View of the south-east part of the *kremlin* with the river Volkhov beyond.

Twelfth-century fresco discovered during excavation of the cathedral of St Sophia, Novgorod.

Twelfth-century silver jewellery discovered during excavation of Old Ryazan.

often iron arrowheads, sometimes more than 100, occasionally 200–400. In the early Scythian period those with two fins and a tang to fix in the shaft and sometimes with a barb are common, but later they became three-sided or three-finned. The horse served its master after death in his life beyond the grave. In the 'ordinary' barrows there are not so many complete horses as in the 'royal' barrows; a piece or parts of the horse's skeleton were placed in the grave to symbolize the sacrifice of a horse.

Women's burials are similar to men's in both ritual and type of construction. Only the objects accompanying a woman are different. Personal ornaments are found in the shape of glass beads, less often gold beads and rings, bronze rings and brace-lets. Loom weights, iron needles and knives, as well as querns (hand mills) of sandstone or granite are commonly found.

The history of the Scythians in the Crimea is a subject on its own. They appeared here at the same time as in steppes on the mainland, and led a nomadic life up to the beginning of the third century B.C. From this century onwards they built towns and fortified sites, settling in the river valleys, and around the lakes and sea. They were engaged in agriculture and stock-rear-ing and had developed crafts. A trade in wheat and raw materials grew with the ancient cities of the Black Sea and Medi-terranean. On the western shore of Crimea in Eupatoria a sig-nificant number of fortified Scythian towns have been traced, the majority belonging to the third century B.C. and later. All these sites are surrounded by defensive walls made of rough stone blocks. The smallest of these has an area of 55 by 44 m. while the largest measures 120 by 90 m. and is surrounded by a double line of walls.

The settlement at Kara tobe (west coast of Crimea) is similar to the hill-forts described above both in time and by the charac-ter of its cultural remains. It is distinguished by the absence of defensive walls or banks. A special type of hut structure was found here consisting of a circular tent 3·6 m. in diameter. Its base was dug into the clay, and above this two walls of inclined poles resting against each other were erected. The whole struc-ture had the appearance of a tent designed for prolonged occu-pation. Flat hearth stones lay in the centre of the sunken floor. Next to the tent a grain-storage pit was situated.

F

In the third to second centuries B.C. the Scythians disappeared from a large part of the Black Sea steppe zone. The territory of their former broad empire was now confined to the Crimea and the lower regions of the Dnepr and Bug. The Scythian capital was transferred from the Dnepr to the Crimean steppes. This was the town of Neapol (to distinguish it from other Neapols it is referred to as the Scythian Neapol). Its territory adjoined present-day Simferopol on the east. The town was surrounded by a wall of large undressed stones set in clay mortar, which was originally 2·5 m. thick but was later thickened and strengthened by reinforcements. It was made higher and very strong so that the full final width reached 8·6 m. or in some places 12·4 m. The passage through the principal town gates was in the middle of the southern line of the wall. It was protected on the east and west sides by towers. Besides these gates the town had two others.

Inside the town residential stone buildings were excavated. Many were roofed with tiles and had walls up to one metre thick, carefully built. The insides were plastered and sometimes painted. Many of the houses of wealthy people had several rooms and annexes for stores with adjoining courts containing grain storage pits in which grains of wheat, barley, and millet were found. Both agriculture and stock-rearing were practised.

To the west of the main town gates a stone mausoleum of the Scythian aristocracy was found. In it there were seventy-two skeletons, mostly of men. The first burial was probably a king, for whom the stone tomb had been erected, while warriors were buried in large wooden cists. Four horses had been killed and buried with the warriors. Three-finned iron arrowheads, swords, and numerous gold plates in the form of stars, lions, bees, tortoises, and so on were found in the graves. Another find was a cut stone of dark red cornelian in the form of a scarab (Egyptian seal), on the reverse side of which had been skilfully cut the head of a bearded Scythian in a tall hat. There were some 1,300 objects of gold alone in the mausoleum.

Burial vaults hewn out of the rock were also found, although all had been robbed in antiquity. The painted walls illustrated an unfamiliar form of Scythian art. In one of the vaults the paintings were enclosed in ornamental borders of triangles and red arrows. Among the paintings one worth mentioning shows a carpet with a chequered pattern of yellow, black, and red squares, and beside it is a bearded Scyth in a tall hat and soft boots. He wears an ample cloak with hanging sleeves and is playing a Greek harp. In the middle of the wall a Scyth is shown riding out on horseback to hunt; in front of him are a black and a red dog. They fling themselves on a wounded wild boar. In one of the niches a Scythian house is shown, with a gabled roof crowned with what appear to be two horses' heads carved in wood.

Archaeological work in the Crimea has made a significant addition to our knowledge of the late Scythian period. Formerly this period in the history of the Scythians was regarded as one of decline of the state and its subjection by the incoming Sarmatian tribes, but now Soviet archaeologists have proved that after the second century B.C. the development of Scythian society continued. [The Sarmatians were a people who moved in from the east at this period and conquered the area formerly held by the Scythians. T.]

Outside the Crimean peninsula the area around the lower Dnepr formed part of the late Scythian kingdom. A whole series of small fortified settlements has been discovered here dating from the second century B.C. to the fourth century A.D. Their inhabitants were engaged in agriculture and stock-rearing. The development of trade with the Greek colonies played a large part in the economy of the inhabitants of this area. In the second century A.D., owing to the decay of this trade and growing pressure from Sarmatian tribes, many of the settlements on the lower Dnepr ceased to exist, but some survived until the fourth century A.D. when the intrusion of the Huns finally put an end to the agricultural settlements of this area.

## THE SARMATIANS

The Sarmatians, who replaced the Scythians in the Black Sea steppes in the second century B.C., had been known in earlier times. From the sixth to the third centuries B.C. they lived between the rivers Don and Ural. By the first century B.C. they had spread as far west as the Danube. They created large united tribal groups with their characteristic culture, and these have an important place in the history of the south European part of our country. They occupied a wide steppe area up to the Caspian, as far south as the Caucasus Mountains and the old Scythian area between the Don and Dnepr. Planned and systematic research on a great mass of Sarmatian remains, earthworks, and burials, especially on the Volga, Don, and Kuban steppes, has been one of the achievements of Soviet archaeologists. At the present time the best studied of the oldest Sarmatian sites lie in the area stretching eastwards from the Don. As a result of field work in the southern area west of the river Ural and in the lower Volga area, hundreds of Sarmatian graves have been examined, dating from the sixth century B.C. to the fourth century A.D. In the Sarmatian barrows beyond the Volga, archaeologists have found confirmation of reports of ancient authors that matriarchal survivals existed among the Sarmatians. Thus in many groups of barrows the central point of the mound is occupied by the burial of a woman warrior or priestess. In these women's graves, weapons and stone altars with legs carved in the shape of animals' heads are found.

In the last fifteen years hill-forts on the north-east edge of the Sarmatian world have been excavated on the banks of the rivers Iseta and Mias and other rivers south-east of the river Ural.

An interesting monument of the Sarmatian period is the hill-fort of Chudaki (the queer fellows) (about 350 km. south-east of Sverdlovsk). The site has an irregular oval shape and is surrounded by a ditch up to 2 m. deep. The houses discovered here consisted of two rectangular rooms at front and back, covering a total area of about 200 sq. m. The floors were let slightly into the ground and the walls consisted of posts driven into the ground reinforced outside by horizontal branches or logs. The roof was conical with a hole in the centre to allow smoke to escape. On the outside the walls and roof were covered over with soil to give greater warmth. The general character of the finds is similar to the finds from the Sarmatian barrows on the south-west side of the river Ural, especially the round-bottomed pots.

In the study of the Sarmatian tribes and their culture one of the intentions of Soviet archaeology has been the formulation of a series of general historical problems, for example the question of their origin and the area where the formation of the tribes took place. The basic territory involved is between the Don and the lower Volga area. Archaeological and especially anthropological material has made it possible to establish a genetic relationship between the early Sarmatians and the bearers of the Bronze-Age Andronovo culture. Soviet archaeologists have worked out a chronological classification of the remains of Sarmatian culture, established the stages of development of the tribes, delimited the areas occupied by various tribal unions, and in several instances have identified local groups of remains with the larger tribal formations known to us from written sources.

In the second century B.C. one of the Sarmatian tribes, the Alans, began to play an important part in history, and gradually their name replaced that of the Sarmatians.

At the same time as the Sarmatians controlled the Black Sea steppes in the western areas, in the middle and east side of the Dnepr there were spreading the so-called 'urn fields'. These belonged to agricultural tribes, descendants of the farmers of the wooded steppe of Scythian times. Among these the most important part was played by the East Slav tribes [the modern Russians, Ukrainians, and White Russians speak east Slavonic languages and are descended from them. See Chapter 9. T.].

## DYAKOVO HILL-FORTS

In the period when the Scythian hill-forts appeared in the south, that is in the middle of the first millennium B.C., fortified settlements appeared also in the forest zone of the European parts of the USSR. They are distinguished from the Scythian sites by siting, dimensions, and finds. These ancient fortified sites are found everywhere in the upper and partly over the central area of the Volga and Oka, on the Valdai heights, and in present-day Estonia. They take their name from the site of this type first examined at Dyakovo, near Moscow. The earthworks are generally found in bends of a river. Their inhabitants were stock-breeders, especially horses. [The Scythians were above all horse-riders and in the Iron Age horse-riding became very widespread. T.] In the hill-forts numerous earth-houses are found. The special peculiarity of Dyakovo sites is the presence of 'textile pottery', so called because on the pots there are impressions of some kind of rough cloth, mats, or nets. Sometimes the ornament was made with a special stamp to produce the mat impressions.

As a result of the work of Soviet archaeologists a chronological classification of these sites has been made, and the remains have been divided into a series of local subdivisions. It has been established that they were in use from *c.* 500 B.C. to *c.* A.D. 500. The Dyakovo earthworks replaced the settlements of the 'pit-comb ware' people (see Chapter 3) and in their turn were replaced by later undefended settlements. . . . [The author explains that the Dyakovo culture can itself be subdivided into two groups with different pottery. Both groups were speakers of languages of the Finno-Ugrian group and ancestors of modern people in the same area speaking such languages. T.].

The excavations at Starshy (oldest) Kashir (about 150 km. south of Moscow) have thrown much light on the character of the settlement in the Dyakovo hill-forts. This hill-fort is on the edge of the modern town of Kashir and can be referred to the fifth to fourth centuries B.C. It is 80 m. long and has an average width of 25 m. It is set on a fairly high promontory with steep gullies on three sides, and joined to more level ground by a narrow neck of land not more than 15 m. wide, which is transected by a ditch. The interior was surrounded by a paling of oak stakes about 35 cm. thick. Twenty-two huts were discovered in the third of the area of the whole site that was excavated. All huts were circular earth-houses, which probably had conical roofs. In the centre of each was a hearth, and there was a plank sill around the edge. Domestic utensils were neither rich nor varied, and the most common finds were sherds of hand-made pots with impressions of cloth on the side, or with smooth undecorated sides. Besides pots there were spindle whorls, loom-weights, crucibles, beads, and so on. One of the most characteristic finds was the weights of the so-called Dyakovo type whose purpose has still not been decided. They are conical clay weights with an opening in the middle and denticulations around the edge.

The bone-work from this site was of especial importance. Among the bone items found in the hill-fort were pins, needles, arrowheads, and harpoons. Amongst the iron objects were two axes, four knives, one sickle, and two awls. Two altars were found shaped like large elliptical plates 1·1 –1·6m. long with a flat bottom and raised edges. These altars stood on a raised dais in the corners of which were remains of posts probably supporting a roof. [The author then describes two successive cultures of the river Kama lasting from the eighth century B.C. to the fifth century A.D. Both used hill-forts and the first is known by rich graves. T.]

SIBERIA

In Siberia, the Early Iron Age is best known by the antiquities of the Minusinsk (upper Yenisei) and Altai areas.

*The Tagarskaya Culture*

On the Yenisei antiquities of the Karasuk Bronze-Age culture are replaced by those of the Tagarskaya culture (named after an island near Minusinsk). The Tagarskaya period begins roughly in the eighth century and finishes in the second century B.C. Only in the middle of this period (fourth and third centuries) can the Iron Age be said to begin. This is not due to the backwardness of Siberia but to the natural abundance of copper and tin, so that iron was not needed until later than elsewhere.

Tagarskaya settlements are often situated on riverside sand dunes, and so the cultural deposits have in most cases been destroyed by the wind. A few settlements have been studied on the steppe, but finds are poor, as they were only tribal refuges where people did not live permanently but gathered in times of danger. The principal remains of the culture are barrows, large and small, enclosed in a rectangular setting of stones with tall stones at the corners and sometimes along the sides as well. More than 200 barrows of this culture containing over 600 burials have been excavated.

Below the mound of the barrow a timber frame is set in a shaft covered by stone slabs, or less often stone cists are found. They are usually family mounds with a man and one or two women buried in them, and often with children buried in special cists. The corpse was richly adorned and lay with its weapons and tools beside it. In the later barrows a change in the burial rites can be seen. Then large numbers of people (up to 150 individuals) were placed in spacious timbered chambers. Instead of tools and weapons small models of them are found carelessly made of bronze or iron specifically as grave goods. In 1954–6 an enormous barrow ($\frac{1}{2}$ km. in circumference) was excavated at Salbyk which had been known since 1739 when its great setting of stones (some weighing 20–30 tons) was described. Unlike other late Tagarskaya barrows which contain numerous interments, in this one a rich grave (robbed in antiquity) consisting of the burial of one family of seven people was found. Over the burial chamber a square-based pyramid of logs had been erected, 2·5 m. high.

The Tagarskaya people were a settled agricultural people with only some supplementary measure of nomadic pastoralism. Agriculture was carried out in fields, and a complicated irrigation system of this time in the valleys of the rivers Erba and Tesa has been explored by archaeologists. Although the settlements are little studied, rock drawings give some information about them. The well-known drawings in the Boyar hills, near Minusinsk, show a series of log-built houses, and one of beaten clay, roofed with thatch with a fireplace inside. On the edge stands a bell-shaped felt tent, and round about roam herds of goats and deer. People are standing by the houses.

The art of the Tagarskaya tribes is very similar to Scythian art. Especially close are decorations in the so-called 'animal style' and the form of several objects in the material culture. The cause of this evidently was not only the similar conditions under which the two cultures developed but also the reception by both cultures of new types of objects from each other.

Remains of the same period as the Tagarskaya culture have been found in areas bordering the Yenisei region: as in the Krasnoyarsk district and in the Altai Mountains. Probably the Tagarskaya culture can be identified with a people whom Chinese historians of the first millennium B.C. call the 'Dinlin'.

## The Altai Mountains

In the Altai Mountains no hill-forts or any remains of permanent settlement dating to the Iron Age have so far been found. Only burials in barrows are known here. A series of burials covered by small cairns contain grave goods scarcely distinguishable from the preceding period. Of especial interest are large barrows in which tribal chiefs were buried. The barrows are extraordinarily rich and remarkable finds abound in them. Even in the eighteenth century, gold objects in the Scythian animal style reached St Petersburg.* The exact provenance of these objects is unknown; they were obtained by rapacious digging of barrows somewhere between the river Ural and the Altai Mountains in southern Siberia and saved by the Governor of Siberia by order of Peter the Great. In the second half of the nineteenth century excavated barrows yielded objects of Scytho–Siberian gold artistically resembling the objects found earlier.

Renewed excavation of such large barrows in the Altai Mountains during Soviet times has produced remarkable discoveries.

The large cairn at Shibe was examined in 1927. The mound was made up of rock fragments and was 2 m. high and 45 m. in diameter. Under the barrow a shaft 7 m. deep came to light. On the bottom a double framework of wood was found which had a log cover and a plank floor. In the burial chamber stood a coffin hollowed out of a large tree trunk. In the northern half of the shaft the skeletons of fourteen horses were found. Above the timber frame stretched transversely right across the shaft were massive beams, and above them were piled thirteen layers of logs. Unfortunately in ancient times robbers were able to cut through the log cover and had ransacked the burials.

* Objects of the animal style, that is stylized representations of various animals, were very widespread in antiquity. They are found in Siberia, central Asia, northern, eastern, and western parts of the Black Sea area, and in the steppe and wooded steppe zones of eastern Europe. The animals are usually shown in movement: intertwined struggling animal bodies, scratching paws, hurtling deer, and so on. Some stylistic resemblances have led to the inference that this animal style originated in one of the early civilized centres (Assyria, Iran) and spread from there to the Scythians. The animal style is found far beyond the borders of the Scythian area where the people had nothing else in common with the Scythians. It is now established that this style was widespread during the Early Iron Age among indigenous tribes, and a number of circumstances show that it was of local origin. As a result of the growth of mutual relations between the tribes this style was carried over a large area.

In 1934 a cairn near Karakol (about 400 km. south-south-east of Novosibirsk) was excavated, under which the burials of an old man and young woman were found together with three horses placed in the northern part of the tomb. The body of the woman was covered with a red silk shroud, over the whole of which had been sewn little circular and square gold plates. Around her neck she wore a torque (*grivna*) decorated at either end with leopards' heads. By their heads was a casket with gold decoration, a mirror, and a needle with eye; the casket contained a stone censer.

The richest burials are the famous group of barrows at Pazyryk (about 600 km. south-east of Novosibirsk) in the Altai Mountain Oblast.

In 1929 the Altai Expedition of the State Ethnographical Museum started excavation in the valley of Pazyryk at a height of 1,650 m. above sea-level in the depths of the mountains far from all through roads. Here five large cairns were found. The first excavated was also the largest, measuring 47 m. in diameter and 2·2 metres in height, and in constructing it 1,800 cubic metres of stones had been used. In 1947 an expedition led by C. I. Rudenko excavated a second barrow, in 1948 the third and fourth, and in 1949 the fifth. In 1950 two more large barrows were excavated at Bash-Adar in the northern part of the river Karakol (about 400 km. south-south-east of Novosibirsk). With the exception of some details the structure of the barrows was uniform (Fig. 15). Under the cairn was a tomb shaft in which there was a log-framed burial chamber 9–24 sq. m. in area and 1·2–1·9 m. high. The log walls were as a rule of double thickness, as was the roof covering. The floor was paved with thick blocks. The timber roof was covered over with several layers of birch-bark with branches of shrubs or sometimes felt above this.

Within the burial chambers against the southern wall stood the coffin hollowed out of a tree-trunk, up to 5 m. long and 1 m. across. The outer surface of the trunk in the first Pazyryk barrow was decorated with drawings of rows of cockerels incised into the bark, in the second barrow deer were shown. The upper face of the coffin in the second Bash-Adar barrow was covered by incised figures of tigers one following another (Pl. 7). On the lid of this coffin were incised four tigers, and beneath them two

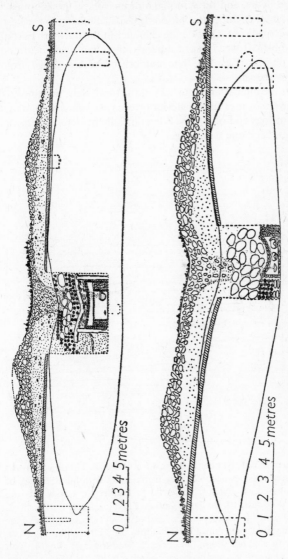

15. Section of Barrow 3, above, and Barrow 4, below, at Pazyryk. *The part of the ground that is frozen is enclosed in a continuous line*

elk, two boars, and three mountain rams. In the northern part of the burial chamber the various objects belonging to the dead man were laid out. Outside the chamber in the northern part of the tomb-shaft were placed horses with riding equipment and other objects (Fig. 16). The number of horses varied from seven to sixteen.

After the interment of the horses, the tomb shaft was filled up with layers of logs (up to eleven or even sixteen layers), or by layers of logs and of stones. Sometimes there were as many as 300 logs, each one 6 m. long.

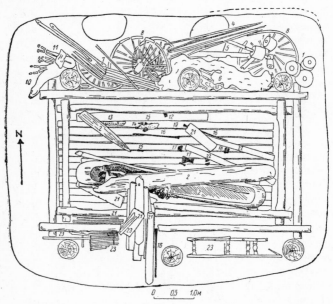

16. Plan of burial chamber in Barrow 5 at Pazyryk. The objects found within are: 1. Cartwheels. 2. Tree-trunk coffin with lid. 3. Bodies of the entombed. 4. Poles from carts. 5. Ladder. 6. Large felt rug. 7–9. Parts of cart. 10. Bodies of horses. 11. Pile carpet. 12. Potsherd. 13. Goatskin. 14. Sheepskin. 15. Legs of small tables. 16. Shafts for supporting six-legged tent. 17. Horn drum. 18. Felt cushion. 19. Horn vessel with wooden spoon. 20. Female headdress. 21. Boards with leather bindings. 22. Beams from chamber roof. 23. Parts of carts.

In the barrows at Pazyryk and Bash-Adar objects survived which normally leave no trace in tombs. Numerous objects of wood and skin, wool and silk, fine clothes of fur, and even the embalmed human bodies and the bodies of the horses survived. This was due to peculiar local conditions. In the barrows the ground the base of the burial shaft had become permanently frozen (Fig. 15). The Altai Mountains are outside the area where the ground is permanently frozen, but under the cairns ice formed because of the severe high altitude climate and special conditions connected with the construction of the barrows. Although all the barrows were robbed in antiquity, the thieves in the majority of cases only took the valuables, so that a great quantity of interesting finds remained to throw light on various sides of the life of the ancient inhabitants of the Altai Mountains. They were stock-rearers who had reached a high level of economic development and lived in the stage when clan society was breaking up. The splendour and magnificence of the chiefs' burials is evidence of the significant accumulation of wealth. In the opinion of most scholars they belong to the third to first centuries B.C., but the excavator, Rudenko, dates them two centuries earlier.

The frozen barrows of the Altai Mountains give exceptionally full information about the species and varieties of the domestic animals kept at that time. Besides the bones of large- and small-horned cattle, the skins of sheep and goats and wool of yaks were found. In so far as tombs were regarded as houses for the dead and to a certain extent had to correspond to real houses, it may be assumed that the general type of that time was log houses. From the tomb, domestic conditions can be reconstructed. There was no special furniture apart from small tables, so they evidently sat on a floor covered with felt. Vessels were of wood, clay, and skin. The walls of the houses of the nobility were hung with carpets. The oldest short-hair teased carpets in the world were found in the Altai. In the fifth barrow at Pazyryk a large multi-coloured carpet with a velvety pile and decorated with complicated designs was found (Pl. 6a). It was about 4 m. square. The central field is square and filled with radiant rosettes, while the broad ornamental borders show figures: fantastic aquiline griffins, deer, horses and riders. The thick felt carpet of large dimensions (4·5 by 6·5 m.) found in the same barrow was remarkable. The whole field of the carpet is filled by two horizontal rows of a repeating motif of a rider and a seated woman. Evidently this represented a tribal chief before a female deity who is conferring his authority on him. In the barrows there were found clothing, footwear, head-dresses, and numerous objects connected with horse-riding such as bridles, saddles, and fantastic adornments in the form of masks covering the horses' heads. There was woollen cloth from Hither and central Asia, and silk from China. All the objects were decorated with numerous peculiar representations of plant and geometric patterns, animals and fantastic monsters. All this was carried out with a variety of technical devices and on different materials. There were sculptures in the round and in low relief, outlines and flat polychrome designs cut out of wood, or sewn on to felt or skins with coloured felt, fur, skin, thread or hair, leaf gold and tin, and mineral colouring matter. There were remarkable scenes of animals fighting, the attacks of tigers or leopards on deer or oxen, made for decorating saddle covers, elegant sculptured figures of deer standing on spherical supports and so on (Pl. 6).

Exceptionally interesting are figures of lions with human bodies, winged and horned sphinxes of the Altai type, griffins, and fantastic animals with the head of a griffin and body of a lion, which played an important role in the mythology of the tribes of the Altai.

In the excavations of 1948 tattooing was observed on the body of a man in the second barrow at Pazyryk, which he had had a long time previous to his death. It had been carried out by pricking and rubbing soot into the pricks. The basic motif of the tattooing was drawings of fantastic animals. The chest, back, and both legs were tattooed (Fig. 17). The tattooed man, a tribal chief, died in battle, for his skull had been broken by strong blows. The enemy had scalped him but the tribesmen had sought out the body of their chief, embalmed it, and interred it together with that of his wife or his concubine, also embalmed. The chief's body had been brought to burial in a wagon parts of which were found in one of the barrows. This wagon had four wheels with numerous spokes and a diameter of more

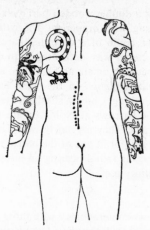

17. Barrow 2 at Pazyryk. Back
of the tattooed man.

than 150 cm. The harnessing showed it was intended to be
pulled by four horses. It consisted of several hundred different
parts secured to each other by wooden tenons and connected by
leather straps, for no metal at all was used in its manufacture.

The finds from the Altai Mountains are of great interest.
Although remains of the later intervening periods (the first half
of the first millennium A.D.) have still not been found, so that
we cannot trace a continuous line of development from the
period of the Pazyryk barrows up to today, yet it is necessary to
point out that the contemporary population of the Altai Mountains Oblast as well as the Kazakhs and Kirgiz use similar
equipment and vessels, and also apply the same motifs in their
representational art as we have seen on the objects taken from
the icy chambers of Pazyryk.

### Noin-Ula

Burials examined in Noin-Ula (well south of Irkutsk across
the frontier into north Mongolia) are similar to those of the
Altai barrows. Seven large and five small earthen barrows were
excavated in all. Under the large barrows there were tomb
shafts up to 7 m. deep. A long corridor (*dromos*) led into these.

In each shaft was a double wooden burial chamber, the inside of which was hung with draperies. The coffin was made of planks. Under the coffin of a very rich barrow a carpet was spread out. The carpet was decorated with appliqué designs showing a fight between an elk and a griffin, a yak and a beast of prey, and stylized plants. In the same burial were found various parts of clothing, Chinese sunshades (*zonty*), and sets of horse bridles. The barrows at Noin-Ula are the remains of a Hunnish aristocracy. They are fairly well dated to about the beginning of our era, for in one of the barrows a small Chinese lacquered tea-cup was found bearing an inscription attributed to the second century B.C.

## The Huns

Hunnish barrows contemporary with those above have been excavated at Ilmovoi Padi (south of Lake Baikal near the Mongolian frontier). These were large square piles of stone, 18 to 20 m. across, formed of blocks of granite almost like cyclopean masonry. At a depth of 6 m. were found log frameworks covered over by a roof and containing plank coffins with burials. In the tombs which had been robbed in antiquity were found the remains of objects, many of them of Chinese origin: silk cloth, small lacquered tea-cups, bronze mirrors, objects of white nephrite, large pots of grey colour with narrow necks, iron bits, and weapons (three-finned iron arrowheads and bone clasps from bows).

Of the few settlements of the Hunnish period that are known a hill-fort near the outlet of the lower Ivolga 14 km. south-west of Ulan-Ude (near the south-east shore of Lake Baikal) was excavated in 1949–50. It is surrounded by a defensive belt of four banks and four ditches. The inside area measures 348 by 208 m. and the remains of several dozen huts excavated into the ground and with channels of stones in the walls for heating were found. Traces of metal-working (slag), weapons, pottery, and so on were found. Bones of domestic animals, querns, and storage pits are evidence that besides stock-rearing (which was the basis of the Huns' economy) agriculture was practised, probably by conquered tribes, and also by Chinese captives. The researches of Soviet archaeologists have made it possible to unfold the history of the economy and life of the nomadic Huns, whose raids of pillage played such a destructive part in the history of the peoples of Asia and Europe. These researches have shown that culturally the Huns were more retarded than the peoples they conquered, so that in the long run they fell under the cultural domination of the latter.

## The Tashtyk Culture

On the Yenisei the Tagarskaya period was followed by the Tashtyk period, extending from the first century B.C. to the fourth century A.D. Settlements are as little known from this period as from the preceding. [The author then describes the various types of grave known from this culture. Among the more interesting grave goods are death masks of clay found in some of the graves. T.]

A large quantity of imported Chinese objects found their way to the Huns, and the people of the Altai and Tashtyk cultures, and the extent of Chinese influence is remarkable. Eight km. to the south of Abakan (about 350 km. south of Krasnoyarsk) a large multi-roomed beaten-clay house of Chinese type has been found. It was covered by a two-tiered, hipped, tiled roof. Under the floor there were heating channels through which hot air passed from a central furnace. On the tiles there were hieroglyphs of the Han dynasty, and one Chinese inscription read: 'To the Son of Heaven (i.e. the Emperor) 10,000 peaceful summers, and to the person whom we desire (evidently the Empress) 1,000 autumns of joy without grief.' Into the great central hall of the building led seven doors. Bronze door knockers were found in the shape of masks of human persons with animals' ears and cows' horns. All the equipment found in the house was Hunnish or Chinese. It is assumed that this house was the palace of the Chinese tribal general Li Lin, who according to the story of the Chinese chroniclers lived in the first century B.C. and was viceroy of the Hunnish rulers on the Yenisei.

*

In the northern areas of the European parts of the USSR, in the *taiga* and tundra zones of Siberia, there was no proper Iron Age. In the period when high civilizations, cities, and states had already appeared in the south, the hunter–fishers and reindeer herders of the north still used stone tools. Iron objects found their way into the north accidentally, but there was no change in the economy or forms of life. Only in the sixteenth and seventeenth centuries after the infiltration of a Russian population into the north did the majority of these tribes and peoples adopt the general use of iron.

So if by the term Early Iron Age is meant the original spread of the use of iron, this extends over a substantial period of time in our country. The unevenness of development in different parts did not diminish, but grew in proportion to the development of the productive forces.

The successes of Soviet archaeologists in the study of the history of the tribes and peoples in the Early Iron Age, the discovery of a series of remarkable remains, the establishment of important historical facts, should not conceal the shortcomings and difficulties which still exist in this field of science. The Iron Age is the period closest to the historical period known to us from written sources. The connexion of ancient archaeological cultures with people known to us from historical sources is much clearer in the Iron Age.

The lack of study in a series of problems connected with the history of the Scythians, the unexplained nature of the tribes and peoples of the Scytho–Sarmatian period, the inadequate study of large cultural groups and their internal subdivisions, all this hinders the understanding of the part played by these tribes in the formation of the contemporary peoples of the USSR and the formation of their cultures.

For example, thorough examination is required of the whole question of direct connexions between the remains of material culture of Scythian times in the central Dnepr area and the culture of 'urn fields', and between the latter and the Slav remains of the sixth to seventh centuries A.D. in the same area. This is important in order to settle the question of the origin of the Slavs. If the earlier view of the Scythians as the ancestors of the Slavs was wrong it is now necessary to explain their true relationship. There can be no doubt that in the next few years not only will there be new discoveries in this field but also the final settling of important theoretical problems.

## Chapter 6

# CLASSICAL CITIES
# ON THE NORTH COAST OF
# THE BLACK SEA

IN the sixth and fifth centuries B.C. numerous towns founded by the Greeks came into being on the north coast of the Black Sea. This was part of a general process of Greek colonization that began in the eighth century. The basic causes of this colonization were rooted in changed historical conditions connected with the development of a slave-holding society and state among the Greeks. ... In the eighth to sixth centuries B.C. the Greek city-states undertook active colonization on an expanding scale. Thus to Miletus alone several ancient authors attributed up to ninety colonies. Colonization took place in a large number of the lands that encircle the Mediterranean. Greek sailors, merchants, and predatory slave-traders penetrated to the north coast of the Black Sea. Here trade factories were founded at first and later urban colonies that played an important part in the history of the southern part of our country. Between the seventh and fifth centuries B.C. colonization expanded over practically the whole of the north coast of the Black Sea between Belgorod–Dnestrovsk and Novorossiisk, and into the area of the Azov Sea and delta of the Don.

Amongst the colonies founded by the Greeks, the most important were: Tyras (7) (now Belgorod–Dnestrovsk),* Olbia (8) on the Bug estuary, Chersonesus (13) near Sevastopol, Theodosia (14) (bearing the same name today), Panticapaeum (26) on the site of modern Kerch, Tanais (36) at the mouth of the Don, Phanagoria (30) on the Tamansk peninsula, Gorgippia (35) (now Anapa). The Greek colonies only occupied territory immediately adjoining the sea; they did not penetrate deep inland. Beyond the limits of the coastal area lived the native

* These towns have Greek, Latin, and Russian versions of their names; in this translation the usual Latin spelling is used. The figures in brackets refer to the position of the towns on the map (Fig. 18). T.

inhabitants, who were barbarians in Greek eyes. Soviet archaeologists have shown that Greek colonization took place not
only on account of certain socio–economic conditions in
Greece, but also on account of reciprocal conditions among
the native tribes in the Black Sea coastal area. In other words
the socio–economic state of the native population had been
already raised to a level where a development of trade with the
Greeks was possible. The trade connexions already slowly
developing assisted subsequent Greek colonization.*

Russian scholarship of the pre-Revolutionary period achieved
significant successes in the study of the ancient cities of the
north coast of the Black Sea. The archaeological material had
great importance, for without it it would not have been possible to work out their history. The material remains, particularly the inscriptions, are the most important source for the
history of Olbia, Chersonesus, and other towns.

The evidence of ancient authors and the numerous inscriptions were examined by various workers, who made it possible
to trace the political history of the north coast of the Black
Sea. Excavation of the ancient sites yielded some information
about their plan, urban industry, the development of crafts and
trade and other sides of their culture.

The most important deficiency of pre-Revolutionary classical
archaeology, as in many other branches of this subject, was the
disproportionate attention paid to artistic remains with a lack
of study of the great mass of material throwing light on the
life of the population. The brilliant civilization of antiquity
completely covered up the history of the local population
in the work of bourgeois scholars. ... Soviet archaeologists
studying classical towns devote special attention to forming a
picture of the life of the whole population of the town and above
all of the working masses. ...

### OLBIA

... The area first colonized was around the mouths of the
Dnepr and Bug. Olbia (8 on Fig. 18), founded in the first half
of the sixth century B.C., became one of the richest and largest

* The argument is ingenious but not wholly convincing. T.

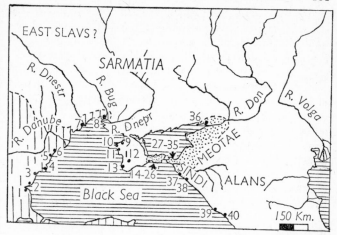

18. Greek cities on the north coast of the Black Sea.

cities of the north Black Sea coast. It lies on the right bank of the Bug estuary (38 km. south of Nikolaev). The greater part of the immigrants were citizens of Miletus, with whom came citizens from other Greek cities. The fortunate situation of Olbia placed it centrally for successful trade with the native tribes who received the finished and other industrial products of the town. In an extensive agricultural zone adjoining the city a large area was occupied by wheat fields and many animals were kept. Pottery-production was well developed at Olbia, as well as the textile, metallurgical, and other industries. The social system was slave-holding. Olbia was a republic – a *polis*, that is an autonomous city with a sovereign government.* In the second half of the fourth century B.C. Olbia reached the climax of its power and wealth. At this period the relations of the city with the surrounding Scythian tribes were comparatively peaceful, but in the third century B.C., owing to the pressure of Sarmatian tribes from beyond the Don, a movement among the

* In contemporary terminology the Greek *polis* should be called not autonomous but sovereign. Greek colonies after their foundation rapidly became completely independent state organisms, being neither politically nor economically dependent on the metropolis. Each colony had its own constitution, laws, courts and officials, minted its own money, and so on.

Scythian and Sarmatian population against the Greeks gathered strength. The local tribes continually bore down on the city walls and forced the citizens to pay a heavy tribute. Olbia gradually began to decline. In the middle of the second century B.C. the town was brought under Scythian control, and a century later it was taken by storm and destroyed by a tribe of Getae. For some decades the city lay in ruins. The part of the city that grew again occupied only a third of the original area.

At this time there was a substantial influx into Olbia of the local population, who began to play a large part in the life of the city. People of the local tribes entered the ruling groups. During the time of the Roman Empire Olbia remained a comparatively small town acting as a trade centre. In the second century A.D. a Roman garrison was stationed there, and at the end of the century it became part of the Roman province of Lower Moesia. At this time the city was strongly fortified, the old defensive walls being dismantled and rebuilt. In the third century Olbia's life as a large trade centre was disrupted by an invasion, possibly of Goths. In the fourth century life in the town died out completely.

From the evidence supplied by excavation it has been established that the city was of triangular shape with an area of about 33 hectares (80 acres) bounded by the estuary of the Bug on the east and deep gullies on the west and north. The city was divided into an upper town and a lower riverside town. It was enclosed by strong defensive walls up to 4 m. thick, with tall towers. The city was densely built over with public buildings, houses, and industrial and storage buildings. The streets crossed each other at right angles forming rectangular blocks. Outside the walls a necropolis has been found covering an area of 500 hectares (1,200 acres). To the south and north of Olbia are dozens of earthworks and settlements both Greek and native.

The position of Olbia was identified by Russian scholars 150 years ago and the first excavations were made in 1801. In the nineteenth century excavations were undertaken seven times on the site. Systematic excavations began in 1901 on both the city and the necropolis and continued without interruption until 1915. They are associated with the name of one of the greatest of Russian archaeologists, B. V. Farmokovsky. He carried out excavation on a carefully prepared plan, trying to work out the history and topography of the ancient city: its boundaries, system of defence, character of town planning, and so on. An interesting feature of the fieldwork was the beautiful final publication of the result, which has made the excavations at Olbia a model for the excavations of Classical towns. Apart from the interruption by the two wars the excavations have continued annually, up to 1928 under Farmokovsky and after his death by other workers. . . .

A very interesting area in the north-eastern part of the upper city dated to the fourth to second centuries B.C. was excavated in 1928–36. On both sides of a narrow street paved with stone flags houses were found. North of this street the remains of two adjoining houses came to light, consisting of eleven rooms and three courts. On the south side of the street one of the houses had three little courts paved with stone flags of irregular shape. North and west of the courts were four living-rooms (one with a cellar below) and several small compartments for storage. The houses had tiled roofs. The main street of the upper town was 10 m. broad and was designed for movement in both directions by pedestrians, and goods. It was crossed by a series of transverse streets, 2–3 m. wide. On both sides of the main street numerous public buildings have been discovered, and residential houses with storage annexes, among which were houses of rich citizens. These houses were distinguished by their large dimensions and finely-jointed walls of dressed stones. (Not all the houses were constructed in a uniform manner. A peculiarity of construction technique at Olbia was the laying of the stone walls on a prepared bed of alternating layers of clay and soil. In some cases the foundations only were of stone, and for the superstructure sun-dried bricks were used.)

In the central part of the upper town parts of the great city square (the Greek *agora*) were discovered by excavation. A series of public buildings opening on to the *agora* has been excavated in the last few years. The basement of a range of commercial buildings consisting of seven rooms was revealed. Many fragments of rich ornamentation from the upper floors were found, two rooms of which were obviously used for cult purposes (as evidence of this were pieces of marble plaques, statues, decorated vases, and so on). About 700 coins were found which had come from the commercial floor above. The inscriptions from Olbia, more than fifteen of which have been found in the *agora* in the last few years, are noteworthy. In 1952 a monumental altar was found in the centre of the *agora*. This striking monument of architecture is evidence of the high level of artistic and structural craftsmanship in Olbia. Another interesting find was a great reservoir, the walls and bottom of which were of stone blocks laid dry without mortar.

In the lower town an area dated to the first to fourth centuries A.D. has been excavated. Outside the part of the stone defensive wall discovered here a pottery was found, in which there were two large and two small kilns. The large kilns were intended for the baking of large vessels and tiles, the small for baking kitchen and table ware. Against the inside of the city wall were six living-rooms adjoining each other. One of the largest buildings of the lower town was a bakery consisting of six rooms, in three of which were large ovens.

On the vast area of the necropolis at Olbia a substantial number of graves have come to light. This has made it possible to establish the basic types of tomb construction. The first were simple rectangular holes in the ground. Then there were passage tombs, which had a niche for the corpse and grave goods in one of the long walls. The third type was the vaulted tombs constructed for the upper classes. They were made of earth and stone and consisted usually of two divisions, the entry or corridor (*dromos*) and the grave chamber. As the population of Olbia was composed of Greeks and natives, so in the necropolis there were a series of burials showing native grave rites, for sometimes the dead were buried in a flexed position.

A large quantity of objects have come from the excavations at Olbia. Especially numerous are *amphorae* with pointed bottoms used as containers for storing and transporting liquid and dry fluid products, and red and grey glazed kitchen and table ware. Rich people owned thin-walled vessels painted with ornamental designs and mythological scenes. In the sixth and first half of the fifth centuries B.C. the figures were painted in with black varnish against a red background (for this reason called 'black-figure vases') (Pl. 9b), while from the end of the sixth to the beginning of the third centuries B.C. the background was in black but the figures were left in the natural red of the clay ('red-figure vases'). Many everyday objects, ornaments, coins, and so on have been found. The artistic remains most frequently found are small terracotta statuettes of baked clay representing either gods or goddesses worshipped in Olbia, or the inhabitants themselves. Finds of marble sculptures are comparatively rare. Very important are the finds of remains of Greek inscriptions, fragments of ancient decrees, inscriptions on tombstones, and so on.

The basis of the prosperity of Olbia was the wheat trade. Small Greco–Scythian agricultural settlements have been excavated near the city. [The author then mentions three sites of this type. T.]

## CHERSONESUS

Three kilometres west of contemporary Sevastopol on the west side of the Bay of Karantin lie the ruins of the largest of the Hellenic cities in the western part of the Crimea, Chersonesus (in Greek the word means peninsula) (13 on Fig. 18.) It was founded in 421 B.C. The Hercules Peninsula on which the city was built had been occupied by the warlike and unfriendly tribes of Tauri. It is believed that the Tauri, a people related to the Cimmerians, who lived in the mountainous part of Crimea, maintained their primitive and isolated form of life up to late times. In the first century A.D. the Tauri merged with Scyths to form the Tauro-Scythians. Chersonesus was founded by emigrants coming from Heraclea Pontica, lying on the southern shore of the Black Sea, to the land of the Tauri, and evidently they remained surrounded by these tribes for a long time. Excavations in 1936–7 to the north of Chersonesus revealed a necropolis of the fourth to third centuries B.C., in which forty per cent of the total number of burials were skeletons in a flexed position belonging to the local population, probably Tauri.

Growing in strength, Chersonesus very soon became a state with influence beyond the town walls. Already in the third century B.C. the city exercised control over a large part of the western Crimea. The inhabitants of Chersonesus were not only traders but also energetic farmers, gardeners, vinegrowers, and craftsmen. Chersonesus was a democratic slave-owning republic [i.e. only free citizens enjoyed full rights. T.]. In the second century B.C. the Scythians in the area grew stronger and King Palacus made war on the city. The citizens turned for help to the king of Pontus, Mithridates Eupator. The latter destroyed the Scythians but the city now passed under his control and after his death became part of the kingdom of the Bosporus. Later on Roman garrisons temporarily occupied the southern shore of the Crimea, and in the second century A.D. the centre of Roman occupation was Chersonesus. In the Middle Ages it became one of the cities of the Byzantine Empire, for unlike Olbia its life did not end with the close of the Graeco-Roman period. In the Middle Ages Chersonesus remained a large trading and political centre in the Crimea and played an important part in the economic and cultural life of the population of the Crimea, the Black Sea area, and medieval Russia. The city survived until 1399 when it was destroyed and burnt in a Tartar invasion.

The first excavations at Chersonesus were undertaken in 1827 and continued at irregular intervals through the century. From 1888 the Imperial Archaeological Commission took charge of the excavations and dug there regularly every year up to 1914. The defensive walls bounding the city were uncovered, as well as a number of areas (amounting to about a quarter of the walled town); the plan of the medieval city was established; several Christian churches and public buildings were excavated, and over 4,000 tombs were discovered. The central part of the city, the most important archaeologically, had not been tackled in pre-Revolutionary times, for it was occupied by a monastery and its gardens.

After 1917 the Chersonesus museum was converted into a scientific research foundation undertaking intensive research on Chersonesus and sites in the Hercules peninsula. In Soviet times prolonged examination of the city fortifications has been undertaken. These developed gradually and in the course of many centuries they were completed and later altered. Three tiers of wall have been discovered; Greek, Roman, and Byzantine. The medieval tiers and new parts of the walls along the sea were constructed mainly in the sixth century A.D. In this form the fortifications served the city up until at least the end of the tenth century. The wall enclosed the city on all sides, and its total length was about 3·5 km. On certain parts it was up to 3·8 m. thick. The technique of construction in the different periods was distinct. The oldest wall consisted of small blocks with a rubble filling set in clay. The work of the Hellenistic period [i.e. after Alexander the Great. T.] was distinguished by accurate and monumental facing, consisting of large blocks laid without mortar and with a rusticated surface. The powerful towers were crenellated, and along the top of the wall were arrow slits.

The town within the walls covered about 38 hectares (95 acres). From the beginning it was laid out on a strict plan, straight streets crossing at right angles, and now excavation has been carried so far that one can walk along the ancient streets. The majority of surviving houses belong to the medieval not the classical town. Excavations from 1934–53 on the shore in the northern part of Chersonesus revealed areas occupied in the third to second centuries B.C., but where occupation had continued throughout the Middle Ages up to the fourteenth century. The classic building units normally consisted of two houses. A narrow corridor led from the street into a central court open to the sky, and residential and storage rooms were arranged around the courtyard. Nearly every courtyard had a well or cistern for storing rain water. The discovery in 1938 of a mosaic floor of the second century B.C. in a small domestic bathroom was of interest. It was made of small coloured stones (beach pebbles). In the central part there are two standing naked female figures and between them a tall washing vase. One figure is shown against a dark blue background, the other against a yellow cloak. This remarkable example of a classical mosaic might have been made by local craftsmen.

Evidence has emerged that throws light on the economic life

of the city, which was based on trade in products of specialized agriculture and of craftsmen's work. Wine-making occupied one of the most important places in the economy. Outside the city walls in the Hercules peninsula lie the ruins of several dozen ancient Greek farmsteads. Excavation of one of these has determined its plan and the dimensions of the buildings, and established that it existed in the third to second centuries B.C. The farm was square and enclosed by stone walls with a square tower in the eastern corner. In the farms of the peninsula vine cutters and the stones of wine-presses have been found. Also on the farms there survive long straight banks dividing up parts of the ground which are the remains of stone walls.

In the northern part of Chersonesus two wine-manufactories dated to the second to fifth centuries A.D. have been found. These consisted of a cement area on which the pressing of the grapes took place and three tanks into which the grape juice flowed. Beside the press was a wine store, where the rock had been hewn out to form several dozen circular holes into which *pithoi* were fitted. Wine-making required a substantial quantity of pottery containers for storage and transport. In Chersonesus and its surroundings the remains of large potteries have been found, one in the north-east part of the town being dated to the third century B.C.

Besides viticulture and wheat-farming there were extensive fisheries. The numerous cisterns in the town dated to the first century A.D. and used for salting fish are evidence of this. The cisterns are rectangular, or less often pear-shaped, and are 3 m. or more deep with a capacity of 60 cu. m. or more. They are hewn out of the solid rock, lined with stones, and carefully plastered with a mortar of mixed lime, sand, and finely pounded pot sherds. The plaster was impermeable, so that ground water could not infiltrate into the tank or the brine or vinegar leak out. Beside the cisterns there are storehouses containing *pithoi*. Partial excavation showed three large rectangular tanks side by side and two storehouses with *pithoi*. One cistern had a thick layer of fish on the bottom, and in one storehouse there were nine well-preserved *pithoi* containing fish remains.

Archaeological finds and inscriptions provide evidence of an active trade with Greece, Asia Minor, the Black Sea area, and especially cities on the opposite shores of the Black Sea : Sinope, Heraclea Pontica and elsewhere.

The excavations in the necropolis at Chersonesus have yielded very interesting results. They showed a clear picture of the social stratification of the population. Burials in family tombs made of stone blocks or in tombs hewn out of the rock have a varied and rich inventory. Gold jewellery, necklaces, rings, glass vessels, and much else are found there. The poorer graves are simply dug into the soil and usually contain no grave goods.

A number of remains of the Roman period have been discovered at Chersonesus, including large buildings. In 1936 baths were discovered, distinguished by their huge size, their monumental walls, and the adoption of new techniques such as the arch and the vault. Exceptionally valuable monuments of local work dated to the end of the second century A.D. are the great marble reliefs discovered in 1935. They were all found during the excavation of a Christian basilica of the sixth century, in which they had been used for paving the floor. Originally plaques decorated with reliefs were used for ornamenting mausolea and also as the sides of sarcophagi. The plaque illustrating the labours of Hercules is of very great interest.

Amongst the numerous medieval remains of Chersonesus one group discovered in the northern coastal part of the city where it has been eroded by the sea is noteworthy. The original occupation in this area belongs to the middle of the fourth century B.C. Life continued here without interruption through many centuries up to the fifteenth century A.D. In the early Medieval Period (fifth to seventh centuries) large Christian basilicas were erected here. One was discovered in 1932, another in 1935. Study of the residential areas of the Late Medieval Period shows a process of gradual impoverishment and decay, dislocation of trade and economy reducing Chersonesus in the thirteenth and fourteenth centuries to an insignificant settlement rather than a city.

## THE BOSPORAN KINGDOM

Around the straits of Kerch called the Cimmerian Bosporus in classical times several Greek city-colonies grew up, amongst which the most important were Panticapaeum (on the Crimean side of the straits) and Phanagoria (on the opposite side of the straits in the Tamansk peninsula). Close to Panticapaeum was the city of Myrmecium (the present Cape Karantinny), farther south along the coast Tyritace and Nymphaeum. South of Phanagoria were two large cities, Hermonassa (probably the present Taman) and Corocondame. Besides these towns there were a number of settlements of less importance. (The towns are Nos. 14–37 in Fig. 18.)

These were independent city states to begin with, but they soon united into an extensive Bosporan state whose capital was at Panticapaeum. The unification was evidently a voluntary one, and as much as economic its purpose was the rallying of the Hellenic settlers for self-preservation because they found themselves surrounded by powerful warlike tribes. The united cities formed a strong political force which not only defended the Bosporus from encroachment but also began aggressive action against its neighbours.

The birth of the Bosporan state took place in 480 B.C., when the aristocratic family of the Archaeanactids began to rule the state. After forty-two years they were replaced by a new dynasty, the Spartocids. Under their rule there was a remarkable expansion in the state's boundaries with the annexation of Nymphaeum, Theodosia, and land belonging to a number of local tribes. The fourth and third centuries B.C. were the most flourishing period of the kingdom. It owed its prosperity in this period in large measure to the trade in wheat. The crafts reached a high level of development. In the second century B.C. the economic and political circumstances were less favourable for the Bosporan kingdom; the competition of Egypt undercut the wheat market, while in the Crimea a powerful Scythian state arose threatening the Bosporus. At the end of the second century B.C. there was a rising of Scythian slaves under the leadership of Saumacus against the Bosporan King Paerisades. Saumacus was able to seize Panticapaeum and Theodosia, but the rising was quickly crushed by the Pontic king Mithridates Eupator, who united the Bosporan towns to the Pontic Kingdom. He suffered defeat at the hands of the Romans and fled to Panticapaeum, where he committed suicide. From then on the Bosporus was more or less dependent on Rome. The dynasty of Bosporan kings continued until the fourth century A.D. Its later history is little known.

In the last period of life in the Bosporus, from the end of the second century A.D., an economic crisis and the decline of external trade which was connected with it led to a diminution of population and impoverishment of the towns. There was a general crisis in the slave-holding system, and feudal relationships were ripening. Weakened and wrecked by internal contradictions, the Bosporan kingdom was not in a state to protect its possessions from the barbarians, and the attacks of the Huns that burst upon it in the seventies of the fourth century A.D. brought about its final collapse. After it had been crushed by the Huns, life over a large part of the Bosporan kingdom completely ceased. Only after some time had elapsed did the inhabitants return to the ruins of the half-destroyed cities.

The history and culture of the Bosporan kingdom became the subject of systematic study from the beginning of the nineteenth century. The first excavations were undertaken in 1816 at Kerch, and from 1830 systematic excavations were carried out annually both on the Kerch and Tamansk peninsulas, thanks to which remarkable architectural and inscribed remains were unearthed. However the main efforts of pre-Revolutionary archaeologists were concentrated on the excavation of the cemeteries lying close to the cities. Soviet archaeologists have turned their attention above all to the examination of occupied sites.

The Bosporan Archaeological Expedition, organized by GAIMK and continued by IIMK, has carried out great work in the study of the Bosporan cities, especially on the 'little towns' and settlements on the Kerch peninsula.

The assembling of all this material has shown the general features of the economic and social life of the Bosporus. Material collected over dozens of years has made it possible to study its trade, agriculture, and crafts. The Bosporus produced a large quantity of wheat and marine fish and also animal products (skins and wool), as well as slaves. Bosporan merchants, shipowners, and landowners accumulated substantial wealth which allowed them to buy a large quantity of finished articles and luxuries from Greece, Asia Minor, and other places. The varied finds make it possible to form a picture of the trade connexions of the Bosporus. Thus for example an important source for settling the question of where wine and oil were imported from are the *amphorae* with pointed bases in which the products were carried, for on the *amphora* there is often a stamp showing the place where it was made.

Goods coming into the Bosporus or produced there were carried by traders far beyond the limits of the kingdom.

Corn, the main trading item, formed a special industry organized by the Greeks, and was bought or taken as tribute from the native population. The Bosporus was a country where farming was the chief occupation of the inhabitants. The basic implement was the plough, the form of which can be judged from representations on coins of the second century B.C. from Panticapaeum. Grain was usually stored in pits in the ground or in *pithoi*. Corn was ground with stone querns, mortars, or hand mills with stone millstones. Excavations on Bosporan settlements carried out in the last decade have provided evidence of a significant development of vine-growing and wine-making here. Fishing on a commercial scale had developed in many places, but one of the most important areas for this was the Kerch straits; the basic implements were the seine net and bronze fish hooks.

In the Bosporan cities the most varied metal objects were produced, from tools to artistic jewellery. In the production of objects of precious metals the representation and decoration on the coinage holds an important place. Craftsmen of the Bosporus made artistic vessels of gold and silver, and plates on which complicated compositions (ritual scenes, drawings of animals, etc.) were shown. In their workshops a number of magnificent objects were made, in which scenes of Scythian life were shown with expressive realism. The production of clay vessels and tiles in the Bosporus began on an extensive scale in the fourth century B.C. In the cities other crafts developed.

*Panticapaeum*

The leading town of the Bosporus was Panticapaeum, where ancient buildings stood on the slopes and at the foot of the present Mt Mithridates in Kerch. The top of the mountain served as the acropolis (the highest point and fortified part of an ancient Greek town and the protection and refuge for the inhabitants from an enemy). A substantial part of the ruins of Panticapaeum has been built over by buildings of contemporary Kerch. During digging for foundations they often came across ancient remains, tombs, and suchlike, but very few systematic excavations were undertaken until 1945.

Excavations have established that on the terraces of Mt Mithridates lie the ruins of sumptuous public and private buildings. On the outskirts of the city were the houses of the poor and of craftsmen; the lower part, the port, was the scene of much activity. Houses of the sixth and fifth centuries B.C. have been revealed by excavation on the mountain. The use of terracing on the hillside in the planning of Panticapaeum has been proved to be as early as the fourth century B.C. Information has been collected not only about the town plan but also about its life, crafts, culture, and art (Pl. 11a).

One of the most important results of the work of the last years may be considered the discovery of the existence of a pre-Greek settlement on the mountain and the presence of a Greek emporium there in the seventh century B.C. An 'Archaic' house was excavated that had been constructed in that century.

## Myrmecium

Not far from Panticapaeum on the northern side of the bay was the port town of Panticapaeum: Myrmecium. It came into existence about the middle of the sixth century B.C., and in the fifth century even issued its own coins bearing a picture of an ant (an emblem corresponding to the name of the town). Systematic excavation began here in 1939. In the beginning of the fourth century B.C. Myrmecium had grown to its greatest size and was surrounded by a strong stone wall, 2·5 m. thick, with towers. Over several centuries up to and including the third century A.D. the population was occupied in fishing, stock-rearing, and trade, but chiefly in wine-making. Gradually the town developed as an industrial and commercial suburb of Panticapaeum but primarily as a vine-growing and wine-making centre. Several large wine manufactories have been found here.

G

In the area near Myrmecium a farm of the third to first centuries B.C. belonging to a large wine-maker has been excavated. The farm was extensive, and consisted of residential and storage rooms grouped around paved courts drained by gutters. Three large wine presses were discovered, with areas for treading the grapes and great tanks for the grape juice. A deep cemented tank dug for storing wine was discovered. In the storage rooms remains of grain stores, mill stones, and grinders were found. The living-rooms of the owners were luxuriously decorated, for in the excavations a great quantity of painted plaster was found that had covered the walls. Interesting finds in the farm were terracotta statuettes (especially of Hercules) and also examples of varied artistic pottery of the Hellenistic period. From the destroyed roof of the farm a large number of stamped tiles survived that had been made in the Bosporus. Several hundred stamps of royal and private tile factories were collected. The farm perished in the stormy events of the time of Mithridates Eupator, and traces of a large conflagration came to light, together with remains of people who perished in it.

## Tyritace

Eleven kilometres south of Kerch lie the ruins of the town of Tyritace, which formed part of the Bosporan kingdom and was a thickly populated coastal town in the approaches to Panticapaeum. . . .

Tyritace emerged as a Greek settlement about the middle of the sixth century B.C. The ruins of a house of the second half of this century, found on the western edge of the town, are of great interest. It consisted of two or three rooms almost square in plan. The lower parts of the wall were of stone, the upper part of sun-dried brick. The roof was covered with clay over a wooden framework. Below the burnt collapsed roof were found numerous and varied objects. Amongst these were various pots, and also painted terracotta statuettes, three of which represented a goddess sitting on a throne. The remains of this house in Tyritace are among the oldest examples of architecture in the Bosporus so far revealed by excavation.

In the fifth century B.C. a stone defensive wall was built

around the town which underwent considerable alterations in the fourth to third centuries B.C. In places the thickness of the wall was doubled and reached 3 or 4 m.; towers were also added. As at Myrmecium one of the basic features of the economy was vine-growing and wine-making. A wine manufactory of the third to second centuries B.C., consisting of an extensive stone building, came to light in 1946. The north-western part was occupied by a treading area (5·25 by 2·7 m.) consisting of a smooth surface of layers of white mortar underlain by small stone blocks. The pressing of the grapes was done here by slaves trampling the bunches of grapes underfoot. Adjoining this area was a quadrangular vat (2 by 1·75 by 1·55 m.) dug into the ground. The sides and bottom were carefully faced with stone and plastered over. The vat could hold 5,000 litres of grape juice. This juice was then baled out in vessels, *pithoi*, and *amphorae*.

In the Roman period the wine-manufactories were of more complicated construction. In an example of the third to fourth centuries A.D. excavated in 1946 a press had been set up in the treading area. The juice from here could flow into four vats arranged in pairs. There was a complicated system of channels and sluices by which the juice could be directed as needed into each vat.

In the first to third centuries A.D. the fishing industry and the salting of fish was of great importance. The eastern and southern parts of the town at this time were completely occupied by wine and fish-salting 'factories' consisting of groups of cemented vats and tanks. The fish salted here were chiefly herring and *khamsa* (a Black Sea fish). A substantial part of the town was occupied by these industrial structures. One long main street passed through the middle of the town and on both sides were residential houses, while behind them and partly between them lay wine presses and fish-salting tanks. No especially rich houses were found. We can envisage the character of the houses of the well-to-do part from the large courtyard house of the third to fourth centuries A.D. excavated in the town (Fig. 19). This belonged to a fish merchant. The central part of the house consisted of a courtyard paved with limestone flags which was entered from the street. Around the courtyard were grouped

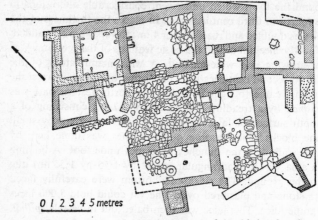

0 1 2 3 4 5 metres

19. Tyritace. Plan of courtyard house of the third to fourth
centuries A.D.

domestic and storage rooms, some of which had an upper
storey. The walls of the houses were built of rubble and roughly
dressed stones. Clay was used as a binding material. The rooms
were lit through windows opening into the court. The house
was destroyed at the time of the invasion of the Huns in the
fourth century A.D.

After the destruction of Tyritace by the Huns life was renewed, but on nothing like the same scale as before. Houses
and a Christian basilica belonging to the sixth to eighth centuries have been excavated.

*Nymphaeum*

Six kilometres south of Tyritace on the coast lies the city of
Nymphaeum, whose ruins lie near the modern village of
Geroevek. Excavations have shown that it was founded in
about the middle of the sixth century B.C. as one of the Ionian
colonies. The presence of a good harbour led to a rapid growth
of the town and made it into an important trading centre. The
excavated ruins of the sanctuary of Demeter situated on the
shore at the foot of the cliff are interesting. The sanctuary had
been in use for several centuries from the sixth century B.C.

onwards and underwent several reconstructions. Remains of
the perimeter wall and the sanctuary wall survived, as well as
the foundations of an altar on which offerings were made. A
large number of such offerings were found, mostly terracotta
statuettes representing Demeter, or maid-servants carrying
vessels full of water, or girls performing ritual dances, and so
on (Pl. 10b).

Research has shown that life in Nymphaeum continued until
the third century A.D.

## Cytaca

South-west of Nymphaeum on the high cliff of the shore lie
the ruins of the Bosporan town of Cytaca. Archaeological work
was carried out here by the Kerch Museum in 1927-9. The
town was encircled by a ditch and strong walls with towers of
a strength justified by the military importance of the town. Big
grain stores were found containing large *pithoi* and grain pits.
Economically the town flourished in the fourth to third centuries B.C., and later in Roman times.

The fortified town of ancient Cytaca has been definitely
identified from an outstanding inscription found there. In 1918
a stone plaque from a temple table with a Greek inscription of
the third century B.C. was found on the seashore, where it had
fallen from the cultural deposit. The inscription records the
construction of the communal temple of the city of Cytaca,
which was dedicated to the nameless 'god that thunders'.
Amongst the finds illustrating the high level of prosperity of the
ruling classes of the population may be mentioned a marble
sun dial of the second century A.D. decorated with the relief
head of an ox. Burial chambers dug out of the rock cliff of
Chetyr-Tau which have been excavated preserved traces of
painting on their walls.

## Cimmericum

The Bosporan town of Cimmericum lies 50 km. to the south
of Kerch on Mt Opuk on the Black Sea coast. The Greek city
with its acropolis was situated on the hills on the west side of
the mountain. The defences of Cimmericum formed the southern limit of the system of defence of the most important and

highly populated part of the Bosporan kingdom, its centre and capital. This system of defence comprised a bank and ditch transecting the Kerch peninsula in a north–south direction. Excavations in the town have brought to light remains of the first centuries A.D. and of the last period of its existence. It has been established that the town perished abruptly as a result of being laid waste and burnt by pirate raiders at the end of the third century A.D. On its southern slopes traces were found of a Bronze-Age settlement (beginning of the first millennium B.C.) in the lower layer, and of the sixth to fifth centuries B.C. in the upper layer. Evidently Cimmericum was born as a settlement in pre-Scythian times and retained as its name the ethnical name of the first settlers [that is, Cimmerians. T.].

## Iluratum

North of the Chyrybashkoe Lake in the village of Ivanovka lie the ruins of the city of Iluratum. This settlement, almost rectangular in plan, was defended by strong walls and towers. The defensive enceinte consisted of two concentric walls with towers, with an average thickness of 6·4 m. From the inner side of the wall project the well-preserved ruins of buildings of the first centuries A.D. Iluratum is one of the classical towns in which a large area has been excavated. These excavations revealed extensive urban blocks, including domestic buildings and a very interesting barbarian sanctuary of the third century A.D. in which a stone altar came to light.

The population of Iluratum was basically Scythian but partly Sarmatian. Numerous Scytho-Sarmatian handmade pots were found decorated with incised and other ornament. The indigenous population of Iluratum was strongly Hellenized but yet retained its individual culture. So for example finds of ritual terracotta figures of the goddesses of fertility are evidence of local religious observances. Together with the cult of Aphrodite, which was popular on the Bosporus, in Iluratum there continued worship of the special form of goddess of the animal and plant kingdom in the form of a woman with a radiant halo whose arms are shown outstretched, one of them taking the form of a branch of a tree. She is shown thus on a clay stamp of the third century A.D. The excavations at Iluratum give a clear picture of Greco–Scythian culture that was the basis of the Bosporan state.

The westernmost town of the Bosporan state was Theodosia. Excavations began here only in 1949.

*Phanagoria*

No less thickly settled than the Kerch peninsula was the part of the Bosporan kingdom lying opposite the Kerch promontory, especially within the bounds of the Tamansk peninsula. The most important trading town here was Phanagoria. This defended site lies on the shores of Tamansk Bay, 3 km. to the south-west of the modern hamlet of Sennai, and it covers an area of about 35 hectares (about 80 acres).

The cultural deposits have an average thickness of 4–5 m., in places much more, and were accumulated during many centuries of occupation in classical and medieval times (twelfth to thirteenth centuries). Excavations began at Phanagoria in 1936, and, interrupted by the war, have subsequently been resumed. Digging has established the exact place of the ancient town, its boundaries, and the sequence of the layers in the deposit. As a result of the sinking of the land and flooding of the coast, the waters of Tamansk Bay now cover the northern part of the town. Piles of masonry survive underwater, which evidently are remains of an ancient defensive wall passing round part of the town that is now covered by the sea. In Phanagoria various craftsmen's workshops existed in which pots, tiles, terracotta statuettes (Pl. 11b), metal objects, and so on were made. Numerous examples of imported black and red blazed ware and fragments of wine *amphorae* indicate an active trade in the town. Among the pottery finds are objects from Attica, the cities of the western shores of Asia Minor, Chios, Rhodes, Delos, Heraclea Pontica, Crimean Chersonesus, and elsewhere.

In Phanagoria remains of monumental public buildings and luxurious private houses have been found. Houses, as is usual in Greek construction, were small and had inner courts. In one of the courts a mosaic paving with a pattern of greenish sea pebbles came to light. The internal walls of the rich houses were covered with painted plaster or faced with marble plaques of different colours. First-class examples of such wall decorations were found in 1939–40.

Among finds of the last few years a stele of fine-grained limestone, bearing a relief on both sides and an inscription, deserves mention. The stone is a monument set up, as the inscription shows, in A.D. 179 by Agathus in memory of his father and grandfather who were members of an aristocratic family of the city holding an important position. In the engraving the buried pair are shown, as well as two figures on horseback.

The thick cultural layer covering the remains of the classical town contains foundations of medieval buildings, on which rested the walls of sun-dried brick that no longer survive.

## Patraeus

In the northern part of the peninsula there were several settlements mentioned in classical sources, but their exact positions have not yet been identified. There are some grounds for thinking that one fortified site is the remains of Patraeus. In 1931 excavations were carried out here and showed that this settlement arose in the sixth century B.C. The ruins of a large wine manufactory of the first centuries A.D. with three vats similar to those already described were found in the town. In 1948 a second large wine manufactory of the second century A.D. with several pressing areas and vats was discovered here.

## Hermonassa

After Phanagoria the second town in importance on the 'Asiatic' side of the Bosporus was Hermonassa. (The Greeks used the term 'Asiatic' to describe the Tamansk side of the straits.) This lies on the site of the modern capital of Tamansk, which was also the site of the ancient Russian town of Tmutarakan. Systematic excavations only began here in 1952, although there had been trial excavations in the town and on the acropolis before. The lower cultural layers lie 10 m. below the modern surface, and the layer of classical times is 6·5 m. thick.

During excavations in 1930 in the coastal part of the town, part of an excellently paved street or square of classical Hermonassa was revealed. A temple or sanctuary of Aphrodite was found in the city. It is possible that the fragments of a marble structure and relief found here, showing the struggle of Hercules with giants, embellished this building.

## Gorgippia and the Sindi

The Bosporan town lying farthest from the Kerch promontory was Gorgippia, which lay on the Black Sea coast on the site of modern Anapa. Excavations have never been carried out here, but during the archaeological survey in 1927 traces of the ancient settlement were found. During various excavations for the foundations of buildings Greek inscriptions, coins, pottery, and sculptured objects have very often been found. Amongst finds that deserve special mention is a beautifully finished marble statue of a governor of the town dating to the second century A.D.

Gorgippia lay in the land of the Sindi and until it was incorporated into the Bosporan kingdom there had been a native town and harbour here (Portus Sinducus). The Sindi were a people who occupied the Tamansk peninsula as far as Gorgippia before the arrival of the Greeks. Under the influence of Greek civilization and as a result of internal socio-economic development the Sindi achieved important successes in the economic and cultural fields. At the end of the fifth century B.C. they began to mint their own money, but they were rapidly absorbed into the Bosporan kingdom. A special expedition set to work in 1950 to study them as well as the Bosporan rural agriculture, and a number of Sindian settlements have been surveyed. A comparatively small number of urban centres had existed in the country with a whole series of small village settlements.

Proportional to the distance from the important centres of the Bosporan kingdom was the growth of the local non-Greek contributions to life, into which the elements of Greek culture only partly penetrated. Nevertheless this was not the case everywhere. Some remote settlements have emerged as completely Greek cities. Such a settlement was a fortified town recently partly excavated on the lower Kuban 12 km. west of Varenikovska, near the famous Seven Brothers' barrows.

This Sindian town sprang up in the sixth century B.C. and reached an impressive level of development before its incorporation into the Bosporan state. In the first half of the fifth century

B.C. it was surrounded by a permanent stone defensive wall and so converted into a powerful fortress. The population were farmers, fishermen, craftsmen, and traders. Of especial interest was a house revealed by excavation and referred to the third and second centuries B.C., which probably belonged to a prosperous landowner. The house is quadrilateral in plan, 22·5 m. long by 19·5 m. broad. The entry on the south side leads into a court which contains a well faced with stone blocks; on three sides of the court are grouped the internal rooms. The massive thickness (1·7 m.) of the walls is striking. Excavations in the house brought agricultural tools to light.

### Elizavetinskaya

The purely native Maeoto–Sarmatian settlements on the river Kuban are sharply distinguished from the Bosporan Greek towns. They are generally small and encircled by a ditch and earth bank. The houses of the inhabitants were constructed of wooden posts, reeds, and twigs, smeared over with clay mixed with straw. One of the largest of such settlements of the Classical Period was examined at Elizavetinskaya, 17 km. west of Krasnodar on the right bank of the river Kuban. The fortified site was distinguished not only by its large dimensions but also by the exceptionally common occurrence of imported objects. During the excavations here besides the local pottery a great quantity of black glazed and other imported ware was found, coins of the fourth to second centuries B.C. from Panticapaeum, and stamped *amphorae* from Rhodes, Sinope, and Thasos. In all probability Elizavetinskaya was the site of an agricultural and craft settlement of the Maeoto–Sarmatians and at the same time a large trading centre through which Bosporan merchants carried out extensive trade and barter in the area around the Kuban.

### Tanais

At the point farthest north of the Bosporan kingdom lay the city of Tanais, near the estuary where the river Tanais (now the Don) flows into the Sea of Azov. The ruins of Tanais lie on the steep right bank of the northern branch of the Don delta near the village of Nedvigovka. To judge by the archaeological evidence life in the town began only in the third to second centuries B.C. Before this the Bosporan colony on the lower reaches of the Don was at another settlement, possibly also called Tanais, whose ruins are surrounded by a large barrow cemetery and lie near Elisavetovskaya, 17 km. to the south-east of the first site. The older of the two towns of Tanais covered a very extensive area (almost 40 hectares, about 100 acres) and had concentric stone defensive walls. The more prosperous people lived in the central part of the town where traces of stone houses have most frequently been found, while on the edge of the town between the inner and outer walls such structures were rare. Here beaten clay houses were found, constructed of a skeleton of branches and twigs and then smeared over with clay. The stone houses with tiled roofs belonged to Greek colonists and prosperous native inhabitants who had adopted the material culture and way of life of the Greeks.

In 1923–8 an expedition of GAIMK examined a series of fortified sites on the lower reaches of the Don which had preceded the arrival of the Greeks on the Black Sea. In the fourth century B.C. these settlements died out but were resettled in the first century A.D. From then on the influence of the more advanced classical culture everywhere shows itself with increasing clarity in the life of the population of these Sarmatian settlements. Evidently an important part was played in this by the growth of the trade operations of Tanais with which the native settlements were linked.

As the main attention of Soviet archaeologists has been concentrated on excavating the Bosporan towns, so the cemeteries have been examined on a more modest scale than in pre-Revolutionary times. However, thanks to the care exercised in the work, it has been possible to elucidate a number of details of the burial ritual, and this way distinguish native from Greek burials, which has assisted in the study of the history of the local population.

## ROMAN CHARAX

In the middle of the first century A.D. Roman troops appeared on the southern shore of the Black Sea. There were Roman garrisons in Chersonesus, and from time to time in Panti-capaeum. The military camps were regular Roman settlements in the Black Sea area. The camp of Charax on the promontory of Ai-Todor, near Yalta, has been studied by Soviet archaeologists. (Excavations were undertaken there in 1849 and 1896–1911 but no reports were published and much of the material has been lost.) Fundamental results emerged from the excavations of 1931–2 and 1935.

These excavations helped to show that Ai-Todor arose in pre-Roman times as a 'refuge' for Tauri. The Romans occupied this area and drove the Tauri away from the coast. The cyclopean wall built already by the Tauri served as part of the defences of Roman Charax, but the chief defence consisted of two lines of roughly coursed stone walls. Most of the buildings were concentrated within the highest wall on a fairly restricted area of not more than 1½ hectares (4 acres). Here were found small stone and brick houses, supplied by water through clay pipes, and a water tank, on the floor of which there was a mosaic showing an octopus. Bricks and tiles were found bearing the stamps of military units which had made them. Charax was a modest settlement occupied by soldiers and craftsmen, and the only luxurious buildings were the bath-houses. These were used as a sort of club by the Romans, and in large towns were sumptuous buildings. This example was comparatively small (25 m. long by 15 m. broad), but nevertheless it was an important building during a fairly long time and was subsequently enlarged by the addition of annexes. It had special rooms for cold and hot baths, a steam chamber, a dressing-room with stone benches, and lavatories. Large rooms adjoined the baths, one of which was evidently used as a *palaestra* (sports area). The walls were built of stone set in lime mortar with a bonding of brick and broken tile, while the bath was warmed with the help of a system of clay pipes, laid under the floor, through which hot air passed.

After the Romans had left the southern shores of the Crimea in the middle of the third century A.D., life on the hill at Ai-Todor did not cease. The fortifications of Charax evidently continued to serve the local inhabitants as a refuge in time of danger. The poor native population of farmers, fishermen, and craftsmen interred their dead in the necropolis which was started in the fourth century A.D. outside the outer wall of Charax.

## TYRAS

In 1946 the Institute of Archaeology of the Ukrainian Academy of Sciences began work on the Greek town of Tyras (7), whose remains lie at Belgorod–Dnestrovsk on the shore of the Dnestr estuary. Tyras was founded in the sixth century B.C. and has existed from then to the present day. Three thick levels of deposits (classical Tyras, Slav Belgorod, and medieval Akkerman) allow the many centuries of the town's history to be disentangled. In the excavations of the ancient Tyras the remains of stone domestic and industrial buildings have been discovered as well as roadways, street drains and the like, besides a large quantity of objects.

*

The thousand years' existence of the classical cities had immense significance for the advancement of culture and for the whole historical development of our country.

The Greek cities stimulated social development and the growth of the economy, culture, and art among the inhabitants of the south Russian steppes. The native peoples borrowed much from the Greeks and the latter in their turn from the native population. The Classical Period in the history of the north coast of the Black Sea is actively studied by Soviet archaeologists.

Attention must be drawn to several shortcomings of classical archaeology in the USSR. They really amount to this: that the majority of archaeologists follow the path of accumulating and collecting purely source material for their researches. Together with the profound archaeological study of the classical cities it is necessary to study in detail the native tribes living around these cities, to extend research to the agricultural areas around the Greek towns, and to resolve the problem of production in conditions where slaves were used and the problem of the relationships of the classical states of this area with the different parts of eastern Europe on the one hand and with the Mediterranean countries on the other. The profound study of these questions will bring Soviet scholars studying the Greco–Roman period to a proper understanding of the process of historical development of slave-owning society in the Black Sea area, and to a full revelation of the picture of its birth, development, and decay.

## Chapter 7

# ANCIENT AND MEDIEVAL STATES OF
# THE CAUCASUS

ARCHAEOLOGICAL study of the north Caucasus and Transcaucasia held a prominent place in pre-Revolutionary Russian scholarship. Publications dealing with the different archaeological monuments appeared in the *Materials for the Archaeology of the Caucasus,* and discoveries and studies of inscriptions, architectural remains, and so on created a whole subject of its own – Caucasian studies (*Kavkazovedenie*).

After 1917 the best traditions in this field of study continued and were carried forward by Soviet archaeological scholarship. Surveys and excavations followed one another over all the different parts of the Caucasus: Armenia, Georgia, Azerbaijan, Kabardia, and Osetia. Almost all the important archaeological areas of the Caucasus underwent careful study. The history of the ancient cultures and early class societies of the Caucasus has been revealed in exceptionally sharp outlines and allotted an important part in world history.

## URARTU

Researches on the remains of the oldest slave-holding state within the limits of the USSR, Urartu, have been of fundamental importance. Already in pre-Revolutionary times archaeologists and orientalists had conducted excavations in Transcaucasia in the region of Lake Van [this area which formed the heart of ancient Urartu lies in the east of modern Turkey. T.] and had discovered and studied cities and graves of Urartu, and translated cuneiform inscriptions; but in Soviet times the study of the history and cultures of Urartu has substantially increased our knowledge of this ancient state.

Urartu was a powerful slave-holding state of the ancient east lying in the central part of Hither Asia on the Armenian foothills in the basin of Lake Van, and was formed in the middle of the ninth century B.C. (Fig. 20). It soon expanded and

20. Map of Caucasus in the second century A.D.

conquered parts of Transcaucasia, and the fertile valley of Ararat
was united to it. For about two centuries from the beginning of
the eighth to the beginning of the sixth centuries B.C. the
southern part of Russian Transcaucasia formed part of the state
of Urartu. In the Armenian SSR a large number of Urartian
remains survive: cuneiform inscriptions on cliff faces recording
conquests and building works, and remains of ancient fortifications. The kings of Urartu built towns and dug irrigation canals,
but for the native population their power brought terrible misfortune, for a large part of the inhabitants was enslaved.

The warrior king Argistis (778–750 B.C.) constructed the fort
Argistikhinili (west of Erevan) in the first half of the eighth century B.C. Remains of fortifications and inscriptions have been
found there. The latter refer to administrative and economic
regulations and one tablet mentions the construction of the
strongly fortified town of Irepuni. Its site was not identified
until 1950. Then, during reconstruction work on an ancient fort
on the southern edge of Erevan, two stones with cuneiform inscriptions came to light. On one was the following text: 'To the
glory of the god Khaldis, Argistis, son of Menuas, who built this

strong fort, completed and called the town Irepuni, to strength-
en the land of Biainas and to terrify enemy countries ...'
Trial excavations on the site established that there had been a
large building of the palace type there, recalling the Assyrian
palaces.

## Teisbaini (Karmir-Blur)

The extensive excavations on the Urartian city of Teisbaini
have special importance. The remains of its citadel lie on the hill
of Karmir-Blur on the left bank of the river Zanga below Erevan. Adjoining the citadel are the remains of the town covering
an area of about 40 hectares (about 100 acres). Excavations
here have provided the basic archaeological sources for the
northern areas of the kingdom of Urartu.

The citadel on Karmir-Blur was built by King Rusas, who
lived in the middle of the eighth century B.C. and was the son of
Argistis. It was possible to identify the town by the find of a
cuneiform inscription on a bronze door bolt found in the
excavations, which read: 'Of Rusas, son of Argistis, the fort'
('house of arms') 'of the town of Teisbaini.'

The whole hill of Karmir-Blur was occupied by one enormous
building covering about 4 hectares (10 acres) and consisting of
no fewer than 120 rooms. The northern and eastern façades of
the building were tiered and divided up by a large number of
turrets. There were massive towers at the corners. The walls,
built with excessive attention to durability, were of large sun-
dried bricks of clay mixed with straw, and in the lower part (up
to 2 m.) of huge, roughly dressed stones. The rooms were very
high, up to 10 m., and were usually elongated, up to 30 m. long,
but not more than 4 m. broad. The flat ceilings were made of
beams of fir, poplar, or oak. The whole building had a monumental tiered appearance, the central part being higher than
the sides and the windows of one tier looking down on to the
roof of the tier below. This building was the palace of the king
of Urartu's governor.

In the excavated rooms that had been used for storage the
remains of food stores were found: barley, wheat, millet,
sesame, beans, and lentils. Remains of bread were also found
made of millet meal, and pots in which malt was prepared to

make beer. Three large rooms were discovered built for making and storing sesame oil which adjoined two storehouses containing 152 large vessels for storing wine (Pl. 12). Their overall capacity was more than 160,000 litres. Besides rooms with food stores, the citadel had many storehouses in which various objects were kept: iron and bronze tools and weapons, objects of adornment, wooden articles, and textiles. The stores were under the care and responsibility of certain officials. Massive doors made of squared wooden beams were locked with bronze and iron locks and sealed with seals. On the floor of several store-rooms were tablets with cuneiform inscriptions, remains of receipts, details for work, and so on. Not all the store-rooms of Karmir-Blur have yet been examined, and future excavations may yield much that is interesting and unexpected.

In the excavations at Karmir-Blur first-class examples of Urartian art have come to light. The best of them was the helmet of King Argistis, found in 1950. The helmet is of bronze with chased decoration. On the front side there are eleven sacred trees arranged in two rows, and by each tree stands a winged god in a horned helmet. These are overlooked by long-necked dragons with lions' heads, four monsters set on each side. The monsters have a magical significance: protection from evil forces. The back part of the helmet is decorated by two rows of war chariots and horsemen, the latter holding in their hands small circular shields and javelins. On the lower is engraved the short inscription reading: 'Argistis, son of Menuas, presented this helmet to the God Khaldis, his Lord.' Earlier, in 1947, a second such helmet was found on which there was an inscription of King Sarduris, son of Argistis, stating that it had been given by the king of Urartu to the temple of his god (Fig. 21). Drawings of horsemen and chariots similar to those on the helmets also occur on two bronze quivers on which there are cuneiform inscriptions of kings of the eighth century B. C.

In 1953 a bronze shield of King Sarduris was found decorated with drawings of lions and oxen set out in three concentric bands. On the edge there was a cuneiform inscription.

Amongst artistic productions the bronze figure of the god of war and storm, Teisbas, is interesting for the town, Teisbaini, was named in his honour. The statue shows the god in a head-

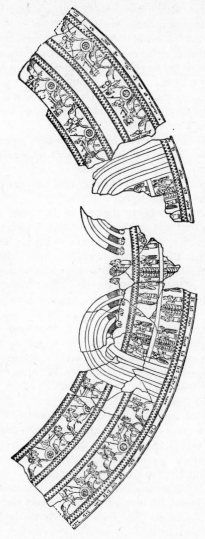

21. Karmir Blur. Decoration on bronze helmet of King Sarduris.

dress decorated with horns holding a mace and battle-axe. Urartian art is similar to the Assyrian in style.

During the excavations of the citadel at Teisbaini many bronze vessels were found, richly ornamented cups, goblets, and so on. In 1949 in one of the jars in the wine store ninety-seven bronze feasting cups placed inside one another were found. At the centre of each cup the name of a Urartian king was inscribed, and sometimes there was a drawing of a fortified tower with a tree and a lion's head below it.

The excavations at the city of Teisbaini have given information about the relations of its inhabitants with neighbouring countries. In the palace seals and beads of Assyrian origin were found, amulets with Egyptian hieroglyphs, gold ear-rings from the Mediterranean, and so on.

An older settlement lay by the edge of the ravine of the river Zanga to the west and south of the citadel. Urartian warriors with their families, numerous artisans doing the extra work necessary to pay the large tribute exacted from Teisbaini, and also farmers working in the fields and gardens belonging to the state lived here. They all lived on state allowances and had no private livelihood to support themselves. So in the excavated houses there are no rooms for the storing of food, or cattle sheds. The houses were built of roughly dressed stone and usually consisted of three rooms communicating with each other by narrow doorways with raised thresholds. The roofs were flat and supported by vertical posts. The main room in the house was lit by a hole in the ceiling which also served as a chimney, while the secondary rooms were lit through the doorway and were half dark. The whole town consisted of such houses adjoining one another over an area in which three straight streets about 6 m. wide were visible with one intersecting street. The settlement was surrounded by a strong stone wall joining the bends of the river to the fortified citadel.

The Urartian administration centre in Transcaucasia, the 'city of the god Teisbas', fell in the early sixth century B.C. under the blows of the Scythians. The circumstances of the destruction of the fort have been established even to the smallest details by archaeological excavation, and are described by the director of the excavations B. B. Piotrovsky in the following way:

The siege of Teisbaini, judged from the condition of the food stores in the houses of the besieged (full grain pits, small vessels with grain), was short. By a decisive attack carried out suddenly by night in the first half of August the Scythians seized the citadel and destroyed it.

Before the attack the citadel was subjected to a barrage from the direction of the side gates and bombarded with burning objects. The temporary houses in the courtyard of the citadel caught alight, and their roofs, constructed only of branches and twigs, collapsed and covered everything inside as if the real storming had begun. The inhabitants only succeeded in escaping from under the burning roofs and were not able to retrieve anything. The finds in these temporary houses have made it possible to establish the time of the year when the destruction of the fort took place. The wheat had been harvested but the grapes were not ripe, and in a surviving tuft of grass the flowers were those of the end of July and first half of August. During the attack the Scythians set light to the citadel and the wooden roofs of the rooms were reduced to ashes. The Scythians dug into the burning storehouse and in the midst of the fire tried successfully to retrieve booty. In the blinding smoke they rushed to the storage jars, looked into them, and believing them empty stopped further search there. However, if they had been able to look less hastily and more carefully at all the jars, they would have found valuable objects. The plunderers ransacked the temple treasure-house, but various objects were hidden at the bottom of the jars in its store-rooms. The Scythians would have found here ninety-seven bronze cups, shields, a helmet, and quivers.

After the destruction of the town at Teisbaini life was not renewed. The excavations at the site are continuing and are giving a whole mass of interesting material.

In 585 B.C., while the Scythians were sacking the northern administrative centres of Urartu, the Medes were taking possession of its central area, and so passed the oldest state impinging on the territory of the modern USSR. After its collapse, the Transcaucasian tribes formerly subordinated to Urartu emerged as the peoples of Armenia and Georgia.


## ARMENIA

The archaeological evidence bearing on the history of Armenia from the sixth century B.C. to the first century A.D. is very slight, not because the remains of this period have survived poorly, but because these remains have not been examined. The period of the struggle of the Armenians with the Iranian conquerors has not been investigated nor the creation and history of the first Armenian states. Already in the second century B.C. Armenia emerged as a single state, and it flourished in the next century. At that period there were more than fifteen flourishing cities famous for their palaces, temples, and other buildings whose ruins have still not been excavated. The ruins of town walls with towers and buildings have survived to the present day at the city of Tigranocerta and the fort of Garni.

## Garni

Researches at Garni have yielded some of the clearest evidence about the level of local Armenian culture developed in close connexion with classical civilization. From the first century B.C. Rome repeatedly tried to subject Armenia to its power. For a time Armenia was even included in the Roman provinces but the troops occupying it were soon forced to withdraw beyond the frontiers. After this Armenia was ruled by local kings, whose summer residence and army headquarters was at Garni up to the fifth century A.D. The fort at Garni was first mentioned by the Roman historian Tacitus as existing in the middle of the first century A.D. but it had evidently arisen long before this as the latest excavations have shown, probably in fact in the third century B.C. Garni lies 27 km. east of Erevan on the foothills of a range of mountains. The remains of a remarkable classical temple survive constructed of local basalt. On a high spur at whose foot flow the two streams of Azat and Gegard stand the remains of the fort walls and gates. The temple ruins tower up at the edge of the cliff, and scattered about are architectural fragments richly decorated with ornament. The site was excavated in 1909–10 but the results were fully published only in 1933.

The temple at Garni is the best surviving classical temple in the Soviet Union. It is a rectangular building surrounded on all sides by an open peristyle of twenty-four Ionic columns. Soviet workers who have thoroughly studied the material of the excavations have been able to make a reconstruction of the building and to date it. Most scholars favour the view that the temple was erected by King Tiridates I in the first century A.D. In 1945 a Greek inscription of this king was found at Garni in which the construction of a fort was mentioned. Excavations have continued since 1949, and the defensive wall has been cleared and a cemetery excavated. Within the fort six layers have been distinguished: one eneolithic, one Bronze-Age, one classical, and three medieval. The entry into the fort was defended by two strong rectangular towers. The towers and the whole of the fort wall are built of huge basalt blocks (weighing 5–6 tons) fastened together by iron clamps whose ends were turned in and fitted into special sockets filled with lead. Three hundred and fourteen metres of the wall have been excavated, and fourteen strong rectangular towers were found, spaced at 10–13 m. intervals. In its time the fort must have been almost impregnable.

The excavation of the cemetery showed that the majority of burials were of the native Armenian population with only a small number of Roman soldiers.

In 1953 near the temple a small room was found which evidently belonged to the palace complex. The floor was decorated with a splendid mosaic showing mythological figures of the Hellenistic world. In the centre were Oceanus and Talos, on the side nymphs, Thetida and others. This mosaic belongs to the first century A.D., and is the first find of a Hellenistic mosaic in Transcaucasia. Among the Armenian aristocracy and urban population the influence of Greco–Roman culture was strong. The remains of the material culture of ancient Armenia possess the same general features as Hellenistic remains in other countries, but are distinguished by certain characteristics peculiar to them alone.

The excavations of the temple at Garni have revealed a fairly high level of culture in ancient Armenia in the fields of structural techniques, metal-working, pottery- and glass-making, and textile crafts. The fort and settlement survived into the Middle Ages. Excavations are giving valuable material on the history and culture of Armenia right up to the Late Medieval Period.

The study of medieval remains in Armenia has been uneven. The history of the period has been interpreted through abundant written sources, but these give little information about economic life, the manner of living of the population, and the material culture. Excavations of medieval sites should fill in this gap.

## Dvin

The excavations at Dvin (south of Erevan), begun in 1937 and renewed in 1946, are now yielding much interesting information about an early medieval town of Armenia.

Dvin was a very large politico–administrative and cultural centre of medieval Armenia for almost a thousand years, from the beginning of the fourth to the middle of the thirteenth centuries A.D. Armenian historians of the fifth century record that Dvin was founded in the first half of the previous century. Through the fifth and sixth centuries, owing to favourable historical circumstances, the town flourished and became a large trade and craft centre. During this period the town walls and a number of monumental ecclesiastical and secular buildings were erected. In the middle of the seventh century Armenia fell under the control of the Arabs, and they held it for 250 years. In this period, grievous for the country, Dvin became the capital of the Arab rulers and retained some of its economic importance, although it suffered a sharp decline. From the middle of the ninth century the Arab caliphate began to decay, and the struggle of the Armenian people for independence and freedom concluded with the birth of an Armenian state. A growth in the economy and culture is now observed. After experiencing a severe earthquake in 893 Dvin flourished again. Its growth continued until the middle of the eleventh century, but in the first half of the tenth century a new capital had arisen, the city of Ani. Dvin gradually yielded its first place, and as a result of raids by Turkic tribes ceased to exist in 1236.

The ruins of Dvin lie on the modern hill of Toprakh-kala and excavations have shown that this hill had a very long history. The earliest settlement here was at the end of the third millennium B.C. during the Eneolithic Period. The place was settled also in later times including the Urartian period. In classical times the hill was converted into a fortress, but it was only when, in the thirties of the fourth century A.D., Dvin became the capital of Armenia that its history began as a trading and manufacturing town and not a mere village.

Excavations have revealed a series of important buildings. In the upper town the ruins of palace buildings of Armenian rulers of the ninth to thirteenth centuries A. D. have been found. Below these ruins at a considerable depth (up to 8 m.) the remains of other palace buildings of the fifth to ninth centuries have been found. In the central part of the town the main church measuring 58 by 26 m., the palace of the *Catholicos* (archbishop), part of the fort wall and its gates, the water supply, a smithy, storage buildings, and wine cellars were discovered. In the upper town and lower fort, houses and a princely hall, baths, a workshop for making pottery and faience objects, and others for cloth and jewellery were found.

The most interesting find was the cathedral. It was built in the third century A.D. as a pagan temple, and was converted into a Christian church at the beginning of the fourth century. From then on it underwent alterations in conformity with the changing styles of Armenian architecture until 893, when it was completely destroyed in the earthquake. To the north-west of the cathedral lay the palace of the *Catholicos* built in A.D. 461 or 485. This palace consisted of three ranges, of which the northern and southern were subdivided into small rooms, while the middle range consisted of a spacious aisled hall divided into bays by four pairs of columns.

Numerous iron objects were found in the excavation such as ploughshares, spades, axes, adzes, and so on. Jewellery-making had reached a high level. Gold objects were widely exported to other countries. The best quality pottery of Dvin is distinguished by the exceptional variety of form and decoration. Many glazed pots with decorations of animals and stamped patterns were found, as well as faience objects, for the most part white, sometimes blue or greenish monochrome cups. Valuable faience dishes were made, with fantastic animals drawn under the glaze. Several kilns, including one for the baking of high-quality pottery, were found. The glazed pottery from Dvin belongs to the eleventh to thirteenth centuries (Pl. 13a) and is analogous to similar pottery from other urban centres of Transcaucasia, and to pottery from several remoter places (Chersonesus in the Crimea and elsewhere) with which the medieval Caucasus had cultural and trade connexions.

Besides locally manufactured pottery, first-class examples of faience imported from the east have been found. About 600 coins (several hundred in hoards) from Byzantine, Sassanian, and Arab rulers as well as those of the local Arab emir have come to light.

The excavations at Dvin, one of the largest centres of medieval Armenia, have made it possible to study the material culture of the fourth to tenth centuries, previously little known, as well as that of the tenth to thirteenth centuries, partly known already thanks to the excavations at Ani (about 150 km. north-west of Erevan), capital and real cultural centre of Armenia at that time. There had been extensive excavations on the latter site in pre-Revolutionary times.

## Anberd

In 1936 one of the most important forts of medieval Armenia, Anberd, was excavated. The ruins lie 40 km. from Erevan on a triangular spur between two rivers. The main objective of the work was the exploration of the castle of the feudal lord, surviving as a three-storey building with every provision for a long siege. In the eleventh century the castle as well as the whole fortress belonged to a prince Pakhlavuni. There were a number of churches in the town and one of these constructed in 1026 survives to the present day and constitutes a remarkable monument of Armenian architecture.

Besides religious and domestic buildings, baths, two reservoirs, and a water main were found in the fort. The twelfth-century baths consisted of two little rooms beneath cupolas which had circular apertures. The floor of each room was paved with stone flags resting on stone pillars. The area beneath the flags was for heating supplied from a third small room in which the water was heated. The smoke and hot air from the furnace circulated beneath the flags and found their escape from these through thick clay pipes placed in each corner of the rooms under a stone facing. The walls were built of dressed stone and covered by polished impermeable plaster. Water entered the bath through iron pipes. In a small annexe to the bath-house, the furnaceman's quarters, various toilet articles were found, including three massive bronze mortars for grinding aromatics, censers, and other objects normal in the bath of a rich oriental feudal lord.

Under the floor of one of the rooms the grave of a jester was found, a terribly deformed man. His face had been altered by a special operation so that it was perpetually laughing. The jester was buried with a cockerel, the invariable companion of jesters in the east and the west.

A great quantity of architectural fragments was found in Anberd decorated with reliefs, as well as numerous glazed clay objects (many of which were found in the castle) with paintings beneath the glaze. Many things turned up which had undoubtedly been imported from eastern countries, for example a Chinese vessel, and from the south, including Egyptian or Syrian painted glass.

In Armenia numerous architectural monuments have survived to the present day. They are the work of remarkable artists who created their own style. The investigation of these sites will help us to understand more fully and clearly the artistic side of the medieval culture of Armenia.


## GEORGIA

The time when class-society and the state emerged in west Georgia is not accurately known. Already in the seventh century B.C. the Greeks carried on active trade with the population of the Caucasus and in the sixth century founded the towns of Phasis, Dioscurias, and Pityus on the coast (see Chapter 6).

The growing external trade and internal barter were responsible for silver coinage minted in this area (Colchis) from the beginning of the sixth century B.C. These coins are found in substantial numbers in west Georgia. The burials show already growing property and social inequality in the population. In the rich burials large quantities of weapons, gold, and silver are found; in others a small number of cheap things. Noteworthy among the finds of this period are gold, silver, and bronze ornaments: belts, necklaces, bangles, ear-rings, brooches, and little figures of animals. Especially favoured in this area were broad bronze belt plates with stylized drawings of animals and ornament. The corpses were commonly interred in large pitchers or sometimes in clay coffins.

Antiquities from Colchis [the classical name for west Georgia. T.] had been known previously for the most part from chance finds or amateur excavations, but in recent years the Georgian Academy of Sciences has undertaken systematic research in the area.

## Kldeeti

At Kldeeti (about 200 km. north-west of Tiflis) a rich cemetery of the second to third centuries A.D. has been excavated. The burials were in pits without barrows and the skeletons were contracted, sometimes accompanied by horse bones. In many there were parts of silver and bronze bridle equipment. Among the items in the graves of warriors there were iron weapons: long swords in scabbards decorated with silver, spearheads, and so on. Many bronze and clay vessels were revealed, including silver cups and a bronze ladle with a sculptured stone ram's head in the handle. The ornaments were gold bracelets, brooches, and ear-rings, and silver and bronze objects decorated with enamel. Some of these things were imported from Rome or the Roman provinces, others were the work of local craftsmen.

## Armazi

In eastern Georgia a state called Iberia by the Greeks arose at the beginning of the third century B.C. (Fig. 20). The capital of Iberia was the town of Armazi, which has been shown by excavation to have been begun around the fourth century B.C. and which remained the capital until the second century A.D. Later the capital became Mtskheta while Armazi remained as its acropolis. The remains of Armazi lie 20 km. from Tiflis, the fortress town being on the summit and sides of a hill, a strategically well-situated point.

From 1937 large-scale excavations have been carried on at Armazi-Mtskheta. At the same time excavations have been conducted north of this site on the largest cemetery in the Caucasus at Samtavro.

The interments here took place from the end of the second millennium B.C. to the seventh to eighth centuries A.D. They are so numerous that the area of the cemetery of almost 14 hectares (over 30 acres) seemed cramped, and sometimes the graves were constructed one on top of another in two or three layers. In Soviet times a substantial part of the cemetery at Samtavro has been discovered and more than 1·5 hectares (3·5 acres) has been examined, in which over 1,800 ancient graves of different periods have been discovered. Some of the graves, as already mentioned, belonged to the Bronze and Iron Ages, but the majority are contemporary with the flourishing period of Armazi-Mtskheta. Over the long period of time that the cemetery was in use the method of burial changed several times: up to the middle of the first millennium B.C. plain burials in the ground; from then to the end of the first millennium B.C. the corpses were usually interred in large clay jars; in the first centuries A.D. they were in cists, which were constructed at first of tiles and flat clay plaques, and later of stone flags. In the graves there were many valuable objects: weapons, utensils, jewellery and ornaments, coins, and so on. . . .

In the citadel at Armazi remains of strong fort walls and palace buildings have been discovered, as well as the town water main and other buildings. A large quantity of building material was found here: beautifully dressed and decorated stone blocks, well fired and painted tiles, bricks, etc. In Samtavro a burial stone was found bearing a Greek inscription in which mention is made of the 'chief artist and architect Akhol'. This Akhol was apparently a leading architect of Mtskheta.

Four km. to the west of Armazi, where the stream Armaziskhevi meets the Kura, on a terrace on the right bank of the latter the ruins of a pagan temple have been discovered as well as the remains of palace buildings and baths. All this was part of a suburban residence of high dignitaries of the Iberian state, *eristavi* or *pitiakhshi*. On this terrace was a necropolis that was in use until the seventh to eighth centuries A.D. The most ancient group of tombs dating to the second to third century A.D. were of exceptional interest. These were in a family vault built next to the palace buildings. The *eristavi* and members of their families were interred in stone coffins or cists of stone flags, sometimes on stands with silver feet. The stands were made of walnut and the corpses covered with gold-woven shrouds with little gold plates and buttons of various shapes sewn on to them. In the graves in this family vault numerous objects were found: gold ornaments, weapons for display, gold and silver coins, and silver utensils of local and foreign make, often with donors' inscriptions. Among the silver vessels deserving mention are a large decorated dish presented to *eristav* Bersum by King Faldad, two cups with engravings of a sacred horse standing before an altar, cups with the sculptured bust of a man, and the high relief figure of a goddess with a cornucopia (Pl. 13b). Especially interesting and varied were the artistic works in jewellery (ear-rings, finger-rings, bracelets, buckles, etc.), made of pure gold with precious stones inset, smalt and gems (cut stones), with portraits of the *eristavi* and their relatives named in Greek inscriptions (Pl. 14). The rich grave goods from the grave of *pitiakhsh* Asparuk have survived entirely, and the portrait gem is distinguished by the fineness of its workmanship and realism of its drawing.

## Mtskheta

The grave structures of Mtskheta are very varied. In 1947 at Bagineti the remains of a tomb of the second century came to light, which had evidently been a royal mausoleum. It was constructed of regular courses of large sandstone blocks joined by iron clamps embedded in lead. The top was covered not by a true vault but formed by corbelling. A tomb that is a unique monument in view of its almost intact state of preservation was discovered at Mtskheta in 1951. It also was made of large sandstone blocks and covered by a semicircular vault of dressed stone, while its gabled roof was covered with tiles decorated with red colouring. The tomb is referred to the end of the first century A.D., but had been robbed in antiquity. However, amongst the surviving objects there is much of interest: the remains of a coffin stand, four silver and nine gold coins, numerous and varied vessels, dozens of gold beads and buttons, a small bronze hollow statuette of a naked beardless boy, and so on. The composition of the grave goods indicates that the person was a woman of the ruling aristocracy.

Very remarkable inscriptions have been found at Mtskheta. Besides several in Greek and two in Hebraic, there were inscriptions in some local language written in hitherto unknown characters of Aramaic origin and called after the site 'Armazi script'. In 1940 a stone plaque with a bilingual inscription was found in the Armaziskhevi necropolis. The text is written in Greek and in the local language in 'Armazi script'. The inscription is dated to the middle of the second century A.D.

This bilingual inscription has made it possible to decipher a group of inscriptions written in the unknown language which previously could not be read. Thanks to the knowledge of the elements of the language of the Armazi inscriptions it is possible now to read them, or at least to obtain the general meaning. The inscriptions found in the Armaziskhevi cemetery make it possible to work out some details of the political history of Georgia and in particular the lives of the civil servants of the Iberian kings called *pitiakhsh*. No less important is the knowledge gained for the study of the development of the Persian and other alphabets, as well as the Georgian script. [Georgian is written in a script of Oriental origin, not in the Russian script which is of course derived from Greek letters. T.]

Mtskheta was the capital of eastern Georgia (Iberia) up to the sixth century A.D. It was at the end of the town's life that the temple of Jvari was built by a man of genius. It holds an exceptional place in the history of Georgian architecture and survives to the present day. In the sixth century Mtskheta gave up its first place to Tiflis (the modern capital), but it remained a religious centre.

The results of the excavations just described prove that ancient Iberia was a developed class-state distinguished by a high degree of Hellenistic culture, which was the foundation on which many centuries of Georgian culture and statehood later rested.

## Dmanisi

Medieval Georgian towns have in recent years received attention from archaeologists. One of the best studied of these is Dmanisi. This fortified site lies about 100 km. south-west of Tiflis on a high precipitous spur at the confluence of two rivers. Georgian written records first mention Dmanisi in the ninth century A.D. It already played a large part in the political history of the period and its name frequently occurs in the sources. It gradually emerged as a town in the first rank of Caucasian towns, and as an important trade centre on the caravan route joining Georgia with Armenia and the Near East. Its population was mixed Georgian, Armenian, Osetian, and Arab.

In the early medieval period Georgia was split up into a mass of small principalities; the struggle for unification was prolonged and accompanied by civil war. Only during the reign of David the Builder (1089–1125) was the formation of a single powerful feudal state completed under the control of one monarch. After 1123 when David took Dmanisi the town was once again in Georgian hands. At the end of the fourteenth century Dmanisi like other Georgian towns was destroyed by Timur. In the sixteenth century it was occupied by the Turks, at the beginning of the seventeenth century by the Persians. In the middle of the eighteenth century its existence as a town ceased and it was finally deserted.

During the excavation it was possible to distinguish two layers dated by coins; eleventh to thirteenth centuries, the floruit of Georgian culture, and thirteenth to fourteenth centuries, the time of Mongol control.

The town walls and various houses inside are built of the local stone, basalt. An ancient road leads to the town gate and continues beyond as a street into the city itself where it leads to the upper town, separated from the lower by its own wall. At the foot of the upper town were concentrated almost all the religious buildings, of which the chief one was the so-called 'Sion of Dmanisi', built in the seventh century, restored in the eighteenth century, and still surviving. There are also the ruins of two other churches of very late construction here. Several buildings have been excavated and wine cellars and oil-stores have been found. The best example of urban architecture is the thirteenth-century baths in the fort on the topmost point of the upper town The baths consisted of three rooms of which the largest was inhabited. The walls of the bath are built of stone and flat square bricks. The roofs of two rooms were covered by flat cupolas, in the middle of which were circular holes to let in daylight. Each cupola was covered by a double gable of flat tile set in lime mortar. One room was used for undressing and for rest, the bath was in the other. Two pipes passed through the walls to provide hot and cold water. In the centre of the floor was an outlet pipe which took away the water under the floor outside. The bath building is set on rock and the foundations do not go deep. The heating arrangements were underground. A clever arrangement provided constant circulation of water into the hot bath, so that the furnace heated the water quickly and evenly but did not overheat it. In the suburbs stand the ruins of three large baths used by the citizens, and also extensive cemeteries, Muslim and Christian.

In the excavations many copper coins, bronze objects, glass bracelets and other objects were found. Among the coins are some very interesting thirteenth-century ones struck in the local mint with the name of David the Builder. The local pottery is varied, especially the glazed wares with patterns of many colours and drawings of animals.

Dmanisi is a good example of a medieval provincial town, typical not only of Georgia but of the whole mountain region of Transcaucasia. Similar to Dmanisi is another town well known from written sources, the fortress of Rustavi (30 km. south of Tiflis on the river Kura).

## Rustavi

The citadel has survived to the present day on an island between the river and an ancient irrigation canal. At the foot of the citadel a residential area was excavated consisting of dozens of uniform buildings constructed of pebbles set in clay mortar. These houses slightly below ground level were typical of eastern Georgia and had a flat roof with central post supporting it. The area was destroyed by fire when Rustavi was sacked in the thirteenth century. The excavations yielded clear evidence of the sack of the city.

The monastery of Gelati (in Georgia) founded by that outstanding agent of the Georgian state, David the Builder, had great significance as a powerful centre of enlightenment, philosophical thought, and artistic culture. In the monastery lie the ruins of an academy in which were taught geometry, arithmetic, astronomy, philosophy, grammar, rhetoric, and music. Excavations in 1945 revealed the main lecture hall of the academy with its stone benches for the students and a stone seat for the lecturer.

H

The study of the medieval remains of Georgia has clarified the various aspects of its national culture and made it possible to establish a number of historical facts. Archaeological examination of the architectural remains not only provides evidence of a high level of architecture in medieval Georgia but also throws light on those details that are important for the history of culture. Thus in 1936 archaeologists cleared the church at Bolnisi of almost half its accumulated soil. Apart from the fact that this is one of the oldest and most interesting churches of Georgia and could be fully studied during the excavations, a building inscription of A.D. 493–5 was found. This inscription, besides recording the exact date of the construction of the church, is also the oldest monument of Georgian epigraphy. It is written in a beautifully formed majuscule, whose degree of refinement presupposes a long period of development of the Georgian script already before the end of the fifth century.

## AZERBAIJAN

Class-society and the state appeared unevenly at different times in the various parts of Azerbaijan. While in the north primitive society continued, in the south the slave-holding state of the Medes developed at the end of the eighth century B.C. About 550 B.C. this state was destroyed by the Persians and the country became one of the satrapies of the Persian Achaemenian Empire founded by King Cyrus. Later it became part of the empire of Alexander the Great, and in the third century B.C. was subjected to Parthia. The northern part of Azerbaijan was called Albania in antiquity (in written sources from the fourth century B.C.). At the time when Albania became known to classical writers it was inhabited by a league of tribes. Together with the Armenians and Georgians they struggled against the Romans and later against the Sassanian state in Iran. In the second half of the seventh century A.D., after Transcaucasia had been incorporated into the Arab caliphate, Mohammedanism became widespread. . . .

### Mingechaur

The history of Azerbaijan is known to a large extent from

written sources. Archaeological remains are still little studied and only recently have researches allowed historical deductions to be made. There is one region in the country where such a quantity of archaeological remains of all periods is concentrated, from the end of the second millennium B.C. up to the Middle Ages, that their examination supplies the basis for dating all the remains of Azerbaijan. This is the area near the village of Mingechaur (200 km. east-south-east of Tiflis) on the river Kura. Mingechaur is at the confluence of many water and caravan routes, and evidently in antiquity it was an important centre.

Work at Mingechaur began in 1935 and has continued since. As a result of surveys and excavations, it has been possible to distinguish four periods of settlement and several cemeteries with a complex of rich remains representative of the craftsmanship, life, and culture of the population of ancient Azerbaijan from the end of the Eneolithic Period up to the late Middle Ages (fifteenth to seventeenth centuries A.D.). The excavations have yielded more than 20,000 objects. Several ancient settlements have come to light. They have been called 'earthworks' provisionally and given consecutive numbers. Earthwork No. 1 is on the right bank of the river Kura where it joins the Boz-Dag. It belongs to the Bronze Age, to the second and beginning of the first millennia B.C. Remains of huts were discovered here with beaten clay floors, and pottery kilns.

Earthwork No. 2 lay on the other side of the Kura. This was a medieval settlement, whose inhabitants were agriculturalists. Dozens of kilns were found here for baking wheel-turned pots. They were of a different type from the Bronze-Age kilns on the other side of the river. This site contained a pre-Christian temple which was subsequently converted into a church. In the eighth to ninth centuries, evidently as a result of an Arab raid, this building was destroyed by fire. Its walls were built of stone and sun-dried brick, and were up to 1·8 m. thick. They were decorated with polychrome painting on the inside, while the roof was covered with large tiles. Mouldings from an ornamental frieze and column bases were found. On one stone two peacocks were represented with ribbons round their necks and between them a tulip. On the upper part of the stone was a cornice, on three sides of which was an inscription in the native language. Archaeological finds have helped to discover fragments of script of the lost Albanian language that can be read. The cultural deposit at this site covers the period between the fourth or fifth and twelfth to fourteenth centuries.

Earthwork No. 3 is also on the left bank of the Kura on a small hill, and covers an area of 300 by 250 m. In the upper part of the cultural deposit, referred to the tenth to thirteenth centuries, remains of huts were found with walls of intertwined twigs and reeds which were plastered with clay. The upper parts, the ceiling and roof, were supported by special wooden props. The second layer (sixth to tenth centuries) was characterized by numerous finds of hut remains, storage pits, and various objects indicative of an advanced state of agriculture and craftsmanship at this time. The lowest layer belongs to the beginning of the Christian era.

The excavation of the graves in this area on both sides of the river has yielded remarkable material. People were buried here from the first millennium B.C. up to approximately the fourth century A.D. Fourteen types of grave were distinguished, of which the most important are described here. In the lowest layer of the cemeteries there were contracted skeletons with eneolithic pots but without other grave goods. Above were Bronze-Age burials. With these were found large bronze swords, battle-axes, daggers, flint and obsidian arrowheads, bronze ornaments, and grey or black pottery sometimes with white incrustation. Judging by the objects of everyday life found in the graves, the population was in a transitional state from nomadic to settled life.

In the seventh to fifth centuries B.C. we find a culture characterized by extensive use of iron mostly for making weapons. Bodies were interred in an extended position and the graves were sometimes covered with stone blocks. Pottery was red and the usual shape was a round pitcher. Triangular gold, bronze, and silver ear-rings, wide bronze belts, gold necklaces, and so on were found in the graves. There were also seal-rings with intaglios of a man standing before an altar, a man with shield and spear battling with a lion, the head of an ox, a lion, a red deer, a roe deer, a chamois, and various birds. Sometimes three-finned arrowheads with barbs are found of the so-called Scythian type. This culture belongs to the Median Period, a time when written sources throw little light on the events in Azerbaijan. The find of these arrowheads of a Scythian type is evidence of the invasions of the Scythians into Media which Herodotus recorded. Graves with slightly flexed skeletons belong to the fourth or third centuries B.C. The weapons are now almost all of iron, and bronze occurs only as a survival.

From the second or first centuries B.C. up to the first or second centuries A.D. the so-called culture of jar burials is found. In vessels of small size with two handles children were buried. In the larger vessels, from 1·2 to 2·05 m. high and 80 cm. or more broad, adults were buried. Around the interment, pots containing the bones of large- and small-horned cattle are found. In the women's graves abundant ornaments occur: beads, bronze bracelets for legs and arms (one skeleton had thirty-six rings on the legs alone), finger-ring seals with stamps of cornelian and glass, and so on. In the men's graves there are weapons; swords, daggers, spearheads, and knives. In these jar burials painted pottery is found with drawings of birds, plants, geometrical shapes, and so on. The bones of domesticated animals found in the graves testify to stock-rearing; pomegranates, walnuts, and other fruit to orchards; sickles, scythes, querns, and other agricultural equipment to farming. To a later time belong the graves in this area in clay beds, wooden frames, catacombs, etc.

Thus the graves at Mingechaur give a remarkable picture of the sequence of cultures following one after the other, and they have formed the basis of the archaeological chronology of Azerbaijan.

### Yaloilu-Tapa

As well as from Mingechaur, important archaeological evidence for the period from the third to first centuries B.C., which is feebly illuminated by written sources in north Azerbaijan, has come from the excavations on a cemetery at a place called Yaloilu-Tapa. This site has given its name to a culture found in the lower parts, steppes, and foothills of the Great Caucasus, that is the basin of the Kura on the north side of the river. At this site, plain graves without barrows containing flexed skeletons and a large quantity of pottery were found. The pots are of complicated, sometimes even whimsical, shape; for example, vessels on three legs, pitchers with elongated spouts in the shape of a gutter with a grill at the base of the spout for filtering, and so on. Bronze and iron objects occurred in appreciable quantities. Archaeologists have inferred that the people who have left this cemetery and others like it led a sedentary life as agriculturalists and sheep-breeders.

## Albania

To the period of the struggle of the people of Albania with invading Roman troops belongs a Latin inscription found in 1948 at the base of Apsheronsky peninsula on the coast (near Baku). The inscription records the posting in this area of the Twelfth Legion in the reign of Domitian (A.D. 81–96).

Written information about Albania in the early centuries A.D. has reached us in the collected works of a series of Greek and Roman authors who had obtained their accounts from Roman legionaries taking part in campaigns in Transcaucasia. Of the twenty-nine towns and villages mentioned by Ptolemy (c. A.D. 120–70) only one name has survived to the present day: Khabala (Kabala). Kabala was evidently the capital of ancient Albania. Its ruins lie at Chukhur-Kabala. Graves of the first century A.D. and remains of later times have been found here. The town was in existence for a long time.

## Oren-Kala

Recently large-scale excavations have been undertaken at the medieval fortified town of Oren-Kala (about 300 km. southeast of Tiflis). In the opinion of many historians this is the site of the former Bailakan which played an important part in the history of Azerbaijan. The town lay on a basic trade route linking south with north Azerbaijan, Iran with Transcaucasia. There were excavations here in 1933, and again from 1953 onwards.

The town consists of a large rectangular fortified area covering 39 hectares (about 95 acres). The defensive walls were evidently built in the fourth to seventh centuries A.D. Later, in the ninth century, a rectangle within the town was divided off and surrounded by a wall of sun-dried brick with semicircular towers. It became the main fortress and the outer wall fell into decay in the twelfth to thirteenth centuries, although occupation outside the fortress did not cease. The town perished at the beginning of the thirteenth century as a result of a Mongol raid. A series of buildings of the twelfth to thirteenth centuries were discovered, as well as numerous architectural details, including the clay head of a lion. Eleventh-century baths and workshops were excavated where many tools, ornaments and glazed pots, faience, and other vessels were found.

## Ganja

Old Ganja (about 200 km. south-east of Tiflis) is the best studied of the medieval towns of Azerbaijan. Large-scale excavations were carried out in 1938–40 on this town, the home of Nizami, the great poet of Azerbaijan. The first references to the town in written sources occur in the ninth century, but it was evidently founded somewhat earlier. By the eleventh century the town was a large fortress, with suburbs adjoining, inhabited for the most part by craftsmen. The town perished in a Mongol attack in either 1231 or 1235. Later it was re-established, but never achieved its earlier prosperity.

Ganja in the eleventh to thirteenth centuries extended along two sides of a river spanned by three bridges built of brick and stone. The town was encircled by two defensive walls about 6 m. thick with large towers at the corners and smaller ones in between. In the enclosed area there were artisan areas, where houses and workshops have been excavated. The houses were built of brick and stone. The city was well maintained, for the ramifications of clay pipes of the water supply have been found. The main products of the workshops were textiles and pottery, the former recorded in written sources, the latter abundantly represented by archaeological material. Besides production of ordinary wares for the general market, a fine glazed ware was made, which was decorated with geometric and plant patterns as well as animal and human figures. It not only satisfied local demand but was exported to other towns. After the Mongol ravages, pottery production fell into decay both in Ganja and the other towns of Azerbaijan.

*

Important successes have been achieved in archaeological studies in the Caucasus and in Transcaucasia, but the exceptional archaeological richness of this area and its part in world history demand still more extensive research. There can be no doubt that the time will soon come when as yet unturned pages of the history of this area will be revealed.

## Chapter 8

# ANCIENT AND MEDIEVAL STATES OF CENTRAL ASIA AND SIBERIA

THE first Russian scholars of central Asia were primarily interested in the remains of the period upon which light was shed by written sources, that is the Middle Ages, particularly from the Arab conquest onwards. . . .

Soviet archaeologists of pre-Islamic central Asia inherited very little, and it has been necessary to a great extent to begin from the beginning. In order to fill the blank spaces on the archaeological map, and to catch up with other branches of archaeology that had shot far ahead, it was necessary to develop archaeological work in central Asia more quickly than in other areas of the Soviet Union. Thanks to the planned character of the work and its good organization, it has been possible to extend surveys and excavations over vast areas. The routes of special expeditions over tens of thousands of kilometres have formed a network over practically the whole area of central Asia from the Caspian deserts to the glaciers of Tien Shan, Altai, and Pamir.

Over the last twenty years the chronological horizons of central Asian archaeology have been much extended. Instead of a cultural history of eight to ten centuries, within which interest was previously confined, Soviet archaeologists have made known different remains from a period of 50,000 years: from the Palaeolithic Period onwards.

Many years of excavations have revealed to the world monuments of the most remarkable central Asian civilization. . . . Over the course of centuries profound changes took place, clearly reflected in the remains of the material culture. In Soviet scholarship the following interpretation has been agreed upon: in the eighth to seventh centuries B.C. the transformation to class-society took place, and the period c. 500 B.C. to c. A.D. 500 was one of slave-holding states in the southern, mainly agricultural areas. Feudalism only developed c. A.D. 500 and was due to internal social progress, not to foreign conquest. The beginnings of the early states in *c.* 800 B.C. had as their basis irrigation farming in the valleys of the large rivers. The irrigation systems of this area have been studied by Soviet scholars. [Most of central Asia either is desert or suffers from chronic droughts caused by slight and unreliable rainfall. T.]

The ancient states of central Asia are related to the basins of the various rivers. Thus Parthia is partly in the basins of the ancient Atrek and Gurgen; Margiana, valley of the lower Murgab; Chorasmia, basin of the lower Amu-Darya (Oxus); Bactria, basin of the middle and upper Amu-Darya; Sogdiana, the basins of the Zeravshan and Kashka-Darya (see Fig. 22).

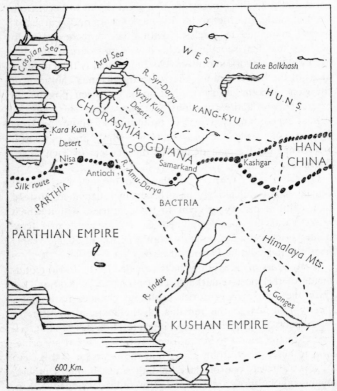

22. Map of central Asia *c.* A.D. 100.

The evidence collected by Soviet archaeologists for the various states is very uneven; some areas are patchily studied, in others a complete picture of the historical development can be offered.

## CHORASMIA

The greatest successes have been achieved in researches in Chorasmia. Among the various expeditions, that of the Academy of Sciences (which has worked there since 1937) has been one of the largest permanently active expeditions in our country. . . . To judge the scale of the work it is sufficient to say that in the first three post-war years aerial flights and motor reconnaissances through the deserts covered more than 15,000 km. The ground was traversed in different directions and over 200 archaeological monuments were brought to light.

The Kara-Kum and Kyzyl-Kum deserts adjoining the contemporary Chorasmian oasis form a peculiar 'archaeological reserve' whose study has yielded remains of 4,000 years from late neolithic to medieval times. The remains of earlier periods have been described above in the relevant parts of this book. To the period of early states belongs the fortified site of Kyuzeli-Gyr.* It is dated from the sixth to fourth centuries B.C.

The whole site is girdled by defensive walls, more than 15 m. thick, built of square sun-dried bricks. In the thickness of the walls are concealed narrow vaulted corridor-like chambers. The roof was defended by a parapet and by archers' slits. The circumference of the walls was 3·5 km. and the chambers in it were 6–7 m. long. The network of ancient irrigation canals of Chorasmia had already been dug by this time and may even have existed more than a century before. At this stage of history this work would have been undertaken by war captives: slaves. It is quite possible that the irrigation system was laid out not by an organized state but by farming communities or unions of such communities.

The powerful Achaemenian Empire was created by Cyrus in the sixth century B.C. As a result of a series of campaigns the

* It has not been considered necessary to indicate the position of desert sites south of the Aral Sea. The termination –*kala* in Turkic place names that frequently occurs in this chapter means 'fort'. T.

Achaemenian kings gained control of a vast territory which included the states of Hither Asia as well as Bactria, Sogdiana, and Chorasmia. The peoples of central Asia resisted the foreign invader but were successful only in Chorasmia, which at the end of the fifth or in the first half of the fourth century freed itself from the Achaemenian rulers, and in the middle of the latter century formed a completely independent state. After Alexander the Great had destroyed the Achaemenians he invaded central Asia in 330–327 B.C. and the peoples of this area again put up a warlike resistance. Chorasmia was not subjugated. The political power of the Greeks was ephemeral and strong empires arose on the eastern side of the former Persian Empire, the Parthian and Greco–Bactrian states with which Chorasmia played an important part in history.

Chorasmia suffered least from foreign conquest from the fourth to first centuries B.C., when it was an important independent state. About 170 B.C. Sogdiana was united to it. Remains of this period have been assigned to the 'Kangyu' culture (the name known from Chinese sources has been tentatively identified with Chorasmia).

One of the most interesting fortified sites and a primary settlement of this time was on the east side of the Amu-Darya. This is the fort of Janbas-Kala. It is rectangular, measuring 200 by 170 m., and is enclosed by double walls of sun-dried brick 10–11 m. high, and 1–1·3 m. thick. The outer wall (Pl. 16a) was furnished with a continuous row of arrow slits but had no towers. So that the archers could shoot along the face of the wall the slits were arranged in threes in semicircular niches. The entry is constructed in the form of a labyrinth with right-angled corners at each of the five gates covered by extra slits on the internal walls. Inside the fort a broad street leads from the gate dividing the town into two blocks, each containing about 200 rooms. The presence of large houses, communal living places, is evidence of the survival of the primitive social system. However there were workshops, internal and external trade was carried on, and irrigation and agriculture were highly developed.

The pottery is distinguished by its high finish and was made on a wheel, operated with the foot. The beads found here provide evidence of trade connexions with Syria, Egypt, and the cities of the north coast of the Black Sea. The art and religion of the people were expressed in numerous terracotta statuettes and clay reliefs. The statuettes mainly show women in sumptuous clothing and men in high boots, short tightly belted jackets with a triangular hole at the collar, and peculiar hats with three horns. The female statuettes probably represent the mother-goddess and protector of water and irrigation, Anakhita, and the male figures a god who was the companion of the great god Siyavush. Among the animals represented are little figures and heads of horses, as well as camels, rams, and pigs.

Rural settlements in the form of separate houses are represented by a series of remains, the most interesting of which is Koi-Krylgan-Kala (meaning 'fort of the dead rams'). The site is in the desert of Kyzyl-Kum (Pl. 16b). The fort is surrounded by a wall with nine towers in the shape of a regular circle. The centre of the circle is occupied by a citadel in the form of a tall, circular, two-storey building 42 m. in diameter. Around the building is an archers' gallery pierced by narrow slits. The interior of the citadel forms a circular area 31 m. in diameter, and contained living quarters and storage rooms. The rooms of the ground floor which survive to their full height are of especial interest. They were roofed with large double brick vaults about 4 m. high. A central vaulted hall along the diameter of the building was 5·5 m. broad, and at right angles to it were set six side chambers. At either end of this hall staircases led to the first floor. The rooms were lit by narrow windows pierced through a wall 6 m. thick. Between the central tower and outer wall were numerous buildings in which slaves probably lived. A number of these building were store-rooms containing enormous painted clay jars, used for wine-storage. Clay rhytons (drinking horns) representing horses and griffins, and flasks decorated with reliefs on the flat side were also found. Finds of various clay sculptures were common, especially of ossuaries in the form of square boxes on which were sitting figures in half natural size. Very interesting was the oldest inscription from Chorasmia (third century B.C.) on one of the jars, written in Aramaic script and evidently recording the owner's name. [Later work has shown the building underwent four stages of development. The excavator considers the central building was used for a burial cult and perhaps also for astrological observations. T.]

A special group of monuments of the first centuries A.D. up to the fifth or sixth centuries was excavated by the Khorezm Expedition in Kazakhistan (on the old course of the Syr-Darya near the Aral Sea). The Kazakh name means the 'Seven Hill-Forts' although in fact there are many more: the surveys in 1941 revealed twelve defended sites forming the heart of the group.

Work was concentrated on Altyn-asar which covers 16 hectares (about 40 acres) and is of an irregular trapeze shape. The remains of a 'great house' were partly excavated in the southern part of the site. Nineteen rooms were discovered in all and the presence of sixteen layers of an overall thickness of more than 10 m. was shown. It was revealed that the building had an extraordinarily interesting spiral plan, being designed something like a gigantic snail shell. The long rooms were arranged at right-angles to the direction of the spiral. In the upper layers were mill-stones, but in the lower hand-querns. This is evidence of great changes in the economic life of the inhabitants in about the third century A.D. However, agriculture played a subordinate part in their lives, for they were primarily herdsmen.

According to classical sources the Tocharians moved southwards in the second century B.C. and overthrew the Greco-Bactrian kingdom. Subsequently the whole of this area was incorporated into the Kushan Empire which had its main centres in northern India (Fig. 22). This huge empire stretched from the Aral Sea to the Ganges, and Chorasmia was absorbed into it in the second century A.D.

In Chorasmia forts have been found in which garrisons of the Kushan Empire were stationed to guard its northern frontiers. One such frontier fort is Gyaur-Kala on the right bank of the Amu-Darya (near the Aral Sea). The fort was built in the second century A.D., probably on the instructions of the Government. It sealed at its north end the passage between the river and the mountains. Excavation was carried out on the north part of the fort adjoining the wall where it was standing to its full height. The rooms in which the garrison lived were found. An interesting large square hall was found, on the walls of which traces of painting survived. In the centre of each wall was a niche while columns with finely moulded bases supported a flat roof. Next to the hall a sculptured male head was found, slightly more than natural size and modelled of clay. The sculpture which portrayed a young man in a sharp-pointed hat of Scythian form is one of the best examples of portrait sculpture of Chorasmia.

Rural settlements of this period in Chorasmia consist of a loose aggregate of large undefended peasant estates, each composed of a large courtyard surrounded by low brick wall, containing probably orchards and gardens. The house contained ten to fifteen rooms each occupied by one large patriarchal family. A fort with watch towers protecting the village stood a little apart.

In c. A.D. 200 Chorasmia freed itself from dependence on the Kushan Empire, and its rulers again began to issue their own coins modelled on the issues of their earlier independence. On these coins the first Chorasmian inscriptions appear, with a picture of the king and an inscription on the obverse and a man on horseback on the reverse.

From the first century B.C. to the sixth century A.D. was the period of active occupation of one of the most remarkable fortified towns of Chorasmia, that is Toprak-kala (a desert site near the Aral Sea). Its lower layers are of the same date as Janbas-kala (Kangyu culture), but its most flourishing period was during late Kushan times. The town forms a regular rectangle surrounded by a strong brick wall furnished with numerous rectangular towers and narrow slits. The town measures 500 m. by 350 m., and is transected by a narrow street which has ten to twelve large houses on either side. Each of the latter consists of dozens of square and rectangular rooms. These houses were inhabited by large patriarchal families of the urban aristocracy, including servants and slaves working in the fields and workshops. A great royal palace of the third century A.D. stood in the north-west corner of the town and occupied about a quarter of the whole area. Below the palace was the town's temple of fire and a large bazaar area connected with the outside world by separate gates.

The palace at Toprak-kala was excavated between 1945 and

1950. It was possible to make an architectural reconstruction of the appearance of the palace. The building was made of large sun-dried bricks and had three massive towers which reach 25 m. in height now and were not less than 30 m. high in antiquity. The first floor consisted of a number of vaulted living and storage rooms and large flat-roofed assembly halls, 12–14 m. above the ground. The ground floor consisted of a system of intersecting beaten clay walls, the space between them being filled up with a foundation of coursed bricks laid dry without mortar but with sand between the courses. The rooms of the second floor only survive to some extent in the north-west corner of the main building, so the main features of the palace plan are only known at first-floor level. A series of room complexes separated by main walls can be distinguished.

The first complex of rooms gave on to the northern courtyard. Domestic and storage buildings adjoined this court as well as an assembly hall. This is where part of the palace guard was posted. From this outer part of the court a corridor led directly into the most impressive hall of the palace, called the 'Hall of the Kings', as sculptural groups thought to represent the kings of Chorasmia with their wives and relatives around them occur in niches covered with grilles along the high part of the walls. The statues, made of unbaked clay and painted, have faces of exceptional realism and are undoubtedly portraits. In two niches large sitting male figures survive of almost double natural size, around which are arranged three to five standing men, women, and children. The wall behind the figures was painted with white and red lilies on a dark blue background with a pink–orange panel below. The discovery of two head ornaments similar to the crown of two kings of Chorasmia known from portraits on coins has made it possible to identify these sculptures as royal portraits.

In the centre of the northern part of the palace was a hall, the wall of which was decorated with plant ornament of sculptured and incised alabaster. South of the 'Alabaster Hall' there was a gallery with rooms on either side. At the beginning of the gallery a door was discovered that led into an internal complex of assembly rooms. Here were two ceremonial halls: the 'Hall of Victories' decorated with sculptures of seated kings, in the company of the goddess of victory, and the 'Warriors' Hall', so called because of the fragments of sculpture showing black warriors in iron chain-mail with cane shields.

In the western part of the palace two more assembly halls were discovered. In the first of these was a frieze with reliefs of spotted deer, and above another frieze of griffins. The walls of the second hall were decorated with dancing couples of which only the legs survive, apart from the head of a dancer and a fragment of another wearing a mask with goat's ears and grotesquely protruding eyes.

Through the western part of the palace the visitor entered the detached southern part where the inner rooms of the royal family lay. East of this lay a workshop for making bows and a storehouse for weapons and war equipment. In this part the uppermost floor, which does not survive, probably housed the court archives.

Besides the sculptures a remarkable discovery at Toprak-kala was that of the monumental wall paintings. During the excavation many pieces of wall painting were found, on clay plaster with mineral colouring matter. In a great part of the rooms, including all the living and assembly rooms, paintings were found. The room on the second floor of the palace looking on to the small northern court was especially richly decorated with paintings of musicians placed among ornamental patterns. One of these survives intact and is a magnificent painting of a harpist. In one room women are shown collecting grapes and pears in their aprons. In the paintings plant ornament is combined with representational subjects and in various rooms pictures of tigers, horses, birds, and so on have been found.

In the excavations many seeds of barley, wheat, and millet have been found, as well as stones and pips of apricots, pears, and grapes, pieces of paper, wool and silk, leather footwear, iron spear- and arrowheads, and so on. The most important finds were documents on skin and wood. These had fallen into the lower rooms from an upper floor that no longer exists. The documents were written in ink in the clear handwriting of clerks with the separate delineation of the letters [i.e. not cursive, T.], and are in the same alphabet as on the Chorasmian coins. They have not yet been deciphered.

The excavations at Toprak-kala have shown the high level of individual character of the artistic culture of Chorasmia. In the opinion of Tolstov the palace was the residence of the shahs of Chorasmia in the third century A.D., and the town itself was the capital until it was transferred to Kyat on the banks of the Amu-Darya in A.D. 305.

In the fourth to fifth centuries the Kushan Empire fell into decline and broke up. The Sassanian Empire in Iran (founded in the first quarter of the third century A.D. and lasting for 400 years) embraced the whole south-western part of Asia. Later on nomadic tribes, called the 'White Huns', from south-east of the Aral Sea seized control in Bactria and in Sogdiana and rapidly expanded almost to the limits of the Kushan Empire. Chorasmia remained independent under its own dynasty of kings. In the early 560s the new empire of the White Huns collapsed under simultaneous blows from east and west. The Turks* of the southern Altai and south-east Kazakhistan created a powerful nomadic state at this time, and central Asia fell under their control. This period was one of remarkable social changes and witnessed the development of feudal relationships replacing slave-holding society. The types of towns, villages, and houses change sharply. The number of towns decreases, many of them falling into decay and being abandoned, as was the case in the sixth century at Toprak-kala. The change from urban to rural settlements gave rise to open undefended villages, while the landowner himself withdrew into a new type of fortification, his private castle. The estates of the aristocrats are distinguished from those of peasants only by their size and lavishness of layout.

The dried-up oasis in the centre of which stands the fortress of Berkut-kala gives a picture of such settlement. In a belt 17 km. long and 2·3 km. wide extending along both sides of a large irrigation canal were scattered about a hundred castles with their estates. Most of these belong to the sixth and seventh centuries. Their size varies but they are all constituted on one principle. Surrounded by high beaten clay walls they have as a rule a 'keep': a residential tower raised on a massive plinth

* Quite distinct from the modern Turks although of course related to them ethnically and linguistically. T.

4–8 m. high and set in the corner or on the line of one of the walls. The walls of the 'keep' have pilasters containing false arrow slits. The raised position of the 'keep' made it difficult to reach in an attack.

In 1938–9 one large and five small estates were excavated. The especial interest of the large estate, the castle of *Teshik-kala*, was the discovery here of coins of the sixth to seventh centuries. The estate covers about a hectare (2·5 acres) and was enclosed by a beaten clay wall with oval towers at the corners. Within was another less thick wall. In the middle of the south-west side of this wall stood the 'keep' on a plinth in the form of a truncated pyramid 8 m. high. Entry was only possible by a drawbridge which was lowered from a tower near the entry. In the rooms wide couches were found while the walls were decorated with friezes of clay reliefs of rosettes and palmettes. On the floor were scraps of carpet, remains of clothing – a dressing-gown, sheepskins, and leather footwear – felt, and sheep's wool. A large number of organic remains attesting agriculture and stock-breeding were found here. In Chorasmia at this time wheat, barley, millet, cotton, beans, grapes, pears, apricots, pumpkins, melons, and cucumber were grown; while sheep, goats, donkeys, pigs, cattle, horses, and camels were reared. Fortified estates evidently came into being, owing to ceaseless wars and the decline of the central authority which could not protect its subjects. Irrigation diminished and the crafts declined.

At the beginning of the seventh century the Arab state came into being and made warlike attacks on its neighbours. The Arabs soon occupied Syria, Palestine, Iran, and, in the beginning of the eighth century, central Asia. They delivered a great blow to the local cultures of the area, in Sogdiana and Chorasmia. . . . With the Arab conquest Islam became widespread and provided further stimulus to the development of feudal relationships. This brought about significant changes in the cultures of the people of central Asia.

In the course of time the rebirth of economic and cultural life in central Asia began. Gradually urban life was restored and new feudal towns came into being. They grew slowly in a dis-ordered fashion; regular planning disappeared. The central

Asian medieval town consisted of a citadel with the palace of the ruler and the administrative buildings with a *shahristan* adjoining occupied by aristocrats, workshops, and so on. The *shahristan* was surrounded by a fortified wall. As the town outside this grew trade and workshop suburbs developed outside. This part is called the *rabad* and in the course of time was also enclosed by a wall.

The early eighth century was the most prosperous period of the shahs of Chorasmia who then controlled a large part of central Asia. After the Arab conquest there was a further revival but in the early thirteenth century central Asia was conquered by the Mongols who destroyed the towns and killed the majority of their inhabitants. Later there was a further revival in some areas and excavations have been carried out at the late medieval capital of Chorasmia, Urgench. Occupation continued here until the seventeenth century.

After the Mongols had enslaved many countries, they created their own towns and cultural values with the help of native craftsmen carried off into captivity. Thus the bright glazed pottery, vessels, and tiles, known from the excavations of the towns of the Golden Horde, were imported from workshops in Chorasmia and above all from Urgench. At the end of the fourteenth century Chorasmia with its irrigation system was destroyed by Timur and the country became a desert.

## BACTRIA

The modern Tajiks and Uzbeks are linked in the past, by long centuries of living together and by a community of culture and way of life, and to some extent also they are ethnically related. The history of ancient Bactria and Sogdiana is to a significant degree the history of the predecessors of the Uzbeks and Tajiks. Large-scale archaeological expeditions have examined the historical remains of the Tajik and Uzbek republics.

One of the most ancient states of central Asia was Bactria. It covered a great part of Tajikistan, southern Uzbekistan, and northern Afghanistan. The antiquities of northern Bactria have so far been little studied, but recently Soviet workers have begun to excavate there.

The campaigns of Alexander the Great led to the spread of Greek culture. The Hellenistic culture that arose after the conquests was a peculiar interweaving of Greek and eastern elements, and the full flowering of central Asian Hellenistic culture belongs to the Kushan period. A remarkable monument of this period is the sculptured stone frieze from Airtarn (about 300 km. south-east of Samarkand) that decorated the outside of a building (possibly a Buddhist temple).* One fragment was found accidentally by a frontier guard in the Amu-Darya, and another seven fragments were found at the fortified site of Airtarn 18 km. upstream from Termez. The frieze shows half-figures of young men and girls, musicians, and bearers of garlands, between acanthus leaves (Pl. 18a). In spite of the presence of elements of Greek and Indian art, the frieze as a whole is distinguished by its special style and technique which suggests the existence of a native school.

In the outskirts of Termez not far from this the remains of an ancient Buddhist monastery have been found, consisting of a large number of artificial caves and subterranean structures of the last centuries B.C. and the first centuries A.D.

After a period of decay in the life at Termez in the fifth and sixth centuries, things began to improve in the seventh century, and in the eleventh and twelfth centuries medieval Termez was most prosperous.

The eleventh- and twelfth-century rulers' luxurious suburban palace, situated on the eastern part of the ruins of Old Termez, has been more thoroughly studied than any other part. The palace occupied an area of about 7,000 sq. m. In the middle of a broad court a reservoir faced with brick was excavated. The large reception hall was richly decorated with incised ornament on gypsum. In clearing out the north side of the pavilion numerous decorative glass medallions with inscriptions and drawings of rosettes, lions, birds, horsemen, and so on were found. On one was the Arabic text, 'For the great, victorious Sultan Bakhramshah', and with this name is associated one of the palace restorations. At the beginning of the thirteenth century the palace was undergoing magnificent restoration but it

* During the first centuries A.D. Buddhism became very widespread in central Asia.

was never completed, for in 1220 Termez was sacked by the Mongols and fell into ruin.

## Afrasiab (*Samarkand*)

One of the most remarkable monuments of ancient Sogdiana in which the cultural remains of many periods have piled up is the enormous hill-fort of ancient Samarkand on the northern side of the present city. It is now called Afrasiab after one of the heroes of an Iranian epic, a legendary king of Turon. This was the site of the town from *c.* 500 B.C. up to A.D. 1220 when Samarkand was sacked by the Mongols and the inhabitants fled.

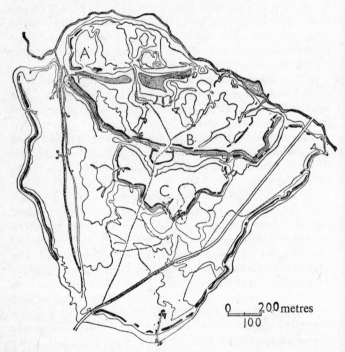

23. Afrasiab (Samarkand). Plan of the town by A. I. Terenozhkin, showing the progressively increasing defences A, B, and C. The heavy black lines are ramparts; the stippled areas, ditches; the hatchet lines, gullies; other dotted lines, ancient roads.

Afrasiab was one of the few central Asian fortified towns where excavations took place in pre-Soviet times and these yielded interesting collections of pottery, terracotta statuettes, and other objects.

The plan of Afrasiab is roughly triangular (see Fig. 23). It is about 1·5 km. across from north to south and roughly the same from east to west, and it covers 219 hectares (about 550 acres). In the middle of the north side rises the citadel. Three lines of defence encircling the city show the gradual growth of the *shahristan*, while a fourth encloses the *rabad* (bazaar area). This plan represents basically the development of Samarkand in the feudal, post-Arab period. Excavations have revealed early levels. A layer belonging to the sixth to fourth centuries B.C. consisted of the remains of houses built of sun-dried bricks and clay, and contained pots which had been produced in workshops, but whose appearance suggests that the wheel had not been in use for very long. From the finds of this period a stone seal showing an Achaemenian king or god with a bow is worthy of note.

In the fourth to second centuries B.C. a high level of urban civilization had been achieved in Sogdiana with the development of crafts and trade. Samarkand at this time had probably extended over the whole area of Afrasiab and so was an enormous town. Numerous clay statuettes and reliefs have been found there, a few connected with classical mythology but most local and connected with the cults of Mazdaism (Zoroasterianism). Especially widespread are representations of the goddess Anakhita with a pomegranate or vessel in her hand (Pl. 17a). In 1948 a pottery was excavated in Afrasiab in which moulds for terracottas of Anakhita were found near the potter's wheel.

The medieval layers at Afrasiab have yielded a vast quantity of finds. In the eighth century there were advances in milling technique and evidence of this was found in the water-mills, with granite millstones up to a metre in diameter, on the irrigation canal of Siab on the northern edge of the town. In medieval times Samarkand was the most important centre in the world for the manufacture of paper although this has left no archaeological trace. In eastern Europe and specially in Russia in the tenth century *dihrems* (silver coins) were widely used that were minted in the central Asian towns (mainly in Bokhara and Samarkand). Pottery production was very advanced and researches in two extremities of the town have revealed pottery areas. Much glazed ware was found. Glass vessels were widely used: tankards, tumblers, flasks, little bottles, and wine-glasses. A workshop where glass beads were made was found as well as many clay water-pipes.

## SOGDIANA

### Tali-Barzu

A very interesting monument of pre-Muslim Sogdiana is the fortified town of Tali-Barzu 6 km. south of Samarkand. The area where it lies was described by Arab geographers as the most flourishing part of ancient Sogdiana. The four sides of Tali-Barzu are oriented almost exactly to the points of the compass. The central tell rises 18 m. above the surrounding locality and its present area of 5 hectares (12 acres) is much smaller than its area in antiquity. Within the town there is an intricate complex of buildings of various types not yet fully studied. Excavations have established the presence of six cultural layers which serve as a guide to its past. In the lowest layers were found terracotta figures sculptured by hand, of camels and other animals, and riders on horseback, and also stamped figures of Anakhita. Drawings scratched on sherds of large pots are noteworthy. One shows a half-human half-bull beast, a mythical being who was one of the demigods of the Iranian pantheon and called Gopat-shah. In the third to fourth centuries A.D. life at Tali-Barzu died out and the castle lay in ruins. In the fourth century an important centre of Sogdiana, Rivdad, was set here, a place visited by the country's rulers. The whole of the town's area was laid out on a planned basis and a strong beaten clay castle was erected with a citadel in its centre. Its corners were defended with towers and arrow slits, and between the towers ran a series of vaulted rooms. The outside walls of the rooms were also the outside of the fort. The rooms, of which there were no fewer than 500, were lit by narrow slits. In the sixth or seventh century the castle belonged to a powerful feudal lord. The Arab conquest brought Sogdian culture to a close; the castle at Tali-Barzu perished in flames.

## Varakhsh

At the other end of the valley of Sogdiana near the oasis of Bokhara (250 km. west of Samarkand), in a desert not occupied for many centuries, several dozen tells are scattered over an area of 500 sq. km. Amongst these, the largest is the fortified site of Varakhsh which was examined in 1947–53. It was the capital of the rulers of the Varakhsh area in pre-Islamic times. In the southern part rise the remains of the citadel with strong walls of sun-dried brick. Beside the citadel were excavated the remains of the palace whose walls were decorated with paintings and beautiful carved plaster (thick alabaster worked with a burin). In the heaps of debris and on the attached columns of the building found on the west side of the palace a vast amount of plaster facing was found with reliefs of various geometric figures, human beings, animals, birds, fish, trees, and fantastic creatures. In the central part of the palace a large chamber came to light furnished with benches made of sun-dried brick along the walls which themselves were covered with painting in a coloured wash over clay plaster. In the upper frieze, which partly survives, there is a procession of animals; in the lower a hunting scene with riders on elephants covered with hangings, struggling with fantastic animals resembling leopards and griffins. East of this paintings were discovered in another room. On its south wall there were compositions with many figures and a king sitting on a throne with his retinue. Several features of these pictures are very similar to those from Pyanjikent described below (see p. 252). On the western wall riders are shown wearing armour and in pointed yellow helmets with chain neck-guards hanging over their shoulders.

Excavation of the palace is not finished and its overall plan not yet understood. Evidently the oldest parts belong to the sixth century A.D. and later it underwent several alterations. The main complex of paintings belongs to the seventh century. Recently work has begun on the citadel and the town which arose in the last centuries B. C. and lasted to the eleventh century A.D. The palace belonged to one of the local potentates, ruler of the lower part of the valley of the Zeravshan. It is a fine example of Sogdian art, showing significant connexions with India and Iran.

## The Mug Mountain Castle

The discovery of the Sogdian castle on Mug Mountain in the upper reaches of the Zeravshan (about 200 km. east of Samarkand) has had great importance for scholarship. It took place accidentally: a shepherd found a basket made of willow twigs containing ancient manuscripts on the mountain. When this became known to scholars in 1933 the Academy of Sciences sent an expedition there.

The castle on the south-west corner of the top of Mug Mountain is surrounded by a wall. It stands on a plinth built of pebbles and loess faced with stone. Up to 80 cm. the walls had an ashlar base but higher up they were faced with sun-dried brick. Five vaulted rooms were excavated in the castle, which were shaped like a series of narrow corridors. Many and various objects were found in the ruins including silver and bronze coins, moulds with the names of Sogdian kings, seal impressions showing people and animals, weapons, cotton and silk cloth, wooden vessels and pots, etc. One of the remarkable finds was a wooden shield lined with skin on which was drawn an armed horseman on a yellow background (Pl. 18b). The rider is wearing a long tunic reaching below the knees and sits on a stationary horse. He is armed with a long sword, a dagger, two bows, and a quiver full of arrows.

The most important find on Mug Mountain was eighty-one documents from the archives of the owner of the castle. The documents are written on paper, skin, and wooden staffs. Eight are in Chinese, one in Arabic, one in a Turkic language, and the remainder in Sogdian. Not all the Sogdian manuscripts have yet been deciphered. They consist of a business list and business notes of the castle's owner, and there are manuscripts dealing with other matters, one of an astrological nature (a calendar). The document in Arabic has been read and has given the name of the owner and of the castle. It is a letter from the prince of

Pyanjikent Divashtich to the Arab governor Maverannakhra who held the office in A.D. 717–19. The fate of Divashtich is known from a contemporary source. He took part in the rising against the Arab governor in 722 and went from Pyanjikent to the castle of Abargar (this is the one at Mug) but was defeated by the Arabs, taken prisoner, and executed. The castle was sacked, but the objects and manuscripts left there after the looting by the Arabs have been found by archaeologists.

*Pyanjikent*

The town of Pyanjikent that was owned by Divashtich lies 68 km. from Samarkand up the river Zeravashan. Ancient Pyanjikent which ceased to exist in the period of Arab conquest of central Asia in the eighth century lies on the south-eastern edge of the modern town. Medieval Pyanjikent lay on the left bank of the river somewhat east of the modern town. The oldest city has been studied since 1947. On the west side lie the remains of the fortified citadel, on the east is the city itself (the *shahristan*) covering 19 hectares (about 45 acres).

East of the *shahristan* extending along the irrigation canals were the suburban estates, while to the south lay the town cemetery. The *shahristan* was enclosed by a high defensive wall with oval towers and a broad flight of steps led to the wall on its main part. The town was supplied with water from the canals which were replenished by mountain springs. In the town lines of clay water-pipes were found. During the excavation two large buildings were discovered that had been Sogdian temples.

One of these buildings lay on the west side of the great town square, almost in the centre of the *shahristan*. This many-chambered monumental building was of sun-dried brick and had been destroyed by fire in the eighth century A.D. In the centre of the building was a square hall (8 by 8 m.) its roof supported by four columns whose bases survived; the columns themselves had been of wood. The hall had no eastern wall and on this side gave directly into a broad columned porch, a characteristic feature of central Asian buildings where this is called the *aivan*. On the east the *aivan* gave on to a quadrangular court. On the western side a doorway led into a closed chamber, evidently the 'holy of holies' of the temple.* On the southern side of the temple were a series of rooms in one of which were found fragments of wall paintings. These showed a religious procession only three male figures of which survive. Paintings were also discovered in several rooms on the northern edge of the temple. On one of the walls two male figures are shown sitting cross-legged in cloths held in by gold belts from which long narrow swords hang. Evidently these were Sogdian priests participating in some ritual meal. There were also pictures of a priest kneeling before an altar, and in a neighbouring room of a ritual dance.

The second monumental temple lay not far north of the first one. The essential part of the temple consisted of a hall with four columns, a 'holy of holies', and an *aivan* of open branching porticos. The paintings of this temple are united by one central theme connected with the Sogdian burial rites. On the southern wall of the *aivan* are shown riders on horseback, Sogdian nobles. In the four-columned hall is shown a scene of mourning for 'Siyavush', the god personifying the death and re-birth of the forces of nature. Through the arched openings of some kind of pavilion of wood and cloth can be seen the body of the dead boy over whom stand weeping mourners. Below are a group of people of whom six are Sogdians, five probably Turks. Two figures support the twisted handles of the pavilion, another carries a pitcher, the remainder are tearing their hair and cutting the lobes of their ears with knives in order to express their grief. On the left a goddess is shown taking part in the mourning for Siyavush. On the west wall three warriors are shown, evidently from his retinue. On other walls fragments of painting survive showing compositions of many figures and panels with plant and geometric ornament. In the niches that occur in both buildings were placed clay statues that unhappily no longer survive. Only part of a sitting figure and the head of a youth have been found separately.

Near the courtyard of the second temple another *aivan* has been excavated, two walls of which were covered by clay reliefs.

* The 'holy of holies' was a closed room accessible to none but priests, found in ancient temples of Iran and other areas of Hither Asia including Chorasmia; it was connected with the fire cult.

There were figures of people, sea monsters, devils, and fish on a background of waves in low relief, painted with blue colouring. Especially interesting were a triton and a man supporting some kind of grandiose pedestal. The sculpture of the *aivan* was evidently related to a water cult and the deity of the river Zeravshan. In the treatment of the human body in this sculpture there are clear traces of realistic classical art, but the overall schemes in the compositions find their closest analogy in the ancient art of India.

On the eastern site of the town square in the *shahristan* opposite the temples a residential area was excavated, consisting of various structural complexes. The walls of the rooms were built of daub and sun-dried brick and survived to a height of 5 m. and more. Many rooms were two- and sometimes three-storeyed.

In each of the residential blocks there was a special parade or assembly room, a large hall with a flat wooden ceiling resting on four wooden columns decorated with incised ornament. The walls of these halls were covered with colourful paintings. In one room a golden altar is shown, before which a man kneels on a bright carpet. He is dressed in a long tunic (*kaftan*) of patterned silk and holds a gold cup in his left hand. Other fragments survive but these are unfortunately damaged.

A second group of residential quarters is being excavated near the eastern defensive wall of the *shahristan*. In the assembly halls here the wall paintings are preserved fairly well. In one the paintings were done on a dull black background and survive on all four walls. They show a series of separate scenes connected in some way with one subject. The scenes are very varied, a feast with an enthroned king and priests sitting on mats under a luxurious canopy (Pl. 19); a fight between groups of mounted warriors; two champions in single combat; a woman playing a harp, and so on. In other halls there are interesting pictures of a procession with an elephant, a group of people playing with dice, and three musicians.

The residential quarters revealed in the *shahristan* were the houses of the nobility, but workshops have also been found. In one of these several furnaces came to light, funnels, and a mould for casting.

Mention must now be made of the excavations in the necropolis of Pyanjikent which lies 300–400 m. south of the town walls.

In conformity with Mazdaistic religious views that were widely held in Sogdiana and the study of the 'sacred elements', fire, water, earth, and air, a corpse could neither be burnt, nor buried in the ground, nor thrown in the water, nor left in the air. So the Sogdians took the flesh off the bones of the dead man and threw it to the beasts of prey or the dogs, but the bones were stored in special ossuaries. The ossuaries were placed in special vaulted tombs. In the cemetery at Pyanjikent these vaults were built of daub or sun-dried brick in the form of a small single-chambered room. In these the ossuaries are found, consisting of rectangular boxes of baked clay with ornamented fronts and lids. The cemetery was robbed during some period of conquest as all the ossuaries found were broken. In spite of this pots, coins, rings, bracelets, and other objects left by the robbers were found.

## PARTHIA

In the southern part of Soviet Turkmenistan are found the remains of the slave-holding state of Parthia.

The powerful Parthian Empire, the chief rival to the world powers claimed by Rome, arose in the third century B.C. At its most flourishing period it extended from the Indus to the Euphrates, from the Amu-Darya (Oxus) to the Persian Gulf. The Parthian emperors controlled Persia, Media, Mesopotamia, Armenia, and Hyrcania. They maintained diplomatic relations with the two extreme points of the then civilized world: with the great power of the Far East, China, and with the great empire of the West, Rome. The Parthian cavalry, famous in antiquity, more than once inflicted defeat on Roman troops. All the efforts of Rome to curtail the power of Parthia were unsuccessful. The campaign of Crassus is well known · he moved against the Parthians with a substantial army but was lured into the deserts of Mesopotamia by the Parthians who then destroyed his army. What the Roman armies had not been able to achieve was accomplished by the internal development of social relationships. In the course of time the great slave-holding state of Parthia began to decay and in the third century A.D. it collapsed. Parthia was subjugated by a king from south Iran who founded the Sassanian dynasty. The new dynasty did its utmost to destroy all record of the former state, so that even its name was obliterated and a geographical term 'Khorasan' (east) was used to describe Parthia. The state annals of Parthia and the special collected works on it of Greco–Roman writers are lost. As a result almost the whole of the five centuries of Parthian power are very dark in the history of the east. We have only very fragmentary information about them.

## Nisa

In southern Turkmenia on the edge of the desert of Kara-Kum at the foot of the Kopet-Dag Mountains 18 km. south-west of Ashkhabad are two fortified sites now called Staraya and Novaya Nisa (Old and New Nisa). Excavations have been carried out here from 1930 to 1936 and from 1946 onwards.

New Nisa covers about 18 hectares (about 45 acres) and con-sists of the remains of an ancient town, the first capital of the Parthian kings. It was enclosed by a strong wall of sun-dried brick with numerous towers. The gates were situated on the eastern side, and beside them a necropolis for Parthian nobles was in use for several centuries. In the southern part of the town rose the citadel. On all sides it was surrounded by build-ings which in their turn were enclosed by an outer mud wall. Beyond this wall on the north side lies the town of Old Nisa. This contained royal palaces, tombs, and temples. The town covered 14 hectares (35 acres) and was also enclosed by a strong wall, the greater part of which remained unfinished. In New Nisa cemeteries of Parthian nobility with several layers have been excavated as well as houses of Parthian and feudal times.

The largest excavations have been carried out recently at Old Nisa. It has been possible to determine the architectural history of several buildings which were added to and altered in the course of centuries. Thus in the southern part of the town a palace–temple complex was excavated in which a square and a circular hall were revealed. The square hall, covering about 400 sq. m., had four brick pillars quatrefoil in section and up to 12 m. high, with a series of attached columns along the walls. In a second layer circular columns were found, and between them were placed male and female statues, greater than natural size, made from unbaked clay, and painted on the surface. The hall beneath had been covered by white plaster but the columns, half-columns, and surfaces of the walls of the second period were red.

The architectural complex in the northern part of the town contained a large house which with its internal courtyard covered about 3,500 sq. m. It had undergone various alterations. In the first structural period it consisted of a courtyard with porticos on all sides of wooden columns resting on stone bases. Beyond these porticos on each side were large rooms with four columns along their long axis. Later the porticos were converted into long rooms and the arcades blocked up. There had been a treasure house of the Parthian kings in this building but it had evidently been robbed after the collapse of the dynasty in the third century A.D., as only a few objects were preserved. Amongst these were pottery, polished and fluted glass which was painted or gilded, iron weapons, bronze shield bosses, ivory objects, terracotta figures, and metal sculptures, including silver ones embellished with gold, of Eros, Athena, and a sphinx.

The most remarkable objects were of ivory and had been stored in one of the four-columned rooms. Amongst these were the legs of a throne of a Parthian king, the ends of which were carved to represent the sharp claws of a griffin holding bunches of acanthus leaves, and royal rhytons carved from elephant tusks of various sizes (that is, wine horns for drinking and ritual libations). In the upper part of the horn there was usually a frieze of gods, muses, and scenes from Greek mythology. Sometimes the frieze was capped by a cornice of male and female heads (Pl. 20b). The stem of the rhyton was polished and enriched at the edge with polychrome glass, precious stones, and gold, and it finished in a sculptured figure in the form of a horse, a lion-type griffin with horns, a goddess with a vessel in her hands, a winged centaur, and so on. The carving is very skilful and refined. Amongst other finds in the northern com-

plex two marble female statues of the second century are interesting, and there were many fragments including parts of
groups of figures.

A very valuable discovery by Soviet archaeologists in Nisa
was of documents from Parthian archives. These were found in
the excavation of a wine store which had a capacity of 100–
200,000 litres, and consist of sherds (*ostraka*) of thick-sided clay
vessels with writing in black colouring on them. In 1948 seven
such documents were found. In 1951 140 were found under the
floor of a wine-store adjoining the northern complex in Old
Nisa. In 1953 over 500 had been discovered. Scholars were
confronted with the task of deciphering them, a difficult task,
for documents proved to be written in Parthian are only known
by single examples, so that comparative material was rare.
Semitic and Iranian scholars, philologists and historians, had
to collaborate. As the result of the labour of such a working
party of scholars the documents have been partly deciphered.
This language, dead for almost a thousand years, was super-
seded by the Persian and Tajik languages.

The documents from Nisa belong to the beginning of the first
century B.C., and for the most part consist of receipts or copies
from receipts issued in return for quantities of wine from wine-
makers. In view of the extraordinary rarity of evidence about
socio–economic relations in central Asia and the adjoining
countries in antiquity these documents contain valuable information about problems that have long preoccupied Soviet
archaeologists. They have yielded evidence about several
peculiarities of the Parthian administrative system, about its
taxation as well as information on the history of agriculture,
especially wine-growing, in central Asia.

Although the Parthian rulers were the most powerful and
important antagonists of the Hellenistic conquerors, the whole
Parthian aristocracy imitated their opponents. The seed of
Hellenistic culture was sown in fertile ground in the ruling
classes of ancient Parthia. In the courts Greek tragedies were
staged, many objects of art and of everyday use were made in
the Hellenistic style, and the coins were inscribed in Greek.
Nevertheless this did not permeate down into the masses, and
conversation and writing was in Parthian, for they did not write

in Greek but in native Parthian in a script derived from Aramaic. Only the script was Aramaic, for (as the decipherers remarked) the writers of the documents were Parthians. Parthian power evidently rested on the use of substantial numbers of native administrators and civil servants.

Nisa continued to flourish into post-Parthian times and into the period of feudalism; later layers have been excavated on the site.

## THE NOMADS AND SIBERIA

From the western spurs of the Altai Mountains to Pamir and from south-east Kazakhistan to the northern part of east Turkestan there lived in the eighth to third centuries B.C. the Sacae tribes, distinct ethnically and culturally from the nomadic tribes related to the Scythians. Their culture has been studied in numerous barrow excavations and from accidental finds.

Cultural remains of the Sacae and other nomadic tribes were found in the Pamir Expedition of 1950–1. Archaeologists established that the native pastoralists had connexions with different countries. They used wooden arrows made of Himalayan cedar (*deodar*) which grows on the southern slopes of the Hindu Kush, wore steatite beads from beyond Lake Baikal, cornelian and perforated diamonds from India, and used bronze and other imported materials.

In the second century B.C. control fell into the hands of some nomadic tribes known from Chinese sources under the name of Usuni. Barrows of this period have been excavated. In the sixth century A.D. south-east Kazakhistan and Tien-Shan were incorporated into the great nomad empire of the west Turkish Khanate. At this period there is some evidence for settled agriculture started by immigrant Sogdians. In the valley of the river Chu agriculture developed and the oldest irrigation system was constructed. Later the Sogdians settled beyond this valley. The archaeological researches place before us a most interesting picture of the mixing of the nomadic culture of the Turks with the settled farming culture of the Sogdians.

The eleventh to twelfth centuries saw the development of towns and monumental architecture. The lowest level of the ancient city of Taraz excavated in 1936 and 1938 belongs to this period. Taraz (300 km. south-west of Lake Balkhash) is on the left bank of the river Talas on the site of modern Jambul. The *shahristan* was rectangular, covered 14 hectares (35 acres), and was oriented towards points of the compass. The citadel was on its northern side and in this area part of the supply-water system, pavements, wells, canals, and so on were found. One of the most interesting finds was the baths, and in them carved plaster decoration, wall paintings, roofs with many cupolas, niches, troughs, and a hot-water system beneath the floor and walls were found.

The ruins of the capital of central Asia in the twelfth century, Balasagun (about 250 km. south of Lake Balkhash), have been discovered. The original aim of the excavations had been to recover the plan of the twelfth-century Buddhist chapel, but in 1953 an eighth-century Buddhist temple was discovered that had probably been destroyed by nomads in the following century. All the numerous clay sculptures found in the temple were broken, including a gigantic seated figure of the Buddha (up to 4 m. high). The walls of the temple had been covered with paintings whose remains were in the rubble layer on the floor. The temple was very large: 80 m. by 22 m.

The Mongol onslaught was a great setback here (as everywhere) to cultural, economic, and urban development.

The towns of south-east Kazakhistan were never refounded. The towns of Chorasmia were refounded but were later destroyed by Timur. Later on in the time of Timur and his successors Sogdiana made a new economic and cultural advance, and Samarkand became the capital of a gigantic nomad empire. In an uninterrupted series of predatory campaigns the armies of Timur captured and brought here precious things, as well as builders, craftsmen, and artists. Luxurious buildings were erected covered with tile mosaics. Many of these buildings survive to the present time.

In the time of Timur's grandson, Ulugbek, who created a powerful khanate, remarkable buildings were erected – a school of religious philosophy, and an observatory, in which Ulugbek busied himself with astronomy, for he was a very eminent scientist in his day. This observatory has been excavated. It

stood on a rocky hill on the banks of a canal to the north of
Afrasiab (Old Samarkand). Excavations have shown that the
observatory consisted of a tall circular building, accurately
measured and built of brick. The building was planned to contain a gigantic sextant, the chief instrument in the observatory.*
Besides the sextant the observatory contained several large halls,
corridors and passages, and small rooms for the operating
staff. The outside of the buildings was covered with beautiful
tiles, and the lower part dressed with grey marble. The observatory of Ulugbek at Samarkand was the best in the world at
this period.

In Chapter 5 we left the archaeology of southern Siberia at
the beginning of our era.

In the middle of the first millennium A.D. Turkish and Kirgiz
states emerged, and drew together in the sixth century. The
culture of the Altai Turks (the Chinese Tu-gyu) can be traced
back to the archaeological remains at Shibe and Pazyryk (see
pp 170 ff.). The Turks founded in the sixth century a huge state
that extended from Outer Mongolia on the east to the Amu-
Darya (Oxus) on the west. The main part in the foundation
of this state was played by the Altai tribes, but the centre of this
state was soon moved south-eastwards to Mongolia. Written
sources have only partially been filled in by archaeology for
although barrows have been dug settlements have not been
studied.

At Kudyrge (500 km. south-east of Novosibirsk) twenty-one
small stone tombs were dug in 1924–5. In each burial there was a
horse with full equipment with the corpse, together with a
saddle and bridle, richly ornamented with copper plates. There
were also quivers and iron arrowheads, iron daggers and
swords. In the tomb silk, bronze mirrors, and coins imported
into the Altai Mountains from China came to light. The engravings on pieces of horn were remarkable examples of native
art depicting the hunting of bears, red and roe deer, goats,
hares, and foxes. Riders riding at full gallop are shooting from
small curved bows. On the broad end of the flat pieces of horn
large figures are shown standing facing each other. Probably

---

* This type of sextant was invented in the tenth century and was used to
study the movements of the sun, moon, and planets.

Iranian pictures of the Sassanian kings hunting served as a model for the craftsman, although he did not just copy but added local people and did it in a very realistic style. The cemetery belongs to the sixth or seventh centuries, although some of the burials are later, from Mongol times (thirteenth and fourteenth centuries).

## Kirgizia

The culture of the Kirgiz on the middle Yenisei belongs to the period of early states but can be traced back to more ancient cultures. There are grounds for supposing that (as among other peoples) the change to class-society among the Kirgiz coincided with the adoption of plough agriculture. In the Minusinsk Depression many iron ploughshares have been found which were made by local smiths, including Chinese heavy ploughs with mould-board which were used by the Kirgiz. One of these is dated to the fifth century A.D. Irrigation systems with many branch canals were now in use, and rotary mills were substituted for hand querns. Nevertheless stock-rearing remained the most important branch of the economy. The crafts were developed. Smiths lived along the Yenisei and its tributaries, where their settlements have been studied.

Kirgiz burial mounds of the first and early second millennia A.D. were generally made of stones (that is, were cairns). In the ninth and tenth centuries cremation predominated. The small mounds usually contained poor grave goods. The later large cairns, *chaatasy* (*chaatas* means war stone), are very rich in grave goods. The burnt remains of the corpse were furnished with a great quantity of goods, although skeletons, probably of slaves, are found without anything. Of outstanding interest are very rich burials of Kirgiz nobility of the seventh to eighth centuries, the *chaatasy* on the river Uibat, particularly at the village of Kopeny (about 300 km. south-west of Krasnoyarsk) excavated in 1939–40. All the burials had been robbed but in special pits near the graves valuable objects were found that the robbers had missed. In the Kopeny cairn four gold jugs on a silver dish, a gold plate, and many ornaments of gold, silver, and bronze were found. Two of the jugs were smooth but on the base they had inscriptions in the native language (Orkhon). On one was

written: 'Gold ... the gift of Ach' (Ach is the name of one
of the Kirgiz tribes); on another 'We gave *begskoe* silver.' This
evidently refers to a gift to an aristocrat, for *beg* is a title. Two
of the gold jugs are covered with decoration in relief of twigs
and flowers, between which are fantastic birds of prey tearing
at fish (Pl. 20a). On the gold plate birds and flowers are shown.
The remarkable bronze figures are shown in hunting scenes:
galloping horsemen who turn and shoot arrows at tigers that
are springing on them, or wild boar, roe deer, or panthers pur-
sued by horsemen. Evidently these figures were saddle ornaments. These things are graphic proof of the high level of Kirgiz
art. They already indicate the riches accumulated in the hands
of the ruling classes.

Apart from barrows an important source for the study of the
culture and the way of the life of the Kirgiz on the Yenisei is
the numerous inscriptions carved on cliffs and stone slabs.
They are written in the native Orkhon alphabet and have been
studied and published by the Soviet Turkic scholar S. E. Malov.
The numerous drawings on rocks are another indication of the
independent character of Kirgiz art. These depict war and
hunting scenes.

The work of Soviet archaeologists has revealed this remarkable ancient Kirgiz culture, previously almost unknown.

The Kirgiz state was destroyed by the Mongols in the thirteenth century. The irrigation canals on the Yenisei were
abandoned and crafts fell into decay. The Kirgiz lost a most
important achievement of the culture, the art of writing.

The remains of the period of the Mongol conquest and the
period that followed in Siberia have hardly been studied at all.

*Chapter 9*

# THE EAST SLAVS AND THEIR NEIGHBOURS

RUSSIAN archaeological scholarship always devoted special attention to the study of Slavonic antiquities. Soviet workers have in this field, as opposed to prehistoric archaeology, a substantial inheritance. Rich collections of Slavonic antiquities were made in the Moscow State Historical Museum, in the Museum of the Archaeological Institute at St Petersburg, in the Kiev Historical Museum, and elsewhere. The period before Kiev Russia (that is before the ninth century) in the history of the east Slavs, however, remained right outside the field of vision of scholars. The information given by ancient authors soon became familiar to historians, but for a long time they never tried to link this up with the evidence of subsequent events. The archaeological sources for the Slavs in the first millennium A.D. are in general poor, and what was known was attributed to the Goths, Finns, or Lithuanians.

Soviet historical science on the other hand was confronted with the problem of the birth of the ancient Russian state. It was clear that Kiev Russia was not a beginning but the continuation of a long historical process. The study of this period became the prime task of archaeologists: the history of the most ancient East Slavs and the elucidation of their origins.

Problems about the origins of peoples are very complicated and as was explained above (see p. 64) cannot be solved by archaeologists independently, although their opinions will of course carry great weight. In order to establish connexions between tribes known to us from ancient archaeological cultures and contemporary peoples (a decisive matter in settling their origins) archaeologists use a retrospective method, that is, to follow back later-known facts to more ancient times. If, let us say, certain elements (in language, customs, and ornaments)

---

\* The reader is warned that this is a difficult chapter so he may wish to read it only cursorily or omit it altogether. Much of the matter in it is also very controversial. T.

occur in some contemporary peoples and similar elements occur in some ancient people, then on the basis of this evidence archaeologists will try to establish a continuity of culture from the ancient tribes up to the modern peoples, and in the same way they will try and extend this farther back into the past. Owing to inadequacy of material or imprecision of the method used, links in the chain may be found wanting.

On the basis of the studies of Soviet, Polish, and Czechoslovakian archaeologists and philologists it may be considered as established that the ancestors of the Slavs lived from the remotest times in central and eastern Europe, forming part of the general aggregation of neolithic tribes of the fourth and third millennia B.C. It is still uncertain however which neolithic tribes were the Slavs' ancestors, and from then up to the first millennium B.C. many guesses have been made to identify them but none with sufficiently reliable evidence to allow them to be regarded by the reader as scientifically certain. For example some workers consider the 'corded-ware' tribes of the Bronze Age as Slavs who appear at the end of the third millennium B.C. in the basin of the Vistula, in Volynia, and on the middle Dnepr. Only from the middle of the first millennium B.C. for the Slavs in general and even later for the East Slavs can archaeologists distinguish a complex of antiquities that is related to Slav antiquities of the later historical period. Amongst these the most important are the remains of the Lausitz culture and its eastern variants extending over central Europe and the western Ukraine. It is possible that in Scythian times some of the earthworks of the wooded steppe belonged to Slavs in the area regarded as inhabited by the farmer Scythians by the Greeks [that is, in the Ukraine. T.]. An urn-field culture (connected by its burial rite with the Lausitz culture) can be definitely identified as Slav from the end of the first millennium B.C. This culture takes its name from a feature fairly uniform in the cemeteries that cover the area from west Czechoslovakia eastwards to the left bank of the Dnepr (although some of the urnfields do not belong to Slavs). The cremated remains of the dead were placed in a clay pot, an urn, which was buried in a communal burial ground. In the central Dnepr area inhumation was practised as well.

## ZARUBINTSI

In 1901 there was published an account of excavations in the urn-fields of Zarubintsi and Chernyakhovo, two villages in the Kiev district. The excavator distinguished two types of remains: Zarubintsi type dating to the last centuries B.C., Chernyakhovo type to the first five centuries A.D. By 1913 fourteen such sites were known but now the number has increased to over 400 and they have been found in the Dnepr and Dnestr areas, in Volynia and elsewhere. Moreover some settlement sites are known (see Fig. 24).

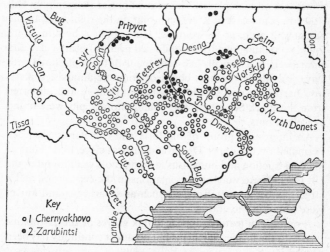

24. Distribution of urn-fields of the Chernyakhovo and Zarubintsi types.

An important contribution of Soviet archaeologists to the study of the early urn-field culture has been the excavation of a large cemetery (more than 100 burials) of a type analogous to the Zarubintsi urn-fields at Korchevaty south-east of Kiev. More than seventy Zarubintsi urn-fields are now known. In the majority of cases the burnt remains are found in an urn or simply put into a hole, and with them occur a few inhumations.

With the burials, brooches, hairpins, pendants, glass beads, and other objects are found, and in the graves there are up to three, occasionally four or even five pots. Some of them evidently contained food, for bones of sheep (or goats), pigs, or more rarely cows and horses are found in them. The pots are hand-made either with a black, shiny, and extraordinarily smooth surface (polished ware as it is called) or of coarse grey ware. On the basis of the latest research these cemeteries date from the second century B.C. to the second century A.D.

Recently numerous settlements belonging to these Zarubintsi people have come to light. They are small agricultural villages covering 2 hectares (5 acres) or less, situated on river banks, sometimes on high places. The excavations at Polipenkovy Hill (100 km. south-east of Kiev) on a spur on the right bank of the Dnepr will serve as an example. Huts about 4 by 4 m. were found containing quadrilateral domed ovens of beaten clay and stone hearths. The walls had been made of twigs plastered with clay, and inside the huts bones of domestic animals, sinkers, iron harpoons, and sherds of pots, both native and imported from the Black Sea cities, were found. Storage pits were found as well as huts.

An interesting group of hill-forts and cemeteries has been examined on the upper Dnepr and Pripyat since 1951. Huts of log construction and numerous farming tools were found in the hill-forts. There were only cremations in the cemeteries, and a large number of metal objects such as spearheads and knives were found in the graves.

A number of features appear to link graves of the Zarubintsi type with the farmer Scythians but no direct continuity has been proved.

## CHERNYAKHOVO

The Chernyakhovo urn-fields chronologically overlap those of the Zarubintsi type. The burial rites, grave goods, and hut construction (log-built huts in the settlements of both were plastered with clay) of the two cultures are similar. The main distinction is that instead of being fortified like the Zarubintsi sites, settlements of the Chernyakhovo people are open and unfortified. A basic and important difference between the two types of remains lies in the wheel-made pottery of the later sites, which testifies to the existence of craft as opposed to domestic production. A significant part of the pottery is grey in colour and highly polished. Besides these high-quality wares a large quantity of rough handmade pots are found as on the other type of site. Very characteristic of Chernyakhovo sites are the widespread finds of Roman coins and objects, including glass vessels, *amphorae*, red-glazed vessels, and ornaments, especially 'cloak fasteners' (safety-pin *fibulae*), called 'provincial Roman' by archaeologists. Roman coins and objects entered Slav lands by way of trade, which to judge by their frequent occurrence was lively. An incomplete list of Roman coins in the Chernyakhovo cultural area comprises 94 hoards and 799 single finds. [A glance at Fig. 24 will show the reader that the culture almost abuts on the area of urban civilization, which may account for some of the points mentioned by the author and possibly also for the more backward state of the more northern Zarubintsi culture. T.]

In several places Zarubintsi cultural remains of the first to second centuries A.D. are replaced by Chernyakhovo remains, but the area of distribution of the latter and more southerly culture is much wider, covering the whole of the wooded steppe from the upper Donets to the upper Dnestr, and even extending south into the steppe proper. As mentioned above all the settlements are open and the huts are arranged in one, two, or three rows extending one or two or even four kilometres. The majority of the huts were built on the surface but semi-subterranean huts are also found. The roofs were evidently gabled and supported by corner posts. Pottery kilns, generally two-storeyed, remains of furnaces, and other traces of craft-working have been found. The latter include jewellery-making, bone- and stone-working, textiles, and so on. Judging by the finds the basis of the economy was settled farming with some stock-rearing and domestic crafts. The topography of the sites testifies to the agricultural interests of their inhabitants: they are situated above the flood terraces of the large rivers, or more often on their tributaries on tillable ground and meadows.

The problem of when the urn-fields came to an end is controversial. Some date this to the fourth or fifth centuries A.D., some later, to the sixth or even seventh centuries A.D. The matter is an important one for definite Slav remains are only known from the sixth to seventh centuries A.D. so that if the Chernyakhovo culture ended in the fifth century a gap of some two centuries is left to guesswork, for it cannot be filled by other remains. If on the other hand the culture continued to the later date then we may regard it as the direct antecedent of Kiev Russia. The latter view however meets the obstacles that not only does there appear to be a chronological gap but that also many cultures are lumped under the name of Chernyakhovo that are not Slav but belong to Sarmatians and other tribes. [The period from the third to eighth centuries A.D. was one of great folk movement. Some archaeologists hesitate to accept even the urn-field peoples as Slavs, and regard them as Germanic tribes who are known to have been in this area at about this time. T.]

## EAST EUROPEAN PLAIN

The first reliable information about Slavs on the east European plain is found in Byzantine and Syriac sources of the sixth century A.D., where they are called Antes and Sclavinae. The Sclavinae are the west Slavs and the Antes the east or more probably a southern part of the east Slavs. According to a sixth-century writer they were previously known under one name as the Venedi. Although the first written references to the Antes occur in the sixth century, some facts are recorded about earlier events (including their war with the Ostrogoth king Vinitar) which have allowed historians to postulate a broad unity of east Slav tribes called the Antes. Judging by the information available they lived in the area between the Dnestr and Dnepr, and there is a further record that they occupied the area north of the Sea of Azov. The written records also speak of the Antes as settled tribes engaged in agriculture and stock-breeding and living in the wooded steppe or forest areas, their small settlements extended along river and lake banks, from which some workers have identified them with the Chernyakhovo urn-fielders.

Already in the fourth century A.D. the Slavs were actively participating in the movement of the European tribes into the Mediterranean world. One of the stages in this struggle was the so-called *Völkerwanderung*, the transference and intrusion of European and Asiatic tribes within the frontiers of the Roman Empire.

In *c.* A.D. 500 the Sclavinae and Antes cooperated in a struggle with the Byzantine Empire and began penetration of the Balkan peninsula, ending in the seventh century with the full settlement of the peninsula by Slavs. The Balkan wars played a large part in the life of the Slav tribes, accelerating the process of decay of the primitive social system and the formation of classes. At the beginning of the seventh century the tribal unity of the Antes came to an end.

The antiquities of the Antes have not been studied, but to them belong numerous hoards found on the area occupied by them. These hoards comprise Eastern and Byzantine silver table ware and other precious things (Pl. 20c), representing no doubt the war booty of Slav chieftains.

Recently the problem of the 'Antic hoards' of the sixth and seventh centuries has received a new interpretation. Two to two and a half centuries after the disappearance of the Antes, Byzantine and Western written sources use a new nomenclature for the east Slav tribes and speak of Ros, Rosy, Rus. Evidently they were originally one of the Slav tribes who later headed a tribal union which gave its name to the powerful state of the ninth to eleventh centuries, Kiev Russia. Rybakov has suggested that the Ros occupied the Dnepr in the basin of the river Ros eastwards to the upper Donets and that the chance finds of the sixth and seventh centuries known from this area be called antiquities of the Ros. Antes and Ros would merely be different names for one and the same south-eastern Slav tribe which later created Kiev Russia.

It must be recognized that, in spite of a number of skilfully worked-out theories, the problem of the identification of the urn-fielders with a race known from written sources, as conversely of the Antes from their archaeological remains, is still unsolved, and remains one of the most important problems of Slavic archaeology.

While the urn-field cultures unfolded in the south some northern forest areas of eastern Europe were evidently inhabited by early Slavs. Urn-fields are known from the upper Dnepr,

Desna, Seim, and Pripyat but do not extend farther north and
east. Here one finds the Dyakovo culture (see p. 165) which is
now regarded as the ancestral to non-Slav east Finnish peoples
(i.e. the speakers of Finno-Ugrian languages).

Undoubted remains of the northern members of the east Slav
tribes are barrows covering cremations found on the uppermost
Dnepr, upper Volga, Oka and West Dvina, and finally in the
basins of Lake Ilmen and Chudsky (see Fig. 25). In the western
part of this area are found the so-called long barrows, in the
eastern, round barrows. These barrows were excavated in vast

Key

1. *Culture of the urn-fields* 2. *Long barrows* 3. *'sopki'*

4. *Hill-forts of the 'Romny' type*

5. *Hill-forts of the Borshevo type and Vyatichi barrows*

25. East Slavs in c. A.D. 500.

26. East Slavs and their neighbours *c.* A.D. 850.

numbers in pre-Soviet times but their mapping and careful study of the finds from them has been one of the achievements of Soviet archaeologists.

These barrows belong to east Slavs subsequently described in a Russian chronicle. The author of *The Chronicle of Contemporary Years* writing of events in the ninth century sketches a general ethnographic picture of eastern Europe. He names thirteen east Slav tribes: Slovene (1), Krivichi (13), Polochane (2),

Vyatichi (3), Severyane (6), Radimichi (5), Drevlyane (8), Duleby (7), Ulichi (12), Tivertsy (11), Khorvaty (10), Polyane (9), Dregovichi (4). [The numbers refer to their position on the accompanying map, Fig. 26. T.]

At the end of the nineteenth century Spitsyn had already pointed out that in Russian antiquities there were as many types and areas as the chronicle had listed tribes and on the basis of excavated barrows one could map the distribution of the ancient Russian tribes with the earliest chronicle. However Spitsyn and other Russian archaeologists were thinking of Slavs as late-comers on the East European plain and so assigned the material to the ninth at the earliest or for a great part from the eleventh to fourteenth centuries. But by that period the tribal groupings of the ancient Slav world had vanished from the historical scene and with the development of class-society tribal divisions were being effaced. Naturally, in view of the resilience of ancient customs, forms of dress, and decoration (especially the latter), materials even of a later period will serve in some measure to establish tribal boundaries. Nevertheless to draw up a real map of the distribution of ancient Russian tribes in the period of the living tribal system and not of its decay, one must turn to the evidence from an earlier period, or more precisely, to the middle and second half of the first millennium A.D.

This is what Soviet archaeologists have done, so that they have been able to trace the archaeological remains of these tribes from the fourth and fifth centuries A.D. onwards. Thus the long barrows mentioned above belong to the largest tribal group, the Krivichi, previously referred to the sixth to eighth centuries but now known to go as far back as the fourth century A.D. These narrow, long, bank-like (sometimes oval) mounds reach up to 50 m. in length and up to 1 m. in height, and contain 5–6 or sometimes 9–10 cremations with sparse grave goods. Evidently these were cemeteries of patriarchal clan families and each time a person was buried the mound was lengthened. In the area north-east of the long barrows where the chronicle places the Slovene (the Novgorod area) another type of burial mound is found, the *sopka*, a tall (up to 10 m. and sometimes 15 m.) conical barrow containing several cremations. Around the base of the *sopka* is a circle built of stones. *Sopki*, like long barrows, belong to the period between the fourth and tenth centuries A.D.

Barrows belonging to the Vyatichi are found by the banks of the river Oka in its upper reaches, at Beseda near Moscow, and elsewhere. This was evidently the homeland of the tribe but settlements and barrows of the eighth to tenth centuries are found on the Don near Voronezh at the village of Borshevo.

In the Borshevo barrows excavations revealed remains of large circular settings of vertical posts (Pl. 22a). In the eastern part of the enclosed area wooden chambers were found in the form of boxes of planks or timber-framed constructions (Pl. 21). Each chamber contained the remains of several cremations, usually placed in pots. Pots not containing cremations were placed in the grave chamber probably with food.

The early barrows of the remaining Slav tribes have not yet been discovered.

In the same district where the Borshevo barrows were excavated a group of hill-forts of the Vyatichi was also examined. The Borshevo 'Large Hill-fort' of the eighth to tenth centuries has earned special fame: this site occupies a spur on the high bank of the Don and is defended by a bank and ditch. The settlement within was very large and inhabited by several thousand people. The remains of domestic huts excavated into the ground were found joined to one another by internal passages to form one large living complex, inhabited by a large patriarchal family. Each hut had several entries. The Byzantine writer, Maurice, living in the seventh century mentioned the existence of such huts among the Slavs. The huts had wooden walls and stone ovens. A group of such huts was surrounded by storage structures, granaries, grain pits, places for grinding corn in which large hand-mills survived, and other structures testifying to the communal character of the inhabitants' economy. In the excavations grains of millet, pots, mostly hand-made, and objects of iron and of other manufactured goods, as well as Arab coins, came to light. Besides agriculture and stock-rearing the inhabitants of the hill-fort were engaged in fishing and hunting. In spite of the fact that the hill-fort belongs to the period of the emergence of Kiev Russia, here in the remote and wooded areas of the upper Don many features of the old life and social system survived. In the tenth century this and other Slav hill-forts on the Don were suddenly abandoned. It can be assumed that there was a retreat north in the face of pressure from steppe nomads advancing into the Don area.

Hill-forts similar in style and time to those of Borshevo area are known from regions assigned by the chronicle to the Seve-ryane (lit. 'northerners').

## Romny Hill-Fort Culture

In 1907–9 Slav hill-forts in the basin of the river Sula near Romny were studied, and from these all similar hill-forts have been referred to as Romny hill-fort culture. They are distinct from the Borshevo forts in the types of hut they contain and in the tribes to which they belonged, so in spite of similarities the two should be given separate names. As opposed to the wooden-walled semi-subterranean homes with stone ovens of the Bor-shevo culture the Romny huts were plastered with clay and contained domed clay ovens. The basic area of distribution of this culture was worked out later. Such hill-forts have been revealed along the whole course of the Desna, on the Seim, Sula, Vorskla, and their tributaries as well as on the upper reaches of the north Don (see Fig. 25).

All Romny hill-forts are situated on promontories of the high banks of rivers or on small hills, and are defended by banks and ditches. In the majority of cases an open settlement adjoins the bank on the inside. The hill-forts occur in groups of three or four, 4–5 km. or sometimes less from each other. Traces of occupation are found dating from the tenth century and later Medieval Period (the eleventh to thirteenth centuries). Romny like Borshevo hill-forts appear only in the eighth century; only recently have settlements of the seventh and eighth centuries been discovered, and these can be regarded as their predeces-sors. These settlements are unfortified and situated right by the rivers as if concealed in the bogs and marshes. In direct associa-tion with the settlements flat cemeteries of cremations in urns are found on higher ground. Semi-subterranean structures with thick clay floors served as huts and were furnished with thick clay walls, ovens on the clay floor, and peculiar storage-pits with sides of intertwined twigs smeared with clay.

Until recently no large-scale excavations had been carried out on Romny hill-forts but in 1952–3 a settlement of the eighth or ninth century was almost wholly excavated at Novotroitsk (about 240 km. east of Kiev). About thirty huts were excavated, all of which had perished in an enemy raid (perhaps of nomads). The huts were semi-subterranean, measured on the average 4 by 4 m., and were up to 1 m. deep. The walls consisted of a framework of posts and planks plastered with clay. The ovens were of clay dug into a part left when the ground was dug out for the hut. The storage structures lay at a little distance from the huts. There were no defensive earthworks at this site as it was situated on a high promontory with steep sides and so had good natural defence.

The basic occupation of the population was settled agriculture and in the houses and storage buildings wheat, rye, and barley as well as farming tools (ploughshares, sickles, scythes, and hoes) were found. Stock-rearing played an important part in the economy, and bones of oxen, small-horned cattle, pigs, and horses were found. Almost all the pottery was hand-made but some of the pots were improved or actually made on a wheel. There was evidence of metallurgy in the form of iron slag. A coin hoard was found on the site including Arab *dihrems* minted from the beginning of the eighth century up to 819. Several coins were found in the huts, the latest dated to 833. Evidently the village was destroyed in the middle of the ninth century and at the time of the attack the houses were burnt and valuable things were buried or thrown away by the inhabitants.

The ancient Slav tribes have been studied very unevenly, so that while information about the Krivichi and Slovene is derived mainly from graves and their settlements are unknown, and the Severyane are known from their hill-forts, there are several tribes including some who played an important part in history whose archaeological remains have not yet been revealed. For example, such is the case with the neighbours of the Severyane, the Polyane, on whose land arose Kiev, the capital of ancient Russia. Summing up the results so far it can be said that although work on the problem of the origin of the Slavs is far from complete the roads that lead to such a solution have been marked out, and the archaeologist has set before him concrete tasks of study of those groups of remains which are related to the most important stages of Slav ethnogenesis. Besides this a very great deal has been done to further the study of the origin of the Slavonic culture of the period of the birth of the Kiev Russian state.

## ANCIENT RUSSIAN BARROWS

For over two centuries Russian scholarship was rent by the fierce dispute between the 'Normanists' and their opponents. The 'Normanists' believed the Kiev state had been created by Varangians or Norsemen who came from Scandinavia, but their opponents denied this and assigned a much greater part to the native Slavs.*

Archaeological evidence should provide evidence to support the 'Normanist' view, and evidence has been invoked from the large cemetery consisting of 3,000 barrows at Gnezdovo near Smolensk, the Mikhailov cemetery near Yaroslavl, and also the barrows in the area of Lake Ladoga and Chernigov, in which objects of Scandinavian appearance have been found. Many of these ninth- and tenth-century barrows are burials of members of the upper class, Russian *druzhiniks*, professional warriors forming the nucleus of the army. The *druzhiniks* were in origin connected with the tribal lords, but by this time they already belonged to the growing feudal nobility whose power was based on the enslavement of the peasantry and on large landowner-ship. On the evidence of burial rite and objects of Scandinavian origin in them these graves have been assigned to Norsemen.

Soviet scholars have continued the work of excavation on the barrows of the *druzhiniks*. At Mikhailov not a single one could be assigned to Norsemen, while out of 700 dug at Gnezdovo

---

* Most of our knowledge of the early formation of the Kiev state is derived from the 'Chronicle of Contemporary Years' (*Povest Vremennykh Let*) written in 1115 and describing events of 200 years before. There is also a little independent evidence from Greek, Arabic, and other sources. These leave no doubt that the Norsemen (Vikings) or Varangians played a very important part in the political and military formation of the Kiev state. This has always given great offence to Russian nationalism and Soviet historians dismiss the chronicle's account as legend, although it is the same chronicle that gives the tribal divisions of the east Slavs. T.

only two were undoubtedly burials of Norsemen, who were in Russian service.

The study of Slav barrows of the tenth to thirteenth centuries has been carried out by Soviet archaeologists by the scientific classification of the material amassed in museums from pre-Revolutionary excavations. Russian workers of the nineteenth and early twentieth centuries (Count Uvarov, Ivanovsky, and so on) excavated about 20,000 barrows. The great quantity of material renders it a very valuable historical source. It must be observed that with the adoption of Christianity burial beneath a barrow gradually ceased. It died out first of all in the towns. All the barrow groups of the eleventh and later centuries are rural cemeteries and so yield evidence mainly of village life, a subject on which the written evidence is poor. Based on this material studies have been made of the economy and social relationships in the countryside, the way of life, tribal areas, and so on. B. A. Rybakov in his book *The Crafts of Ancient Russia* has studied the details of the crafts, established the market areas of the craftsmen, explained the techniques of production which differed somewhat from urban work, and so on.

The study of the Russian countryside not from barrow material but from the actual occupied sites, the villages, has unhappily not received due attention in the work of archaeologists. Only in recent years has this task been assigned a place in the overall plan of work.

## THE NON-SLAVONIC PEOPLES

### The East Finns (Mordvins)

Archaeological researches take on especial importance in the study of past peoples of the Volga and Ural areas. All these people spoke languages of the Finno-Ugrian family and so are often somewhat inaccurately called east Finns [as opposed to Slav speakers on the west and Turkic speakers on the south and east. T.].

On the vast expanses of the western Volga area fairly uniform cemeteries are found, dating from the first and early second millennia A.D., that belonged to the predecessors of the Mordvins and related tribes, who were subsequently russified. It has been established that the people of this area lived in fortified sites up to the fourth or fifth centuries when these were abandoned in favour of open settlements which have not yet been examined. The burial rite remained the same, however, and the cemetery at Ryazan continued in use until the tenth century. At that time the valley of the Oka was settled by Slavs and the older population was partly assimilated and partly pushed eastward.

In the Ryazan graves as well as in the latest Mordvin ones the women's graves are distinguished by the frequent occurrence of metal ornaments, especially rattle pendants, and numerous small bronze plates and tubes which were attached to the headdress, skirts, and shoes. These rattle pendants are a very characteristic feature of all graves of the west Volga area from the eighth to the fourteenth centuries. [The author then gives a list of excavated sites. T.]

In view of the absence of writing among the ancient Mordvins and the rarity of references to them in the Russian chronicles study of the archaeological remains of these people has an especial importance for their history. It has been shown that the patriarchal clan system survived among them until very late. The main features of their economy were stock-rearing (especially of horses and pigs), hunting, collecting of honey from wild bees, and fishing. Agriculture was primitive slash-and-burn cultivation and only of minor importance. [The author then briefly mentions and describes work on other east Finnish peoples. T.]

*The Bulgars*

The Bulgars of the Volga are believed to have had their origin in the following manner. In the middle Volga there are Dyakovo hill-forts, containing mat-impressed pottery, which were occupied by settled pastoralists. Their nearest neighbours on the south were Sarmatian and Alan nomadic pastoralists of the steppes, some of whom moved north and mixed with the people of the hill-forts. In the seventh and eighth centuries Turkic-speaking tribes of Bulgars from the Azov steppes moved into the Middle Volga and subjugated the native population. [A westward movement of other Bulgars gave rise to the name of modern Bulgaria. T.] The older population adopted the new language and so appeared the Volga Bulgars. Their large state had three main centres: Bolgar, Bilyar, and Suvar.

Bolgar (north-east of Kuibyshev) is a triangular earthwork whose surviving banks and ditches are 8 km. long. There were excavations here in the last century but systematic work began only in 1938. In antiquity there was a wooden construction on the banks filled up with earth behind. The original town, occupying only a small area, was the capital from the tenth and eleventh centuries. It was destroyed by the Mongols in the thirteenth century but in this and the following century enjoyed a second flourishing period, the time to which the surviving banks and brick buildings – mosques, minarets, and baths – belong. When Kazan arose in the fifteenth century it lost its importance.

Excavations at Bolgar have revealed two layers: a pre-Mongol layer and a later one of the period of the Golden Horde. In the latter the houses were log-built with domed clay ovens, and there are many storage-pits near them. In the centre of the town were found the remains of an ancient timber roadway and water-pipes dating from the fourteenth century. Bolgar was a large craft centre, and the workshops of smiths, bone-carvers, cobblers, and blacksmiths were found. There were numerous kilns, blast furnaces for smelting iron, and fourteenth-century furnaces for melting iron to make cast iron. The latter are very interesting because they prove that the manufacture of cast iron at Bolgar was the oldest in Europe. Previously solid iron had had to be worked by hammering. The arms-makers produced remarkable objects, for example long narrow battle-axes covered with plant ornament, while the work of the bronze-founders is no less striking, for example, bronze locks in the shape of horses or other animals. An interesting building was the fourteenth-century baths, called the Red Hall because its walls were coloured red. It was built on the plan usual in the Muslim East and consisted of a series of closed rooms separated by thick walls from a central cruciform room, in the centre of which stood a large stone fountain, shaped like a flower with twelve petals. In the central hall and in the side chambers were tanks for mixing the hot and cold water. Clay pipes led from cisterns to copper taps, set in pairs in the wall, one for hot and one for cold water. The furnace was under one of the cisterns.

The capital of the Volga Bulgars in the twelfth century was Bilyar but the site has not yet been excavated.

The town of Suvar (not far from Bolgar) is quadrilateral in shape and is defended on three sides by banks and ditches. It was excavated in 1933–7, and the finds resemble those of Bolgar: defences, huts, storage-pits, etc. There were also beaten-clay as well as timber houses. In the centre a brick palace was excavated which had been built in the tenth century and which underwent several alterations before its destruction in the fourteenth century at the time when life in the town ceased. During its last phase the palace was faced with blue and green glazed bricks.

The descendants of the Volga Bulgars adopted in the fifteenth and sixteenth centuries the name of Tartars, a name belonging to one of the Mongol tribes, who had subjugated their ancestors in the thirteenth century. The modern Tartars and Chuvash are the descendants of the Volga Bulgars and heirs to their civilization.

## The Khazars

The closest neighbours of the Volga Bulgars and their rivals in their early period of history were the Khazars.

In the steppe expanses in the south-east part of our country cemeteries and settlements belonging to the so-called Saltov culture are found. This takes its name from a cemetery of the sixth to ninth centuries, discovered near Saltov on the Donets. The characteristic feature of this culture was burial in special, artificial, subterranean catacomb chambers. It is believed that Saltov culture can be identified with the Alans of written sources. In the second half of the first millennium A.D. the Alans fell under the control of the Khazars. Basically both Alans and Khazars were nomads, but in about the eighth century some of them began to settle on the land and practise agriculture as well as stock-rearing. Besides the Alans the Khazars overpowered several other tribes surrounding their country. The centre of the Khazar state was north-west of the Caspian and on the lower Volga, and its capital, Itil, at the mouth of the Volga. The upper class derived its income by acting as a trade intermediary collecting customs and tributes from dependent tribes. The culture of the Khazars was eclectic and it made use of the cultural achievements of its conquered people without itself contributing anything original.

The main Khazar centres have not been found and the only town excavated is Sarkel on the Don on the western edge of the country proper, whose position was identified archaeologically. Excavations in 1934–6 revealed two layers, Russian above and Khazar below. As the site was later to be flooded to make a reservoir excavations were made as full as possible.

Sarkel was constructed by Khazars in the ninth century with the help of Byzantine engineers. Excavations have shown that the fort was erected on a low riverside promontory in the form of a rectangle (186 by 126 m.). The red brick walls were 3·75 m. thick and 10 m. high and were strengthened by bastions and massive corner towers. The main gateway was found in one of the bastions in the north-west wall. Inside were guardrooms. The fort was divided into two almost equal parts by a transverse internal wall. This wall as well as the disposition of the buildings within was designed to increase the defensibility of the fort. The fortification and the buildings within must have required no fewer than 10 million bricks. These were made on the site, and by the river a little way upstream kilns for baking bricks were found. The plan of Sarkel is surprising in its geometrical regularity, and was evidently a Byzantine conception. The construction technique was, however, local and rather crude, for the walls were built without foundations, and soft lime-and-sand mortar was used.

Apart from the garrison there was a domestic civilian area where the houses were semi-subterranean. Beside these a large granary was found. Ploughs were used in agriculture, and the only crafts of which there was evidence were bone-carving and pottery-making. There were many imported objects from Iran, central Asia, the Caucasus, Crimea, Byzantium, etc.

One of the largest undertakings in the external affairs of Kiev Russia was the campaign against the Khazars begun by Prince Svyatoslav in 954. After defeating them, the Russian *druzhiniks* continued into the north Caucasus and as far as the Kerch Straits. Under the year 965 the chronicler records the capture of Belaya Vezha (White Tower) by Svyatoslav, which is the Russian translation of the Khazar word, Sarkel.

A Russian population made its appearance immediately after the capture of Sarkel by Svyatoslav. It was composed of merchants and craftsmen from the districts east of the Dnepr. The houses continued to be semi-subterranean but the walls were now of wickerwork with both faces plastered with clay, or of a framework of logs. The inhabitants (as in all medieval towns) were engaged in large measure in crafts and trade as well as farming. In the wars of the eleventh and twelfth centuries between Russia and the Polovtsi the inhabitants of Sarkel fared badly, and in 1117 a Russian chronicle recorded their migration to Russia.

An important outpost on the south-eastern edge of Kiev Russia was Tmutarakan (on the Kerch Straits), the capital of a principality of that name. It is believed to have been founded in the tenth century as a result of the campaign of Svyatoslav, and its name occurs more than once in eleventh-century annals. Excavations have revealed two layers: an upper Russian level, and a lower level belonging to the Greek Bosporan city.

## The Balts

The Soviet Baltic area is one of the best studied archaeologically in our country, but work has been uneven in different parts. In Estonia and Latvia excavations have been carried on from the 1870s and 1880s almost continuously, but in Lithuania excavations began only in 1930.

Barrows dating from the second to fifth centuries A.D. with collective interments are found in south Latvia, and in north Latvia and Estonia cemeteries in stone settings. In the sixth century barrows with collective burials give way to single burials and at the same time burials with especially rich grave goods are found. The graves of the sixth to ninth centuries in the Baltic area are cemeteries that with a few exceptions lack any external indication, while considerable property and social inequalities are observable in the grave goods. In the ninth and tenth centuries communal hill-forts were abandoned in favour of more powerful hill-forts situated in the main tribal centres. In the eleventh and twelfth centuries large-scale landowning appears and early feudal relationships were formed. Excavators are now paying more attention to the fortified sites than previously, when barrows were the main interest.

## Chapter 10

# MEDIEVAL RUSSIAN TOWNS

IN pre-Revolutionary historiography there was little interest in the history of Russian towns. Archaeological excavations were unsystematic, casual, and amateurish, and the bad methods applied yielded much less to science than they could have done. Even when in certain cases the excavations were interesting their results remained virtually unpublished.

Nevertheless in the study of the ancient Russian town archaeological researches provide most important source material. Their especial importance arises from the fact that the urban archives of Kiev Russia have not survived, while the records in the chronicles about the towns are extremely irregular and do not give a continuous account. Soviet archaeologists have set out on a plan of excavation of ancient Russian towns. Among the tasks before them are the solution of concrete historical or historico–cultural problems, such as the origin of the towns, the development of urban crafts, art, the evolution of the house, and so on. General works that have helped to mark out the road which researches should follow have already appeared. Thus *Ancient Russian Towns*, the work of M. N. Tikhomirov, had great importance for the study of Russian urban history; in this the written references and most important archaeological material are used. There are also the collective works *History of the Culture of Ancient Russia*, and the first volume of *The History of Russian Art*, and Rybakov's *Crafts of Ancient Russia*.

These works have played a great part in Soviet historiography as they were the first to give a complete and objective picture of Russian culture and especially of urban culture and crafts.

## KIEV RUSSIA

The urban crafts of Kiev Russia reached a high level especially in iron-working, jewellery, copper, gold, silver, casting, enamels, gilding, incrusting and other artistic metal-work, pottery, glass, textiles, books, woodwork, work in bone and stone, sculpture, building, etc. There were more than sixty different craft specialities in the towns, each with its own organization of masters and journeymen. The different products were marketed throughout Russia and beyond its frontiers. There was an especially flourishing period of Russian craftsmanship from the middle of the twelfth century continuing up to the Tartar onslaught. The Tartar conquest in the thirteenth century was accompanied by the barbarous destruction of the Russian economy and crafts, and the carrying off into captivity by the Tartars of the craftsmen, and consequently the disappearance of a whole series of highly advanced crafts. A new rise of crafts and economy began in the second half of the fourteenth century accompanying the active struggle for freedom of the Russian people against the Tartar invaders.

The rise of the towns among the east Slavs was connected with the growth of craft production and the trade accompanying it. Naturally those towns began in different ways: sometimes a small craft centre grew into a feudal town; sometimes the town was founded by a prince; sometimes the town grew as a settlement nucleus around an old trading-place; and so on. In the eighth and ninth centuries large settlements appeared in which developed craft-working and trade are observed. These were the future towns in embryo.

The process of the transformation of a settlement into a real town is at the same time the separation of town from country. Towns grew up gradually as large concentrations of population and as large centres of crafts and trade. Generally during this process the old fortified village became the feudal *kremlin* which was the administrative centre occupied by the prince and nobility, while around the *kremlin* suburbs grew up occupied by craftsmen and merchants. In the course of time the suburbs were enclosed by a defensive wall which formed the outer part of the city's defences. [The reader may compare the medieval towns of central Asia with this, p. 244. T.] During excavation remains of older settlements preceding the towns have been found, and the clearest picture of this is seen at Kiev and Staraya (Old) Ladoga.

*Kiev*

Archaeological work on the oldest capital of the Russian state, 'the mother of Russian towns', Kiev, began more than 125 years ago. Excavations were casual until Khvoika's brilliant discovery in 1907–8 in the centre of Old Kiev of the remains of princes' palaces, houses, workshops, and so on led to systematic excavation being undertaken, which was interrupted by the First World War. In Soviet times excavations have been renewed on a large scale.

As a result of this work many problems of the historical development of the town and its culture have been settled. It is established that in the eighth to tenth centuries on the site of modern Kiev there existed three separate fortified sites (on Andreev Hill, Kiselevka Hill, and in the area of Frunze Street, formerly Cyril Street). Adjoining each of these was a cemetery. In the cemeteries besides graves of artisans there were exceptionally rich burials of warrior *druzhiniks*. The three independent villages united only at the end of tenth century into one city. The legend that has reached us in the *Chronicle of Contemporary Years* about the foundation of Kiev by three brothers, Kii, Shchek, and Khoriv, is probably based on traditions of the existence of several villages of a Slav tribe on the Kiev hills. One of these villages on Andreev Hill became the centre of the town of Vladimir Svyatoslavich. Up to the end of the tenth century it covered only a small part (about a fifth of the plateau on the hill) and was enclosed by a bank and ditch beyond which lay the barrow cemetery. In the time of Vladimir Svyatoslavich (who ruled from 980 to 1015) the ditch was filled in and the cemetery levelled and built over. The town now extended over the whole plateau and was enclosed by new ramparts with stone gateways. On the site of the levelled barrow cemetery was erected the oldest stone construction in Kiev Russia, the Desyatinnaya (Tithe) Church. The ruins of this church were fully revealed in 1938–9 and its original plan and former decoration were exposed. In the excavations capitals, marble and slate cornices, pieces of wall mosaics and frescoes, marble parapets, and fragments from the mosaic floor of the ancient church came to light. Besides several burials in slate coffins found earlier in the church and its walls, in 1939 a wooden coffin containing a burial was discovered. With the skeleton lay a sword in a sheath whose chape was decorated with silver and niello (black matter used for filling the background in silver-work). Around the Desyatinnaya Church several palace buildings of the tenth and eleventh centuries were excavated, although only foundations of some of these survived. Directly adjoining the palace building were workshops. The town very quickly grew beyond the limits of Vladimir's wall.

In 1037 Prince Yaroslav the Wise founded a new city, that is erected a new city wall enclosing an area several times greater than the old 'city of the Vladimirs'. The architectural centre of the new city, the Cathedral of St Sophia, was built at the same time as the new defences. This cathedral survives to the present day and is a masterpiece of Russian architecture. In more than 900 years of existence it has undergone numerous alterations so that its original appearance has been very much altered. For the history of Russian architecture it was very important to decide the earliest form of the monument, and so excavations were carried out inside and outside, as well as other researches. In its original form it was a vast building enclosed by two open galleries. The walls of the church were decorated with mosaics and frescoes, and fragments of an original mosaic floor were found under the later floors. Not far from its northern wall a large eleventh-century kiln was excavated in 1946, intended for firing the bricks used in its construction.

In 1948–50 remains of a strong stone wall were found that had evidently at one time enclosed the palace–castle of the metropolitan of Kiev.

Many other ancient stone buildings in Kiev and its neighbourhood have been examined archaeologically including the church of St Boris and St Gleb in the Upper Town and the great churches in the Zarubsky and other monasteries. All these excavations have made new contributions to our knowledge of the architectural appearance of ancient Kiev and provided solutions to important problems in the history of Russian architecture.

The best evidence yielded by excavations at Kiev comes from the eleventh- to thirteenth-century sites. It is necessary first to

a square hiding-place dug 5 m. down into the natural loess was found. In the lower part a number of human skeletons were found as well as a sword, a helmet, pieces of rich cloth, six silver medallions, and a whole group of other objects, including casting moulds made of shale. (There were sixteen of these for casting various ornaments; ear-rings, bracelets, and pendants.) At the bottom a passage about 1 m. long had been dug into one side and not finished. Here two wooden spades with iron tips, an iron axe, and iron hoops from wooden pails were found. M. K. Karger has convincingly shown that the death of the people in the hiding-place was connected with the tragic events of December 1240. Fleeing from destruction, the people hid themselves in this cellar in the church which previously had been used as a storeplace for church valuables. They wanted to dig a passage out of the church to the hillside but under the barrage of stones from the Tartar siege-machines the building collapsed. Falling vaults and walls buried the hiding-place and the people within it were killed. Amongst them was a craftsman taking his most valuable objects with him – his moulds. He ran to the church from his workshop which was not far away. This workshop lay in the garden of the present Historical Museum where excavations have yielded moulds exactly the same as those from the church. On one mould his name, Maxim, is inscribed.

Seizing and destroying Kiev, Batu pushed westwards, but exhausted by the heavy fighting in Russia the Tartars could not overcome the opposition of the Czechs and their allies, so in 1242 they turned back. On the lower Volga they formed the state of the 'Golden Horde'. All Russia fell under the control of the Tartars. They had destroyed and laid waste Kiev and for a long time it lost its former importance. Its rebirth began considerably later.

## Chernigov

After Kiev Chernigov was the largest city in the middle Dnepr area during the period of Kiev Russia. It is situated on the steep side of the Desna. Excavations on the citadel revealed semi-subterranean houses of the eighth century belonging to the Slav settlements that preceded the town. A twelfth-century

K

house and the remains of the cathedral built in the 1280s came to light. Subsequently further houses and a complex of stone palace buildings of the eleventh and twelfth centuries were also excavated.

## Vshchizh

With the development of feudal conditions in the eleventh and twelfth centuries a multiplicity of tiny princedoms appeared, sometimes consisting of only one or two town districts. The historical fate of one of these, Vshchizh, was clarified by archaeological excavation. This fortified site lies on a high spur on the right bank of the Desna, 50 km. north-west of Bryansk. The site is shaped like an isosceles triangle the equal sides of which are 350 m. long and are formed by the Desna and a small tributary, while the third side defended by a bank and deep ditch is 250 m. long. Within, the earthwork is divided into two unequal parts by a low bank and ditch, cutting off the western part of the promontory. Probably this was the town's citadel and the eastern part the suburb. Vshchizh is mentioned in the chronicles between 1142 and 1167.

Excavations were carried out here in 1940 and 1948–9. These established that in the eleventh and early twelfth centuries Vshchizh was a small fort with a suburb beyond its ramparts. In all probability at this time it formed part of the Chernigov princedom which would have maintained a fortified palace or castle here. In the middle of the twelfth century it was converted from a prince's castle into an independent town with advanced craft-working and an extensive suburb. The old banks were levelled and the ditch filled in. The suburb was fortified with double banks and a deep ditch still measuring 18 m. across. The walls of the citadel (*detinets*) were faced with oak logs and in their centre was placed a massive wooden tower. The houses were set against the bank, the centre of the citadel being left free. A low internal wall separated this from the suburb. At the centre of the latter was a stone church of the mid twelfth century, while on its edges against the banks lived craftsmen. A smithy and pottery were found here. The houses were log-built, horizontal logs supported by vertical corner posts. The chimneys were made of thin brick. In the citadel, besides huts lying close together evidently belonging to servants, a large house was excavated which measured 14 m. along its front face and had probably been two-storeyed. This was the boyar's or prince's house. In 1160 during a civil war of the princes the town endured a prolonged siege and some of the houses were burnt. The excavations revealed burnt houses, and corpses buried in the streets and courtyards. A second cinder layer at Vschizh probably corresponds to its destruction by the Tartars.

## Vyshgorod (lit. 'upper town')

One of the oldest Russian towns first mentioned in the chronicles in 946, Vyshgorod, was examined by an expedition in 1934–7 and 1947. It is 20 km. north of Kiev on the Dnepr. Strong fortifications defending the *detinets* (citadel) survive as well as a double series of banks protecting the craftsmen's suburb. In the centre of the *detinets* the brick foundations of the church of St Boris and St Gleb of the eleventh or twelfth century were revealed. Part of a street was exposed with the remains of semi-subterranean houses. Usually the houses consisted of a domestic room with clay oven and an annex sometimes used as a workshop. In the eleventh and twelfth centuries the town was a large craft-working centre and smiths' furnaces, jewellers' and founders' workshops with crucibles, moulds, an outfit of tools (files, chisels, etc.), bone-carving workshops, and so on were found. Several kilns were excavated. Vyshgorod was destroyed by the Tartars in 1240, and subsequently a village arose on the site.

## Belgorod (lit. 'white town')

This is 27 km. south-west of Kiev. There have been excavations here from 1909–10 onwards. Peculiarities of the construction of the ramparts have been brought to light: it was formed of a timber framework filled in with sun-dried bricks.

## Galich*

This town on the Dnestr was the capital of Galicia in the eleventh and twelfth centuries and one of the largest economic

---

* A number of other towns of Kiev Russia whose excavation is mentioned briefly are omitted in this translation. T.

and cultural centres of Kiev Russia. It lay 6 km. south of modern Galich, and was eventually destroyed by the Tartars. The ramparts of the *detinets* survive and adjoining them is the artisan suburb defended by three lines of fortifications. After the reunification of the western part of the Ukraine with the Soviet Ukraine excavations were carried out here in 1940–1. Remains of numerous residential and storage buildings were found as well as jewellery, smelting, blacksmiths', and pottery work-shops, and foundations and parts of the walls of Uspenski Cathedral of the twelfth century. In the town and neighbour-hood remains of another nine churches were examined. In the fortified upper part of the town a large area where iron-smelting and working had been carried out came to light. A copper-casting workshop was also revealed.

*Raiki*

At Raiki (150 km. west-south-west of Kiev) a small fortified town constructed by some Kiev prince of the eleventh century and built as part of a defensive system against the steppe nomads was excavated in 1929–35 and 1946–7. The 'suburb' and rural settlements adjoining it were dug. The original name of this small town (covering 12,000 sq. m.) is not known from the chronicles but it is the only town of Kiev Russia that has been entirely excavated with its adjoining parts: *detinets*, suburb, and adjoining settlements. The real value of this excavation, apart from its completeness, lies in the fact that the town and the whole of its population was destroyed by the Tartar Mongols and since then no cultural layer has accumulated above that of the destruction layer of the thirteenth century. The burnt houses and domestic property lay untouched, and hundreds of defenders and attackers lay just where they fell in the battle together with the bodies of the slaughtered women and children thrown unburied in the houses. Evidently the Tar-tars made as short work of the inhabitants of this town as the chronicles says they did those of Kozelsk: 'for all the huts and even for the children to the very babies sucking milk there was no mercy.'

All the domestic and storage buildings were joined with the defensive works to form one system of fortification for the town. On the inside the rampart was composed of soil thrown up from the ditch boxed into elongated timber frames (*tarasy*), which on the outside projected downwards into the side of the ditch while on the inside they served as the wall of the house adjoining the rampart. [This is a similar construction to the 'timber-lacing' of west European Iron-Age camps. T.] The defensive systems also included quadrilateral towers and concealed subterranean passages leading out to the bottom of the ditch. The huts against the frames on the inside were arranged continuously along the inner face of the rampart, and this continuous row of buildings was broken only in the north-west corner of the inner town at the entry. A second row of frames was set within the first but spaced at different intervals and against this were cattle-pens and storehouses. Within this ring of houses and service buildings there was a broad court containing several isolated semi-subterranean houses, mostly workshops, smithies, iron-foundries, etc. On the beaten clay floors of the houses by the rampart numerous objects of everyday life were found: scorched wooden vessels, pottery, and tools (spades axes, picks, ploughshares, scythes, sickles, etc.); many weapons (more than 1,000 iron and bone arrowheads, spearheads, swords, sabres, battle-axes, iron and copper maces, helmets, spurs, quivers, etc.); locks, keys, iron hobbles for horses; glass, amber, silver, and gold ornaments; craftsmen's tools (files, hammers, pincers, moulds, matrix mould for decorative stamps); and so on. Outside the area of the *detinets* the 'suburb' where the craftsmen lived and also three rural settlements were excavated.

## Grodno

A strong outpost of Kiev Russia in the twelfth and thirteenth centuries on its western edge was Grodno, excavated off and on since 1932. Evidence for the study of stone architecture was especially prolific. The ruins of two brick defensive towers of the twelfth century and a church in the fort with a hand-carved majolica floor were found. Ancient houses were also excavated. Clearly even here on the western edge of Russia in the midst of a foreign tribal population Russian urban culture is recognizable as something strong and independent.

*Staraya (Old) Ladoga*

One of the oldest and most important of the northern Russian towns was Old Ladoga situated on the left bank of the Volkhov 12 km. from its outlet into Lake Ladoga. There is an older settlement on the promontory formed by the juncture of the river Ladozhka with the Volkhov, but remains have not been found here as it was destroyed by the construction of a stone fort in the twelfth century. On the southern side separated from it by a narrow ditch is the so-called Zemlyanoe (Earthen) town which forms part of the old town. It is enclosed by ramparts and bastions built in the fifteenth and sixteenth centuries and with its ramparts covers an area of 140 by 150 m. There have been excavations here off and on since 1911.

The oldest layer in Old Ladoga belongs to the seventh and eighth centuries. In this period Ladoga was a small village of Slav colonists who had come from more southern areas. The spacious log-houses (measuring 12 by 8 m.) give an indication of the social system. A large patriarchal family, a whole clan community, could have lived in such a house. Around the houses were stalls for cattle and storage buildings. At this stage the basis of life in the town was stock-rearing and agriculture, helped out by hunting and especially fishing. Domestic economy was advanced but craftsmanship had not become a separate profession (except perhaps iron-working).

Hemp and barley grains and especially millet were found. The latter formed the basis of cultivation at Ladoga in that period. Among the agricultural tools iron ploughshares, sickles, curved scythes, etc. were found. The spacious stalls for cattle with half a metre of manure on the floor and the mass of bones of domestic animals (horse, cow, pig, and sheep) are evidence that stock-rearing occupied a large place in the economy.

In the tenth century Ladoga changed from a rural village into a town with trade and craft-working. This was the time of the final break-up of tribal relationships and their replacement by a class society. The development of the productive forces, in the first place the change from slash-and-burn to field agriculture and then the expansion of barter and external trade, led to the weakening of tribal relationships, to the growth of property inequalities, and finally to the birth of feudal society. Here in Ladoga the process was speeded up by the struggle with foreign invaders, the Varangians. Ladoga lay on the 'great water route from Varangia to Greece' and the growth of overseas trade brought about the creation of the town. [Varangians is the Russian name for Scandinavians, Vikings. T.] In the tenth century the great family-houses were replaced by small huts. The normal hut was of wood and measured 4 by 5 m. including porch and heating-place. Storage buildings apart from small pigsties and granaries have now disappeared. The houses are not now set in a small nucleus of buildings as previously but on both sides of straight, narrow streets, almost touching each other. This is an urban type of building. The crafts become an independent branch of the economy and there are traces of trading activities.

With the rise of the Novgorod state Ladoga became an outer suburb of Novgorod the Great and the two towns formed the outer defence of the north-western frontier of Russian soil. The twelfth century saw the main floruit of Ladoga and at this time a stone fort and five churches were built there. The suburbs extended 2 km. along the bank of the river Volkhov.

Although layers have been revealed at Ladoga dating from various periods of its existence up to the seventeenth century and a great mass of material collected, the most important result of the work there has been the study of its lower levels belonging to the juncture of the two periods, the change from a rural village to a town. In this rests the outstanding significance of the archaeological research at Ladoga.

## Pskov

An older village preceding the feudal town has also been discovered at Pskov. On the high cliff at the confluence of the rivers Velikaya and Pskov where the present *kremlin* of Pskov lies there has been continuous occupation from the second and third centuries A.D. onwards, to judge by the results of excavation. The archaeological expedition that worked at Pskov from 1945 to 1949 paid special attention to the *kremlin*. It was established that the northern part of the promontory on which it stands was occupied by an older village not later than the eighth century which had the clear character of a craft centre. There were numerous smelting and smiths' furnaces. From the number of furnaces it appears that the smiths of Pskov supplied a large district with iron and iron objects.

The town itself is situated on a high and precipitous promontory and originally lacked proper defences. In the eighth century a bank was thrown up and surmounted with a wooden wall. In the tenth century the first defensive wall of stone slabs was built; in the thirteenth it was replaced by a new stone wall whose remains survive today. In the eighth century Pskov had already become a trade and craft centre. The houses of this time were timber-framed with a stone oven in one corner and usually with a cellar. In the tenth century timber roadways appear. In the layers of the eighth and ninth centuries several Slav pagan altars have been found. They are all oval in shape filled with clean river sand framed in stone slabs. Besides altars heaps of animal bones have been found. To judge by the number of altars that have come to light Pskov can be considered as a pagan religious centre. Unfortunately the cultural layers in the *kremlin* later than the tenth century were dug away in the eighteenth century and the archaeological study of Pskov in the eleventh and later centuries must be done in other parts of the town.

## Beloozero (lit. 'White Lake')

In 1949 work began on Old Beloozero, one of the Russian towns mentioned in the chronicle in connexion with the events of the ninth to tenth centuries. On the right bank of the Sheksna (about 400 km. east of Leningrad) is a locality bearing the name 'Old Town'. Here there are no fortifications, usual in other ancient Russian towns, but ruins of houses survive over an extensive area covered with turf and stick up as humps. The excavations revealed houses and brought to light a very varied list of objects belonging to the ninth to thirteenth centuries. In the fourteenth century as a result of an epidemic of the Black Death the town was transferred to a new site (modern Belozersk, 17 km. west of 'Old Town').

## Novgorod the Great

The excavations at Novgorod have been the largest in the

scale of work and most interesting in their results. The outstanding part played by Novgorod in Russian history and in the history of Russian culture has ensured that it received corresponding attention from Soviet archaeologists. It should be said that the fact that wooden objects and buildings have survived because of the very wet conditions of the soil has favoured successful results.

Novgorod the Great is situated on the river Volkhov which divides it into two parts; the western or Sofiiskaya (of St Sophia), and the eastern or Torgovaya (commercial). On the St Sophia side there is a *kremlin* (Pl. 22b) containing a very ancient stone building, the cathedral of St Sophia. The city was in antiquity divided into five parts. On the commercial side there were two: Slavensky in the south, Plotnitsky in the north. On the St Sophia side there were three: Nerevsky in the north, in the south Lyudin (or Goncharsky), on the west Zagorodsky (lit. 'beyond the city'). In the Slavensky area on the bank of the Volkhov opposite the *kremlin* lay the important administrative centre of ancient Novgorod, the Court of Yaroslavov.

Systematic excavations began in Novgorod in 1932 and have been carried on annually ever since apart from the five-year interruption caused by the war. An outstanding part in the excavations has been played by A. V. Artsikhovsky, who has directed continuously the expedition of the Institute for the History of Material Culture of the Academy of Sciences of the Soviet Union. Separate excavations in Novgorod mainly relating to research on architectural monuments have been carried out by M. K. Karger and the author.

The problem of the earliest settlement at Novgorod is still not settled. The oldest layers discovered belong to the tenth century and only isolated buildings belong to an earlier time. In the ninth century the city evidently still did not exist and at that time we can postulate only small separate villages. Novgorod's history begins only with the tenth century. Evidently it was called New Town (Nov-Gorod) with reference to some older town, perhaps Old Ladoga. It has been said that the old town lay 3 km. upstream from Novgorod on the right bank of the Volkhov on a hill which is called Rurik's Hill-Fort. From the 1130s princes lived here who had been driven out of Novgorod after a popular uprising. Excavations on the site have revealed deposits of the ninth and tenth centuries. Naturally this is not sufficient grounds for believing that this hill-fort was the predecessor of Novgorod as a town, but the fact of the existence of a very old settlement there is important.

Layers of the ninth and tenth centuries have been discovered elsewhere in the neighbourhood of Novgorod. In the place where the Volkhov flows from Lake Ilmen is a locality called Peryn. Presumably its name records the memory of a pagan sanctuary of the god Perun that was here formerly. Excavations have revealed a construction here consisting of a circular area enclosed by a ditch with eight bow-shaped projections giving a general plan resembling a flower with eight petals. The diameter of the circle including the ditch reaches 33 m. In the centre stood a large wooden post which had evidently served as a pedestal for an idol of Peryn, the whole work being a temple of the heathen deity. At Peryn semi-subterranean houses of the eleventh to fourteenth centuries were discovered and layers of the ninth to tenth centuries with handmade pottery.

Remains of heathendom (that is earlier than the adoption of Christianity in 988) have been found within the area of Novgorod. Such a pagan grave with a cremated burial has been discovered in the centre of the town in the Yaroslavov Court, and traces of pagan offerings have been discovered in the Nerevsky area. Below very old layers there was discovered a hole dug into the natural rock containing nine wooden cups. Seven of the cups were set out in a semicircle, the other two being in the centre. The cups were placed on edge in such a way that their contents would pour out. Artsikhovsky has suggested that nine landowners, heads of large families, made this offering before they settled in this place.

Judging by the excavations, from the very beginning of its existence Novgorod like other ancient Russian towns was a city of craftsmen. Already in the first excavations in 1932 in a locality called Slavno in the Slavensky area three workshops came to light dating from the twelfth to thirteenth centuries. One of these belonged to a shoemaker and in and around it were found several thousand pieces of leather and leather footwear. Attached to the hut was a cist, the so-called ash-pit, in which the hair was removed from the skin with the help of lime. The second workshop belonged to an oil maker, and the excavations yielded five massive crushers or presses. The third was that of a toy maker who made little clay birds covered with bright yellow glaze.

During the excavation of the southern part of the *kremlin* at Novgorod remains of further workshops were studied: of a shoemaker, blacksmith, bone-carver, and a wool-worker.

In all later excavations a mass of manufacturing tools has been found, of carpenters, blacksmiths, jewellers, and other craftsmen, as well as objects made by them. Numerous finds testify to Novgorod's trade with distant countries. It is necessary to draw attention to the curious fact recently established, that some of Novgorod's wooden objects are made of imported

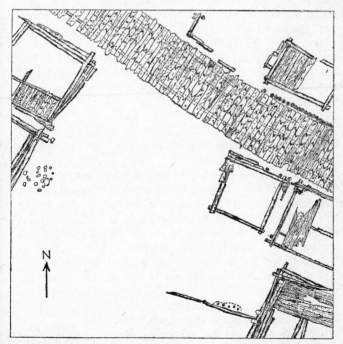

28. Novgorod. Plan of the 13th wooden road, with adjoining houses.

wood of southern species of trees, for example, combs of box tree and tub staves of yew.

The excavations at Novgorod have revealed not odd houses but whole areas and streets; in the *kremlin* the remains of ancient Bishop Street, in the Nerevsky area Serf and Main Streets at their intersection, in the Yaroslavov Court the flooring of the *Veche* area. [*Veche* is the name of a type of popular assembly in ancient Russia. T.] Throughout the period of the chroniclers the streets of Novgorod were surfaced with wood (Fig. 28). The paved area can be 6 m. but is normally 3–4 m. wide. It consisted of wide planks laid transversely on long thin logs lying lengthways. Periodically the streets were re-surfaced with timbers. Thus in Serf Street a cultural layer 7·5 m. thick was revealed and twenty-five layers of such surfaces were cleaned and then taken up. The most interesting feature of urban planning of Novgorod was the system of drains for removing ground water in the constant struggle with the boggy conditions of the residential areas. The drains consisted of large wooden pipes up to 50 cm. in diameter, made in two halves held tightly together by zigzag stitching, while birch-bark was wound around the junctions between pipes. Large wells and barrel sumps joined up to one another were included in the drainage systems.

Not only separate houses but also large log-built (sometimes two-storeyed) buildings and whole estates with their service buildings were fully examined.

Excavations have revealed the ancient defensive structures of Novgorod. In the Slavensky area a stone wall 3 m. thick was found that is known by the chronicle to have been built by the 'mayor' (*posadnik*) Fedor Danilovich in 1335. On the town rampart surrounding Novgorod on all sides the remains of ancient stone towers have been revealed which were built in 1391 and parts of a stone wall 4·6 m. thick. Of the stone buildings discovered by archaeologists besides the town walls the most remarkable was the church of St Boris and St Gleb in the *kremlin*. It was erected in the twelfth century by Sotko Sytinich and was destroyed in the seventeenth century.

In Novgorod remarkable monuments of Russian architecture have survived. During the research and restoration work on and near them excavations were carried out. Excavations (directed by the author) of the porch of the cathedral of St Sophia have made it possible to establish its ancient architectural appearance. Here were found the grave of one of the greatest political figures of Novgorod, the archbishop Basil, and a fragment of a remarkable twelfth-century fresco showing a prince and members of his family (Pl. 23). In the excavations at the cathedral of St George at the monastery of Yurev the graves of important Novgorod figures of the twelfth to thirteenth centuries came to light, the 'mayors' Miroshka Nezdinich, his son Dmitri Miroshkinich, and Semen Borisovich. It is curious that contrary to the prohibitions of the Christian Church vessels containing food and swords were placed in their graves following the pagan rite.

Excavations carried out in Novgorod have made important additions to cultural and art history. In particular a number of objects covered with fine carving (cups, flagons, ladles, batons, etc.) have come to light. Wooden columns almost covered with interlace pattern (so-called wickerwork design) are remarkable finds from an eleventh-century layer, although they may belong to the previous century (Fig. 29). In the pattern were a griffin and a centaur. Sculptures of wood, carvings on bone of a dragon and mermaid, and so on have also been found.

For a long time the opinion had prevailed that only a few Russian people in antiquity could read and write, that writing was an accomplishment of a narrow educated community. The discoveries of archaeologists have refuted this view. In many Russian towns everyday objects with inscriptions have been found showing that a knowledge of writing was widespread among modest citizens, craftsmen, and merchants. In Novgorod many varied objects bearing inscriptions made by the owners were found. But the most remarkable find in Novgorod and perhaps the most remarkable archaeological discovery in general in the last few years is the discovery of birch-bark letters. There had been information that the people of ancient Russia wrote on birch-bark but this form of writing was only found during the excavations at Novgorod in 1951. The objects in question are little scrolls of birch-bark on which the letters have been scratched with a bone implement (Fig. 30).

29. Novgorod.
Carved wooden
column.

30. Novgorod. Transcription of document on birch-bark.

At the present moment (1958) more than 300 have been discovered. Their content is very varied. There are notes of debts, expenditure on purchases, complaints of peasants to a feudal lord, private letters, and others. This is the first time that we have met the colloquial speech of the people of ancient Novgorod. This is not the official language of ecclesiastical books, laws, and acts, or of literary work or chronicles, but the living speech of the people of Russia from the eleventh to fifteenth centuries, never known to us before. One of them (twelfth century) records a family dispute. Gostyata complains to Vasiliya that someone, evidently her husband, has taken away her property inherited from her father and relatives and having taken a new wife into the house has driven her out. Gostyata begs Vasiliya to come and bring peace to the family and mend matters. A letter of Peter to Mary is interesting. Peter has gone to the lake area to mow hay but the local inhabitants have taken his mown hay away from him. In order to prove his right to the hay Peter asks Mary to write a deed of purchase and send it to him. In one or two documents historical personages known to us from chronicles are mentioned. Thus in some found in 1953 the names of the fourteenth-century Novgorod knights Ontsifor Lukich and his son Yury Ontsiforovich are mentioned. In one of these the peasants complain to Yury about the extortion and rapacity of his bailiff (that is the person managing affairs on the lord's behalf).

## Ryazan

The ancient capital of the Ryazan princedom lay on the right bank of the Oka 50 km. from modern Ryazan. All that survive from the once flourishing town are the ramparts. These enclose a ploughed field which forms an irregular quadrilateral in plan and covers overall about 48 hectares (120 acres). An internal bank in the northern part separates a small area where the oldest settlement lay.

Excavations at Ryazan began in 1836 and were continued with long periods of interruption. Several valuable discoveries were made but the scientific level of the work was low. In Soviet times work has been carried out intermittently since 1926. An expedition of IIMK worked there from 1945–50 under the

direction of A. L. Mongait [the author, his most extensive
fieldwork. T.].

Excavations have revealed that the oldest settlement, going
back to the first centuries A.D., lies in the extreme north-western
projection of the town. In the tenth century a mass colonization of the middle Oka by the Slavs took place and the native
Mordvin tribes were assimilated or forced out. On the site of
the small village of Erzyan arose the Russian town of Ryazan
preserving in its name the tribal name of the native east
Finnish inhabitants. Within a short time during the eleventh
and twelfth centuries it grew rapidly and from the small nucleus
developed into a thickly built-over town lying within a monumental earthen rampart. In the eleventh century the northern
part of the town separated off by a bank was probably still the
site of the prince's palace and served as the *kremlin*, but in the
early twelfth century the social topography changed. The
northern part was now occupied by craftsmen and became the
real craft centre of the town while the richer houses and stone
churches were built in the southern part.

Houses of craftsmen and workshops and their fittings were
found; bone-carvers, jewellers (Pl. 24), smithies, several furnaces and kilns. The pottery kilns were of two types, for firing
ordinary wares and for firing glazed wares. The kilns of the
first type were of beaten clay and the upper firing chamber was
separated from the heating part by a horizontal partition with
apertures in it for the heat to pass through. Kilns of the second
type were made of sun-dried brick and the heating chamber was
not below but level with the firing chamber. The houses at Old
Ryazan were of two types: semi-subterranean like those at
Kiev; and surface timber dwellings, sometimes with a plank
floor, with a board or straw gabled roof, and with one or two
storage-pits beneath the floor. The ovens in most cases are of
beaten clay and rectangular with a flat top without pipes or
stand.

As early as 1836 the large twelfth-century cathedral of St
Boris and St Gleb was excavated. Subsequently further work
has been carried out on this building. In 1948 remains of the
Uspensky Cathedral were discovered and examined. From
this it has been established that there was a local architectural

school at Ryazan similar to that of Chernigov. The ramparts have been examined in detail and wooden constructions were found in them, *gorodni*. As at other towns there was confirmation of widespread literacy among the urban population. Recently an inscription on a twelfth-century pot was found which read: 'Dobrilo sent new wine to Prince Bogunka.' Bricks usually had the stamp of a master craftsman on them and on some he put his name, 'Yakov'.

In December 1237 the Tartars besieged and captured Old Ryazan. The town suffered terrible destruction, traces of which appear in the archaeological record. Life was soon renewed. The churches and fortifications were restored and new houses built. In the fourteenth century, however, the capital of the princedom was for several reasons, including repeated raids by Tartars because of its proximity to the steppe, transferred to Pereyaslavl-Ryazansky (renamed Ryazan in 1778). The old town gradually became deserted.

## Moscow

Moscow was studied in pre-Revolutionary times mainly through the museum collections and also by excavations on barrows and hill-forts downstream. There was no important work in the town itself. In Soviet times work has been mainly confined to careful observation of foundation digging in Moscow. During construction work ancient layers have been exposed and many finds made. Thus a large quantity of valuable evidence on the capital's history was obtained by observations made during the construction of the 'Metropolitan' (underground railway) first and second lines. Eminent Soviet historians and archaeologists took part in this. Subsequently mass observations have been made in Moscow at more than 200 points during work on the reconstruction of the city. More valuable information about the city and its population has been obtained from special archaeological excavations carried out since 1946.

In the fifteenth and sixteenth centuries an important artisan area of Moscow, the 'Pottery Suburb', lay on a high hill at the mouth of the river Yauza where it joins the Oka. Three kilns came to light and later potters' workshops which yielded a rich variety of the products of Moscow potteries and full details of the process of production. Excavations in 1949–51 gave further details about Moscow crafts in the Zaryadi district. Buildings of an artisans' suburb were revealed that had existed at least as early as the eleventh or twelfth century. Remains of jewellers', shoemakers', smiths', and bone-carvers' work were found here. The discovery of this suburb has great importance for Moscow's history. The first written reference to Moscow was in 1147, and many historians had supposed that at that time Moscow was a prince's estate or small fort and that it had not a developed suburb inhabited by craftsmen and traders. The excavations at Zaryadi have shown that approximately half a century before the first references to Moscow in a chronicle there had been an artisans' settlement here along a narrow stretch of the Moscow River covering a substantial area of ground that now adjoins the Kremlin.

Later on the town grew and in the fifteenth century the craftsmen moved out of this district which, lying near the Kremlin, was occupied by the feudal aristocracy of the Muscovite state.

The discovery of gardens and estates belonging to various classes has been of great interest during the excavations at Moscow. They yielded valuable evidence on the communal urban economy. Timber roads of the fifteenth to seventeenth centuries came to light, as well as a whole system of drainage constructions that drained the Zaryadi district during the fourteenth and fifteenth centuries. Wooden pipes like those at Novgorod were used for draining away the water.

*

Our summary of archaeological work on ancient Russian towns is far from complete, but enough has been said to indicate how much this work has contributed to the history of crafts, trade, the daily life of the population, and sometimes even to political history.

Archaeologists provide material and themselves study various aspects of Russian culture. So it is necessary to repeat that the work of archaeologists has provided much new information about Russian architecture. In the last few years alone more than twenty-five architectural monuments of the twelfth and thirteenth centuries have been discovered or restudied. From this enrichment of knowledge by monuments of ancient Russian architecture it has been possible to reassess the general history and especially to distinguish the local architectural schools of the period of feudal disintegration.

The auxiliary historical disciplines such as numismatics, the study of seals, and epigraphy are also closely connected with archaeology. In Soviet times they have been brought into the system and frequently recurring coins have been mapped according to the Russian mint of their issue in the eleventh to thirteenth centuries. The occurrence of coin ingots of the twelfth to fourteenth centuries has also been mapped.

Expanding archaeological research on the ancient Russian towns places in the hands of historians a mass of factual evidence which allows it to be concluded that Kiev Russia was an outstanding state with a high level of individual culture.

However important the works carried out in the last few years may have been a series of important questions that have not been answered remains. Many of the most important towns have not been examined at all, others only incompletely, and there are some whole groups of towns about whose ancient history and culture we know nothing (in White Russia for example). The pre-Mongol urban culture is well studied but the fourteenth and subsequent centuries have not been sufficiently represented in the archaeological materials. The study of craftsmen areas and agricultural suburbs of the large towns must be increased. The princes' castles and fortified manors should be studied. A systematic survey of the towns and hillforts must be made and an archaeological map of the ancient Russian towns drawn up.

# CONCLUSION

WE have attempted to acquaint the reader with the wide range of historical problems which occupy Soviet archaeologists and to show their successes and shortcomings in the working out of these problems. The size of the book and its scope do not allow us to touch on all matters. It has been necessary to present many subjects very fragmentarily; about much it was not possible to speak comprehensively. Yet if the reader has gained even the most general impression of how Soviet archaeologists work and what the scientific results of this work have been the aim of publishing this book will have been achieved.

In a general list of works and discoveries it is sometimes difficult to distinguish the important from the secondary, especially if one has to write about recent discoveries for whose evaluation perspective created by the passage of time is lacking. It is possible that many discoveries which we could not or did not consider it necessary to mention will hold a very important place in researches in the future and that sites and researches about which we have spoken in our book will be covered up or pushed into a back place by later discoveries. While trying to satisfy the need for facts about different remains, we have tried at the same time not to lose sight of the most important lines of development of archaeology in our country and to show what archaeologists have done for the study of history in the USSR. Soviet archaeologists plan their work to meet this very important and honourable duty, not casually studying different archaeological sites and museum collections as they may interest scholars but examining in the first instance the material which can help in the solution of the most important problems of historical science. Thanks to this principle the work of archaeologists has been able to hold an important place in the general studies on the history of the USSR.

In the general works on the history of Russia written by pre-Revolutionary historians we do not find attempts to illuminate the whole ancient history of the country. For this they lacked the factual material and were impeded by the view prevailing at that time that outside the great civilizations of antiquity – Egypt, Mesopotamia, Greece, and Rome – lived non-historical people, whose development was uninteresting and insignificant in the unfolding of world history. In Soviet times a systematic exposition of the history of primitive and slave-holding periods within the area of the Soviet Union has been made. This has been due to the cooperative strength of archaeologists and historians.

Carrying out this basic duty, to assist in the study of the history of our country, the young science of archaeology has to work simultaneously upon the advancement and refinements of methods of research and upon the solution of problems of theory and practice in scientific work. As the growing-pains of archaeology were the preoccupation with objects or attempts to regard the main duty of archaeology as the ethnical interpretation of archaeological cultures, or preoccupation with sociological or stadial schemes, so the complexity of problems confronting archaeologists has increased and no one side should be given preference. These include problems of ethnogenesis, social relationships, and economic forms in antiquity, problems of the development of rural economy and techniques, religious manifestations, art, etc. The proper answer to all these many-sided questions of history and the history of culture of ancient societies can be obtained only by mastering a very precise method of research.

The aim of our book has been to demonstrate not only what Soviet archaeologists have done in the study of the past but also what methods of research they used.

# Books for Further Reading

## A. IN WEST EUROPEAN LANGUAGES

There are few books that deal with the results of recent Soviet archaeological work, but the following provide useful background information or deal with Soviet work.

### GENERAL

For Chapters 1–4 there are various articles in the volumes of *Reallexikon der Vorgeschichte*, Berlin 1924–32, edited by M. Ebert. The main article is entitled 'Sudrussland'. For Chapters 6–10 the appropriate chapters in the *Cambridge Ancient* and *Medieval Histories* are useful. The dead periodical *Eurasia Septentrionalis Antiqua* (Helsinki, 1925–38) dealt with Russian prehistoric archaeology during the interwar period.

### MAPS AND LANGUAGES

de Bray, R. G. A. *Guide to the Slavonic Languages*. London, 1951.
Matthews, W. K. *Languages of the U S S R*. Cambridge, 1951.
*The U S S R and Eastern Europe*. Oxford Regional Atlas, 1956.

### IDEOLOGY

Black, C. E. (Editor). *Rewriting Russian History. Soviet Interpretations of Russia's Past*. London, 1957.*
Engels, F. *The Origin of the Family, Private Property, and the State*. Translation of 1891 edition. Moscow, 1948.
Matthews, W. K. 'The Japhetic Theory.' *The Slavonic and E. European Review*, XXVII (1948), pp. 172–97. An account of Marr and Marrism.
Miller, M. *Archaeology in the U S S R*. London, 1956.*
Tallgren, A. M. 'Archaeological Studies in Soviet Russia.' *Eurasia Septentrionalis Antiqua*, 10 (1936), pp. 129–71.

### Chapter 2

Golomshtok, E. A. 'The Old Stone Age in European Russia.' *Trans. American Phil. Soc.*, N.S., XXIX (1938), pp. 191–468.

* These two books were published for the *Research Program in the U S S R* in America and are unsympathetic.

Hančar, F. 'Probleme der jungeren Altsteinzeit Osteuropas, Versuch einer Systematisieurung. *Quarter* (Freiburg), IV (1942), pp. 125–86.

'Paléolithique et Néolithique de l'URSS.' *Annales du Centre d'Études et de Documentation Paleontologiques* (Paris), XVIII (1956). Translation of *Materialy* No. 39.

## Chapters 3–4

Childe, V. G. *The Dawn of European Civilisation*, London, 6th ed., 1957. Chapters VIII, IX, and XI.

'The Socketed Celt in Upper Eurasia.' *Report of the London University Institute of Archaeology*, X (1954), pp. 11–26.

Gimbutas, M. 'Borodino, Seima, and their Contemporaries.' *Proc. Prehistoric Soc.*, XXII (1956), pp. 143–73.

'The Prehistory of Eastern Europe.' *American School of Prehistoric Research, Bull.* Cambridge (Mass.), XX (1956).

Hančar, F. *Urgeschichte Kaukasiens von den Anfängen seiner Besiedlung bis in die Zeit seiner fruhen Metallurgie.* Vienna, 1937.

Tallgren, A. M. 'La Pontide Préscythique après l'Introduction des Métaux.' *Eurasia Septentrionalis Antiqua*, II (1926).

## Chapters 5–6

Herodotus. *The History.* Especially Book IV.

Minns, E. H. *Scythians and Greeks.* Cambridge, 1913.

Rice, T. T. *The Scythians.* London, 1957.

Rostovtzeff, M. *Iranians and Greeks in South Russia.* Oxford, 1922.

Rudenko, S. I. *Der Zweite Kurgan von Pasyryk.* Berlin, 1951. (Translation)

Trever, C. 'Excavations in N. Mongolia.' *Memoirs of the Academy of the History of Material Culture* (Leningrad, 1932).

## Chapters 7–8

Barthold, W. *Turkestan down to the Mongol Invasion.* Translated from the Russian by H. A. R. Gibb. London, 1928.

Ghirshman, R. *Iran.* London (Penguin Books), 1954.

Grousset, R. *L'Empire des Steppes.* Paris, 1939.

Papers presented by the Soviet Delegation at the 23rd International Congress of Orientalists, Akad. Nauk. Moscow, 1954.

Rostovtzeff, M. *The Social and Economic History of the Hellenistic World.* Oxford, 3 vols, 1941.

Tarn, W. W. *The Greeks in Bactria and India.* Cambridge, 2nd ed., 1951.

Tolstov, S. P. 'The Prehistoric Cultures and Primitive Irrigation

Systems of Ancient Chorasmia.' *Report of the London University Institute of Archaeology*, XIII, pp. 8–36.

*Chapters 9–10*

Chadwick, N. K. *The Beginnings of Russian History: An Enquiry into Sources*. Cambridge, 1946.

Cross, S. H. 'The Russian Primary Chronicle.' *Harvard Studies and Notes in Philology and Literature*. Cambridge (Mass.), 1930. This is an English translation of the *Povest Vremennykh Let* with an Introduction.

Vernadsky, G. *Ancient Russia*. Yale, 3 vols., 1943–53.

## B. IN RUSSIAN

### PERIODICALS

The three principal Soviet periodicals published by the Academy of Sciences for I I M K are:

*Kratkie Soobshcheniya o Dokladakh i Polevykh Issledovaniyakh I I M K*. Deals with the activities of I I M K.

*Materialy i Issledovaniya po Arkheologii S S S R.*

This enjoys an international reputation. The volumes appear at frequent but irregular intervals and deal with a single subject like Palaeolithic and Neolithic, Novgorod Expedition, etc. (Abbreviated M I A.)

*Sovetskaya Arkheologiya*. (Abbreviated S A.)

There are several other Soviet periodicals that deal partly with archaeological subjects. Among the pre-Revolutionary periodicals the *Otchety* of the Imperial Archaeological Commission are large volumes containing excavation reports. The volumes for 1897–1900 contain reports on some very exciting Scythian burials and the original account of the famous Maikop barrow.

### GENERAL

The first three are published by the Academy of Sciences for I I M K and contain abundant references.

*Itogi i Perspektivy Razvitiya Sovetskoi Arkheologii* (Materialy dlya Delegatov Vsesoyuznovo Arkheologicheskovo Soveshchaniya), 1945.

Mongait, A. L. *Arkheologiya v S S S R*. 1955. The work translated here. Contains references to sites mentioned, list of Soviet archaeologists, maps of sites. An English edition of Mongait's book was published in Moscow in 1959.

Mongait, A. L., and Tretyakov, P. N. (Editors). *Ocherki Istorii S S S R I., Pervobytno-obshchinny Stroi i Drevneishie Gosudarstva na Territorii S S S R*, 1956. Attractively produced; useful maps; the standard work.

*Bolshaya Sovetskaya Entsiklopedia*. Moscow, 2nd ed., 1949 (in progress).
A mine of information on sites, persons, cultures, etc. The main articles are authoritative with references appended.


SPECIAL SUBJECTS

A few recent books and articles of special interest are given below. Unless otherwise stated they were published by the Soviet Academy of Sciences.

Artsikhovsky, A. V. *Novgorodskie Gramoty na Bereste (iz raskopok 1952 g.)*.*

Artsikhovsky, A. V. i Kolchin, B.A. *Trudy Novgorodskoi Arkheologicheskoi Ekspeditsii, I, M I A* , No. 55 (1956).*

Bondar, N. N. 'Torgovie Snosheniya Olvii co Skifiei VI–V vv. do N.E.', *S.A.* 23 (1955), 58–80.

Bryusov, A. Y. *Ocherki po Istorii Plemen Evropeiskoi Chasti S S S R v Neoliticheskuyu Epokhu,* 1952.

Efimenko, P. P. *Pervobytnoe Obshchestvo,* Int. Arkh., Ak Nauk Uk. S S R. Kiev, 1953.

Karger, M. K. 'Kiev i Mongolskoe Zavoevanie', *S A*, XI (1949), pp. 55–102.

Kuftin, B. A. *Archaeological Excavations in Trialeti,* I. Academy of Sciences of the Georgian S S R. 1941. Russian text.*

Passek, T. S. *Periodizatsiya Tripolskikh Poselenii, M I A*, 10 (1949).*

Piotrovskii, B. B. *Istoriya Kultura Urartu,* Inst. Ist. Ak. Nauk Arm. S S R. Erevan, 1944.

Piotrovskii, B. B. *Karmir-Blur,* Ak. Nauk Arm. S S R, I (in progress). Erevan, 1950.*

Rudenko, S. I. *Kultura Naseleniya Gornovo Altaya v Skifskoe Vremya.* 1953.*

Tolstov, S. P. *Trudy Khorezmskoi Arkheologo-Etnograficheskoi Ekspeditsii,* I (1945–8). 1952.*

Trever, K. V. *Pamyatniki Greko-Baktriiskovo Iskusstva.* Gosud. Ermitazh, Moscow-Leningrad, 1940.*

Yakubovskii, A. Y. i Dyakonov, M. M. (Editors). *Zhivopis Drevnevo Pyanjikenta.* 1954.*

  * With numerous illustrations that may interest the reader who does not know Russian.

# INDEX